CONTEST FAVORITES
40 afghans
TO CROCHET

*I*f you prize originality and style, you'll love these one-of-a-kind creations designed by afghan aficionadas just like you! All of the wraps are so stunning you won't know which to crochet first.

These 40 irresistible beauties were selected from almost 100 entries in the Red Heart® Afghan Design Contest sponsored by Leisure Arts' Crochet With Heart *magazine*. The three winning afghans are included along with personal glimpses of their designers. Offering intriguing twists and turns as exceptional as the designers themselves, the worsted-weight wonders feature basic and specialty stitches and some unusual variations on time-honored motifs.

Among the lovely coverlets, you'll find filet crochet hearts and bunnies; textured lighthouses; angels with popcorn-stitch accents; and rosebuds, ivy, and other florals. Plus there are checkerboard, stained glass, harlequin, Southwestern, and other themes that will suit everyone's fancy. Seasonal designs include granny squares stitched in rows to resemble evergreens, then arranged in a classic Log Cabin quilt pattern; rounds of red-and-white spirals reminiscent of sweet peppermint treats; and a winsome snowman warming up an icy field of wintry grey.

Thrill the special people in your life by surprising them with these state-of-the-heart creations you've crocheted yourself. Warming heart and home, the eye-catching, cozy throws are versatile, decorative — and indispensable, too!

EDITORIAL STAFF

Vice President and Editor-in-Chief: Anne Van Wagner Childs
Executive Director: Sandra Graham Case
Editorial Director: Susan Frantz Wiles
Publications Director: Carla Bentley
Creative Art Director: Gloria Bearden
Senior Graphics Art Director: Melinda Stout

PRODUCTION

Managing Editor: Susan White Sullivan
Technical Editor: Patty Kowaleski
Instructional Editors: Susan Ackerman, Sarah J. Green,
  Valesha Marshell Kirksey, Jeanne Lowes, Frances Moore-Kyle, and
  Katherine Satterfield

EDITORIAL

Managing Editor: Marjorie Ann Lacy
Associate Editor: Debby Carr

ART

Graphics Art Director: Rhonda Hodge Shelby
Senior Graphics Illustrator: Lora Prall Puls
Graphics Illustrators: Katie Murphy and Dana Vaughn
Photography Stylist: Aurora Huston
Publishing Systems Administrator: Cindy Lumpkin
Publishing Systems Assistant: Susan Mary Gray

BUSINESS STAFF

Publisher: Rick Barton
Vice President and General Manager: Thomas L. Carlisle
Vice President, Finance: Tom Siebenmorgen
Vice President, Marketing: Bob Humphrey
Vice President, National Accounts: Pam Stebbins
Retail Marketing Director: Margaret Sweetin
General Merchandise Manager: Cathy Laird
Vice President, Operations: Brian U. Davis
Distribution Director: Rob Thieme
Retail Customer Service Director: Tonie B. Maulding
Retail Customer Service Managers: Carolyn Pruss and Wanda Price
Print Production Manager: Fred F. Pruss

CREDITS

Photography: Larry Pennington, Ken West, Mark Mathews, and
  Karen Busick Shirey of Peerless Photography, Little Rock, Arkansas;
  and Jerry R. Davis of Jerry Davis Photography and Natalie Young of
  Natalie Young Photography, Little Rock, Arkansas
Photography Stylists: Sondra Daniel, Karen Hall, Sandra Hubbard, and
  Christy Myers
Photo Locations: The homes of Nancy Gunn Porter, Jodie Davis,
  Jane Prather, Sammye Taylor, Marilyn Sternberg, Gail Wilcox, and
  Lange Cheek

Softcover ISBN 1-57486-153-0

contents

first prize

Leigh K. Nestor

"Noah's Ark is a popular theme these days, and I just had to try my hand at it!" says First Prize winner Leigh K. Nestor. A crocheter since the age of 16, Leigh has had six of her designs published previously and has "plenty more stashed in my cedar chest." She thoroughly enjoys her job at a local discount store yet admits there's one drawback. "Now, I have more money to buy yarn but less time to crochet!" Leigh lives in Pennsylvania with her husband, Joe, and their 7-year-old son, Brian.

NOAH'S ARK

Finished Size: 45" x 61"

MATERIALS
Worsted Weight Yarn:
  Green - 19½ ounces, (550 grams, 1,100 yards)
  Blue - 13 ounces, (370 grams, 735 yards)
  Dk Blue - 9 ounces, (260 grams, 510 yards)
  Brown - 4 ounces, (110 grams, 225 yards)
  Gold - 3½ ounces, (100 grams, 200 yards)
  White - 1½ ounces, (40 grams, 85 yards)
  Grey - 1½ ounces, (40 grams, 85 yards)
  Rose - 1 ounce, (30 grams, 55 yards)
  Purple - 1 ounce, (30 grams, 55 yards)
  Tan - ¼ ounce, (10 grams, 15 yards)
Crochet hook, size H (5.00 mm) **or** size needed for gauge
¾" Buttons for Giraffes' spots - 12
1" Buttons for Stars - 4
6 mm round black beads for eyes - 16
Sewing needle and thread
Safety pins
Yarn needle

GAUGE: On Panels, in pattern,
3 Shells and 8 rows = 4";
(sc, dc) 6 times and 12 rows = 4"
On all other pieces, 7 sc and 7 rows = 2"

STITCH GUIDE

TREBLE CROCHET *(abbreviated tr)*
YO twice, insert hook in st indicated, YO and pull up a loop (4 loops on hook), (YO and draw through 2 loops on hook) 3 times.
SHELL (uses one st)
Dc in st indicated, (ch 1, dc in same st) twice.
BEGINNING DECREASE
Pull up a loop in first 2 sc, YO and draw through all 3 loops on hook **(counts as one sc)**.
DECREASE
Pull up a loop in next 2 sc, YO and draw through all 3 loops on hook **(counts as one sc)**.
BOBBLE (uses one ch)
★ YO, insert hook in ch indicated, YO and pull up a loop, YO and draw through 2 loops on hook; repeat from ★ 2 times **more**, YO and draw through all 4 loops on hook.

Continued on page 6.

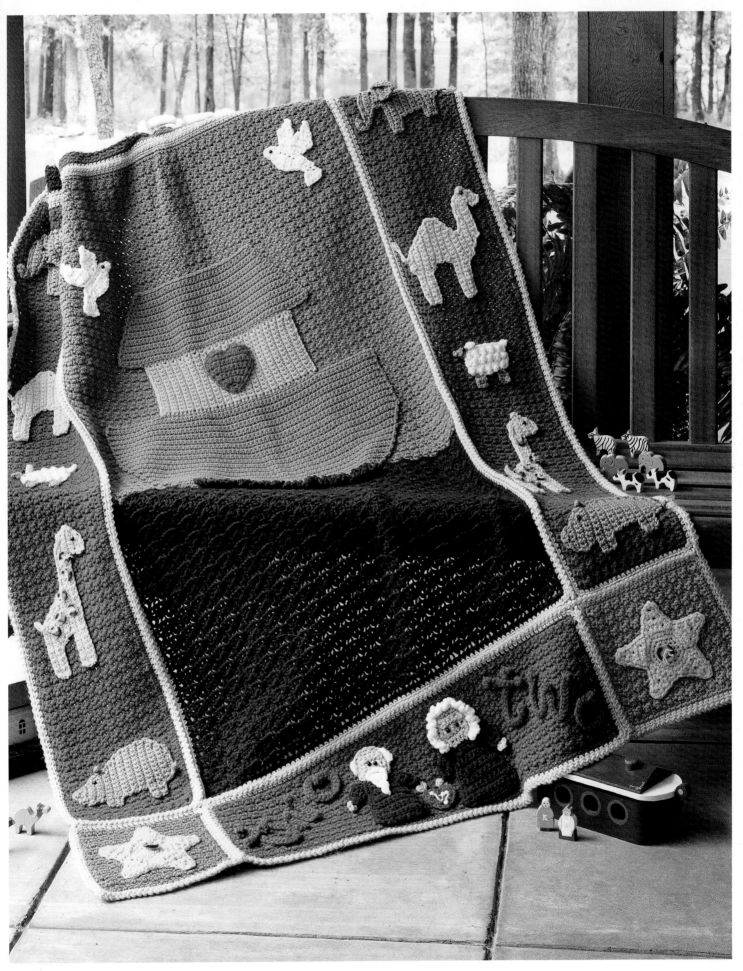

AFGHAN BODY

CENTER PANEL

With Dk Blue, ch 78 **loosely**.

Row 1: Sc in second ch from hook, ★ skip next ch, work Shell in next ch, skip next ch, sc in next ch; repeat from ★ across: 19 Shells and 20 sc.

Row 2 (Right side): Ch 4 **(counts as first dc plus ch 1, now and throughout)**, turn; working in Back Loops Only *(Fig. 2, page 125)*, dc in same st, skip next dc, sc in next dc, ★ skip next dc, work Shell in next sc, skip next dc, sc in next dc; repeat from ★ across to last 3 sts, skip next ch and next dc, (dc, ch 1, dc) in last sc: 18 Shells and 19 sc.

Note: Loop a short piece of yarn around any stitch to mark Row 2 as **right** side.

Row 3: Ch 1, turn; working in both loops, sc in first dc, ★ skip next dc, work Shell in next sc, skip next dc, sc in next dc; repeat from ★ across: 19 Shells and 20 sc.

Row 4: Ch 4, turn; working in Back Loops Only, dc in same st, skip next dc, sc in next dc, ★ skip next dc, work Shell in next sc, skip next dc, sc in next dc; repeat from ★ across to last 3 sts, skip next ch and next dc, (dc, ch 1, dc) in last sc: 18 Shells and 19 sc.

Rows 5-34: Repeat Rows 3 and 4, 15 times.

Row 35: Ch 1, turn; working in both loops, sc in first dc, ★ skip next dc, work Shell in next sc, skip next dc, sc in next dc; repeat from ★ across changing to Blue in last sc *(Fig. 5, page 126)*: 19 Shells and 20 sc.

Row 36: Ch 1, turn; working in Back Loops Only, sc in first sc, place marker around sc just made for Edging placement, dc in same st, ★ sc in next dc, skip next ch, dc in next dc, skip next ch, sc in next dc, dc in next sc; repeat from ★ across: 78 sts.

Rows 37-110: Ch 1, turn; working in both loops, sc in first dc, dc in next sc, (sc in next dc, dc in next sc) across.
Finish off.

EDGING

Rnd 1: With **right** side facing and working in end of rows, join Blue with sc in marked row *(see Joining With Sc, page 125)*; sc in each row across; working across sts on Row 110, 3 sc in first sc, sc in each st across to last dc, 3 sc in last dc; sc in end of first 75 rows changing to Dk Blue in last sc, work 50 sc evenly spaced across end of rows; working in free loops of beginning ch *(Fig. 3b, page 126)*, 3 sc in ch at base of first sc, work 76 sc evenly spaced across to last ch, 3 sc in last ch; work 50 sc evenly spaced across end of rows; join with slip st to first sc, finish off: 414 sc.

Rnd 2: With **right** side facing, join Tan with sc in any sc; sc in each sc around working 3 sc in center sc of each corner 3-sc group; join with slip st to first sc, finish off: 422 sc.

SIDE PANEL (Make 2)

With Green, ch 23 **loosely**.

Row 1 (Right side): Sc in second ch from hook, dc in next ch, (sc in next ch, dc in next ch) across: 22 sts.
Note: Mark Row 1 as **right** side.

Rows 2-125: Ch 1, turn; sc in first dc, dc in next sc, (sc in next dc, dc in next sc) across; do **not** finish off.

EDGING

Rnd 1: Ch 1, do **not** turn; sc in end of each row across; working in free loops of beginning ch, 3 sc in first ch, sc in next 20 chs, 3 sc in next ch; sc in end of each row across; working across sts on Row 125, 3 sc in first sc, sc in each st across to last dc, 3 sc in last dc; join with slip st to first sc, finish off: 302 sc.

Rnd 2: With **right** side facing, join Tan with sc in any sc; sc in each sc around working 3 sc in center sc of each corner 3-sc group; join with slip st to first sc, finish off: 310 sc.

BOTTOM PANEL

With Green, ch 79 **loosely**.

Row 1 (Right side): Sc in second ch from hook, dc in next ch, (sc in next ch, dc in next ch) across: 78 sts.
Note: Mark Row 1 as **right** side.

Rows 2-20: Ch 1, turn; sc in first dc, dc in next sc, (sc in next dc, dc in next sc) across; at end of Row 20, do **not** finish off.

EDGING

Rnd 1: Ch 1, turn; 3 sc in first dc, sc in each st across to last sc, 3 sc in last sc; sc in end of each row across; working in free loops of beginning ch, 3 sc in first ch, sc in next 76 chs, 3 sc in next ch; sc in end of each row across; join with slip st to first sc, finish off: 204 sc.

Rnd 2: With **right** side facing, join Tan with sc in any sc; sc in each sc around working 3 sc in center sc of each corner 3-sc group; join with slip st to first sc, finish off: 212 sc.

TOP PANEL

Work same as Bottom Panel.

CORNER PANEL (Make 4)

Note: Make 2 **each** of Dk Blue and Blue.

With color indicated, ch 23 **loosely**.
Row 1 (Right side)**:** Sc in second ch from hook, dc in next ch, (sc in next ch, dc in next ch) across: 22 sts.
Note: Mark Row 1 as **right** side.
Rows 2-20: Ch 1, turn; sc in first dc, dc in next sc, (sc in next dc, dc in next sc) across; at end of Row 20, do **not** finish off.

EDGING

Rnd 1: Ch 1, turn; 3 sc in first dc, sc in each st across to last sc, 3 sc in last sc; sc in end of each row across; working in free loops of beginning ch, 3 sc in first ch, sc in next 20 chs, 3 sc in next ch; sc in end of each row across; join with slip st to first sc, finish off: 92 sc.
Rnd 2: With **right** side facing, join Tan with sc in any sc; sc in each sc around working 3 sc in center sc of each corner 3-sc group; join with slip st to first sc, finish off: 100 sc.

ASSEMBLY

Using photo as a guide for placement, page 5, join Panels in the following order: Side Panels to Center Panel, Dk Blue Corner Panels to Top Panel, Blue Corner Panels to Bottom Panel, Top Panel section to Center Panel section, and Bottom Panel section to Center Panel section.

To join first two Panels, place Panels with **wrong** sides together. Working through **inside** loop of each stitch on **both** pieces, join Tan with slip st in center sc of first corner 3-sc group; (ch 1, slip st in next sc) across ending in center sc of next corner 3-sc group; finish off.

Join remaining Panels in same manner.

BORDER

With **right** side facing and working in Back Loops Only, join Tan with slip st in center sc of any corner 3-sc group; ch 1, (slip st in same st, ch 1) twice, (slip st in next sc, ch 1) around working (slip st, ch 1) 3 times in center sc of each corner 3-sc group; join with slip st to first slip st, finish off.

ADDITIONAL PIECES

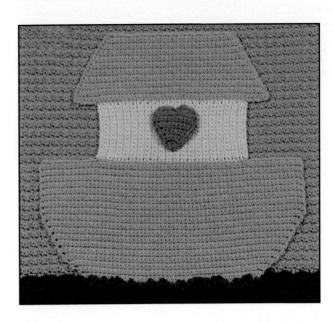

ARK
BOTTOM

With Brown, ch 41 **loosely**.
Row 1 (Right side)**:** Sc in back ridge of second ch from hook *(Fig. 1, page 125)* and each ch across: 40 sc.
Note: Mark Row 1 as **right** side.
Rows 2-8: Ch 1, turn; 2 sc in first sc, sc in each sc across to last sc, 2 sc in last sc: 54 sc.
Row 9: Ch 1, turn; sc in each sc across.
Row 10 (Increase row)**:** Ch 1, turn; 2 sc in first sc, sc in each sc across to last sc, 2 sc in last sc: 56 sc.
Rows 11-20: Repeat Rows 9 and 10, 5 times: 66 sc.
Rows 21-37: Ch 1, turn; sc in each sc across. Finish off.
Waves: With **right** side facing and working in free loops of beginning ch, join Dk Blue with slip st in first ch; ch 1, (sc, ch 3) twice in same st and in next 37 chs, **[**(sc, ch 3) twice, slip st**]** in next ch; finish off.

Continued on page 8.

ROOF

With Brown, ch 51 **loosely**.

Row 1: Sc in back ridge of second ch from hook and each ch across: 50 sc.

Row 2 (Right side): Ch 1, turn; sc in each sc across. *Note:* Mark Row 2 as **right** side.

Row 3 (Decrease row): Ch 1, turn; work beginning decrease, sc in each sc across to last 2 sc, decrease: 48 sc.

Row 4: Ch 1, turn; sc in each sc across.

Rows 5-20: Repeat Rows 3 and 4, 8 times: 32 sc. Finish off.

HOUSE

With Tan and leaving a 20" end for sewing, ch 16 **loosely**.

Row 1 (Wrong side): Sc in back ridge of second ch from hook and each ch across: 15 sc. *Note:* Mark **back** of any stitch on Row 1 as **right** side.

Rows 2-40: Ch 1, turn; sc in each sc across. Finish off, leaving a 20" end for sewing.

LARGE HEART

Row 1 (Right side): With Rose, ch 2, 3 sc in second ch from hook: 3 sc. *Note:* Mark Row 1 as **right** side.

Row 2: Ch 1, turn; 2 sc in first sc, sc in next sc, 2 sc in last sc: 5 sc.

Row 3: Ch 1, turn; sc in each sc across.

Row 4 (Increase row): Ch 1, turn; 2 sc in first sc, sc in each sc across to last sc, 2 sc in last sc: 7 sc.

Rows 5-9: Repeat Rows 3 and 4 twice, then repeat Row 3 once **more**; do **not** finish off: 11 sc.

FIRST SIDE

Row 1: Ch 1, turn; work beginning decrease, sc in next 3 sc, leave remaining 6 sc unworked: 4 sc.

Row 2: Ch 1, turn; sc in each sc across.

Row 3: Ch 1, turn; work beginning decrease, decrease; finish off: 2 sc.

SECOND SIDE

Row 1: With **wrong** side facing, skip next sc from First Side and join Rose with sc in next sc; sc in next 2 sc, decrease: 4 sc.

Row 2: Ch 1, turn; sc in each sc across.

Row 3: Ch 1, turn; work beginning decrease, decrease: 2 sc.

Edging: Ch 1, turn; sc evenly around entire Heart working 3 sc at bottom point; join with slip st to first sc, finish off leaving a long end for sewing.

NOAH
BODY

With Purple, ch 11 **loosely**.

Row 1: Sc in second ch from hook and in each ch across: 10 sc.

Row 2 (Right side): Ch 1, turn; sc in each sc across. *Note:* Mark Row 2 as **right** side.

Row 3 (Decrease row): Ch 1, turn; work beginning decrease, sc in each sc across to last 2 sc, decrease: 8 sc.

Rows 4-6: Ch 1, turn; sc in each sc across.

Rows 7-11: Repeat Rows 3-6 once, then repeat Row 3 once **more**: 4 sc.

Row 12: Ch 1, turn; sc in each sc across.

Edging: Ch 1, do **not** turn; sc evenly across end of rows; working in free loops of beginning ch, 3 sc in ch at base of first sc, sc in each ch across to last ch, 3 sc in last ch; sc evenly across end of rows; working across sts on Row 12, 3 sc in first sc, sc in last 3 sc, place marker around last sc made for Head placement, 2 sc in same st; join with slip st to first sc, finish off leaving a long end for sewing.

HEAD

Row 1: With **wrong** side of Body facing, join Tan with sc in marked sc; sc in next 3 sc, leave remaining sc unworked: 4 sc.

Row 2: Ch 1, turn; working in Back Loops Only, 2 sc in first sc, sc in next sc, place marker around sc just made for Mustache placement, sc in next sc, 2 sc in last sc: 6 sc.

Rows 3 and 4: Ch 1, turn; sc in both loops of each sc across.

Row 5: Ch 1, turn; work beginning decrease, sc in next 2 sc, decrease: 4 sc.

Row 6: Ch 1, turn; sc in each sc across; finish off.

Edging: With **right** side facing, join Tan with slip st in right end of Row 1; work 15 sc evenly spaced around Head, slip st in opposite end of Row 1; finish off leaving a long end for sewing: 17 sts.

HAIR

First Side: With **right** side facing, skip first 3 sts on Head Edging and join White with slip st in next sc; sc in same st and in next 2 sc, slip st in next sc, leave remaining 10 sts unworked; finish off.

Second Side: With **right** side facing, skip next 3 sc from First Side and join White with slip st in next sc; sc in next 2 sc, (sc, slip st) in next sc, leave remaining 3 sts unworked; finish off.

BEARD

Row 1: With **right** side facing, Head toward you, and working in free loops of sts on Row 1 on Head *(Fig. 3a, page 126)*, join White with sc in first sc; sc in last 3 sc: 4 sc.

Row 2: Ch 1, turn; work beginning decrease, decrease: 2 sc.

Row 3: Ch 1, turn; sc in next 2 sc.

Row 4: Ch 1, turn; work beginning decrease: one sc.

Row 5: Ch 1, turn; sc in next sc; finish off leaving a long end for sewing.
Sew bottom of Beard to Body.

Mustache: With **right** side facing and Body toward you, join White with slip st in right end of Row 1 on Beard; ch 2, slip st around post of marked sc on Head *(Fig. 4, page 126)*, ch 2, slip st in opposite end of Row 1 on Beard; finish off.

ARM (Make 2)

Row 1 (Right side)**:** With Purple, ch 2, sc in second ch from hook: one sc.
Note: Mark Row 1 as **right** side.

Rows 2-5: Ch 1, turn; sc in next sc.

Edging: Ch 1, do **not** turn; sc evenly around entire Arm; join with slip st to first sc, finish off leaving a long end for sewing.

Using photo as a guide for placement, page 8, sew Arms to Body.

HAND (Make 2)

With Tan, ch 2, (3 sc, slip st) in second ch from hook; finish off leaving a long end for sewing.

Using photo as a guide for placement, sew Hands to Arms.

MRS. NOAH

Work same as Noah through Row 1 of Head: 4 sc.

Row 2: Ch 1, turn; 2 sc in first sc, sc in next 2 sc, 2 sc in last sc: 6 sc.

Rows 3 and 4: Ch 1, turn; sc in each sc across.

Row 5: Ch 1, turn; work beginning decrease, sc in next 2 sc, decrease: 4 sc.

Row 6: Ch 1, turn; sc in each sc across; finish off.

Edging: With **right** side facing, join Tan with slip st in right end of Row 1; work 15 sc evenly spaced around Head, slip st in opposite end of Row 1; finish off leaving a long end for sewing: 17 sts.

HAIR

With **right** side facing, skip first slip st on Head Edging and join White with slip st in next sc; ch 3, sc in same st, ch 3, (sc, ch 3) twice in each sc around to last 2 sts, (sc, ch 3, slip st) in next sc, leave remaining slip st unworked; finish off.

ARMS AND HANDS

Work same as Noah.

SMALL HEART

Row 1 (Right side)**:** With Rose, ch 2, sc in second ch from hook: one sc.
Note: Mark Row 1 as **right** side.

Row 2: Ch 1, turn; 3 sc in next sc.

Row 3: Ch 1, turn; 2 sc in first sc, sc in next sc, 2 sc in last sc; do **not** finish off: 5 sc.

FIRST SIDE

Row 1: Ch 1, turn; work beginning decrease, leave remaining 3 sc unworked: one sc.

Row 2: Ch 1, turn; sc in next sc; finish off.

SECOND SIDE

Row 1: With **wrong** side facing, skip next sc from First Side and join Rose with slip st in next sc; ch 1, pull up a loop in same st and in last sc, YO and draw through all 3 loops on hook: one st.

Row 2: Ch 1, turn; sc in next st.

Edging: Ch 1, do **not** turn; sc evenly around entire Heart working 3 sc at bottom point; join with slip st to first sc, finish off leaving a long end for sewing.

With White and using photo as a guide, page 8, add straight stitches *(Fig. 10, page 127)* and French knots *(Fig. A)* to Small Heart to form the word "by".

Fig. A

Continued on page 10.

9

RIGHT DOVE
BODY
With White, ch 13 **loosely**, place marker in sixth ch from hook for Wing placement.

Row 1: Sc in back ridge of second ch from hook and each ch across: 12 sc.

Row 2 (Right side): Ch 2, turn; 2 sc in first sc, (sc, slip st) in next sc, skip next sc, 2 dc in next sc, 2 tr in each of next 2 sc, 2 dc in next sc, skip next 2 sc, sc in next 2 sc, 2 sc in last sc: 17 sts.

Note: Mark Row 2 as **right** side.

Row 3: Ch 2, turn; 2 dc in first sc, 2 tr in next sc, leave remaining 15 sts unworked; finish off.

FIRST WING
Row 1: With **right** side facing and working in free loops of beginning ch, join White with sc in marked ch; sc in next 2 chs, leave remaining 5 chs unworked: 3 sc.

Row 2: Ch 1, turn; sc in first 2 sc, 2 sc in last sc: 4 sc.

Row 3: Ch 1, turn; 2 sc in first sc, sc in last 3 sc: 5 sc.

Row 4: Ch 1, turn; work beginning decrease, sc in next 2 sc, 2 sc in last sc.

Row 5: Ch 1, turn; work beginning decrease, sc in next sc, decrease: 3 sc.

Row 6: Ch 1, turn; sc in first sc, decrease: 2 sc.

Row 7: Ch 1, turn; work beginning decrease: one sc.

Row 8: Ch 1, turn; sc in next sc; finish off.

SECOND WING
Row 1: With **right** side facing and working in free loops of beginning ch, join White with sc in next ch from First Wing; sc in next ch, leave remaining 3 chs unworked: 2 sc.

Row 2: Ch 1, turn; 2 sc in first sc, sc in last sc: 3 sc.

Row 3: Ch 1, turn; sc in first 2 sc, 2 sc in last sc: 4 sc.

Row 4: Ch 1, turn; 2 sc in first sc, sc in next sc, decrease.

Row 5: Ch 1, turn; work beginning decrease, decrease: 2 sc.

Row 6: Ch 1, turn; work beginning decrease: one sc.

Row 7: Ch 1, turn; sc in next sc; finish off.

LEFT DOVE
BODY
With White, ch 13 **loosely**, place marker in tenth ch from hook for Wing placement.

Row 1 (Right side): Sc in back ridge of second ch from hook and each ch across: 12 sc.

Note: Mark Row 1 as **right** side.

Row 2: Ch 2, turn; 2 sc in first sc, (sc, slip st) in next sc, skip next sc, 2 dc in next sc, 2 tr in each of next 2 sc, 2 dc in next sc, skip next 2 sc, sc in next 2 sc, 2 sc in last sc: 17 sts.

Row 3: Ch 2, turn; 2 dc in first sc, 2 tr in next sc, leave remaining 15 sts unworked; finish off.

FIRST WING
Row 1: With **right** side facing and working in free loops of beginning ch, join White with sc in marked ch; sc in next ch, leave remaining 8 chs unworked: 2 sc.

Row 2: Ch 1, turn; sc in first sc, 2 sc in last sc: 3 sc.

Row 3: Ch 1, turn; 2 sc in first sc, sc in last 2 sc: 4 sc.

Row 4: Ch 1, turn; work beginning decrease, sc in next sc, 2 sc in last sc.

Row 5: Ch 1, turn; work beginning decrease, decrease: 2 sc.

Row 6: Ch 1, turn; work beginning decrease: one sc.

Row 7: Ch 1, turn; sc in next sc; finish off.

SECOND WING
Row 1: With **right** side facing and working in free loops of beginning ch, join White with sc in next ch from First Wing; sc in next 2 chs, leave remaining chs unworked: 3 sc.

Row 2: Ch 1, turn; 2 sc in first sc, sc in last 2 sc: 4 sc.

Row 3: Ch 1, turn; sc in first 3 sc, 2 sc in last sc: 5 sc.

Row 4: Ch 1, turn; 2 sc in first sc, sc in next 2 sc, decrease.

Row 5: Ch 1, turn; work beginning decrease, sc in next sc, decrease: 3 sc.

Row 6: Ch 1, turn; work beginning decrease, sc in last sc: 2 sc.

Row 7: Ch 1, turn; work beginning decrease: one sc.

Row 8: Ch 1, turn; sc in next sc; finish off.

ELEPHANT (Make 2)
BODY
With Grey, ch 13 **loosely**.

Row 1 (Right side): Sc in second ch from hook and in next ch, 2 sc in each of next 2 chs, sc in each ch across: 14 sc.

Note: Mark Row 1 as **right** side.

Row 2: Ch 1, turn; 2 sc in first sc, sc in next 6 sc, slip st in next sc, leave remaining 6 sc unworked: 9 sts.

Row 3: Ch 1, turn; skip first slip st, slip st in next sc, sc in next 6 sc, 2 sc in last sc: 9 sts.

Row 4: Ch 1, turn; 2 sc in first sc, sc in next 5 sc, decrease, leave remaining slip st unworked: 8 sc.

Row 5: Ch 1, turn; sc in first sc, sc in Back Loop Only of each sc across to last sc, sc in **both** loops of last sc.

Row 6: Ch 1, turn; sc in both loops of each sc across.

Row 7: Ch 8 **loosely**, turn; sc in second ch from hook and in next 6 chs, sc in next 6 sc, decrease: 14 sc.

Row 8: Ch 1, turn; work beginning decrease, sc in each sc across: 13 sc.

Row 9: Ch 1, turn; sc in each sc across to last sc, 2 sc in last sc: 14 sc.

Row 10: Ch 1, turn; sc in first 11 sc, leave remaining 3 sc unworked.

Row 11: Ch 1, turn; sc in each sc across to last sc, 2 sc in last sc: 12 sc.

Row 12: Ch 1, turn; sc in each sc across.

Row 13: Ch 1, turn; sc in each sc across to last sc, 2 sc in last sc: 13 sc.

Rows 14-16: Ch 1, turn; sc in each sc across.

Row 17: Ch 4 **loosely**, turn; sc in second ch from hook and in next 2 chs, sc in each sc across: 16 sc.

Row 18: Ch 1, turn; work beginning decrease, sc in each sc across: 15 sc.

Row 19: Ch 1, turn; sc in each sc across to last 2 sc, decrease: 14 sc.

Row 20: Ch 1, turn; work beginning decrease, sc in next 6 sc, decrease, leave remaining 4 sc unworked: 8 sc.

Row 21: Ch 1, turn; work beginning decrease, sc in next 4 sc, decrease: 6 sc.

Row 22: Ch 1, turn; work beginning decrease, sc in next sc, slip st in last 3 sc, ch 3; finish off leaving a 1" end for tail.

Unravel tail and trim ends as desired.

EAR
Row 1: With **right** side facing, head toward you, and working in free loops of sc on Row 4, join Grey with sc in first sc; sc in same st and in next 5 sc: 7 sc.

Row 2: Ch 1, turn; 2 sc in first sc, sc in next 5 sc, 2 sc in last sc: 9 sc.

Row 3: Ch 1, turn; 2 sc in first sc, sc in each sc across: 10 sc.

Row 4: Ch 1, turn; work beginning decrease, sc in each sc across: 9 sc.

Row 5: Ch 1, turn; work beginning decrease, sc in next 5 sc, decrease: 7 sc.

Row 6: Ch 1, turn; work beginning decrease, sc in next 3 sc, decrease; finish off: 5 sc.

CAMEL (Make 2)
Row 1 (Right side): With Gold, ch 2, 2 sc in second ch from hook: 2 sc.

Note: Mark Row 1 as **right** side.

Row 2: Ch 1, turn; sc in next 2 sc.

Row 3: Ch 1, turn; 2 sc in first sc, leave remaining sc unworked; do **not** finish off: 2 sc.

Continued on page 12

Row 4: Ch 1, turn; 2 sc in first sc, sc in next sc: 3 sc.
Row 5: Ch 3, turn; slip st in third ch from hook (ear), 2 sc in first sc, sc in next 2 sc: 4 sc.
Row 6: Ch 8 **loosely**, turn; 2 sc in second ch from hook, sc in next 6 chs and in next 2 sc, decrease, leave ear unworked: 11 sc.
Row 7: Ch 1, turn; work beginning decrease, sc in each sc across to last sc, 2 sc in last sc: 11 sc.
Row 8: Ch 1, turn; 2 sc in first sc, sc in next 4 sc, slip st in last 6 sc: 12 sts.
Row 9: Turn; skip first slip st, working **around** slip sts on Row 8 and in sc on Row 7, slip st in next sc, sc in next 4 sc, sc in next 5 sc on Row 8, 2 sc in last sc: 12 sts.
Row 10: Ch 1, turn; 2 sc in first sc, sc in next 3 sc, decrease, leave remaining 6 sts unworked: 6 sc.
Row 11: Ch 1, turn; sc in each sc across.
Row 12: Ch 9 **loosely**, turn; sc in second ch from hook and in next 7 chs, sc in next 5 sc, 2 sc in last sc: 15 sc.
Row 13: Ch 1, turn; 2 sc in first sc, sc in each sc across: 16 sc.
Row 14: Ch 1, turn; sc in each sc across to last sc, 2 sc in last sc: 17 sc.
Row 15: Ch 1, turn; 2 sc in first sc, sc in next 6 sc, decrease, leave remaining 8 sc unworked: 9 sc.
Row 16: Ch 1, turn; work beginning decrease, sc in each sc across to last sc, 2 sc in last sc: 9 sc.
Row 17: Ch 1, turn; 2 sc in first sc, sc in each sc across: 10 sc.
Row 18: Ch 1, turn; sc in each sc across.
Row 19: Ch 1, turn; work beginning decrease, sc in each sc across: 9 sc.
Row 20: Ch 1, turn; 2 sc in first sc, sc in next 6 sc, decrease: 9 sc.
Row 21: Ch 1, turn; work beginning decrease, sc in each sc across to last sc, 2 sc in last sc: 9 sc.
Row 22: Ch 9 **loosely**, turn; sc in second ch from hook and in next 7 chs, sc in next 7 sc, decrease: 16 sc.
Row 23: Ch 1, turn; work beginning decrease, sc in each sc across: 15 sc.
Row 24: Ch 1, turn; sc in each sc across to last 2 sc, decrease: 14 sc.
Row 25: Ch 1, turn; work beginning decrease, sc in next 3 sc, decrease, leave remaining 7 sc unworked: 5 sc.
Row 26: Ch 1, turn; work beginning decrease, sc in next sc, decrease: 3 sc.
Row 27: Turn; slip st in first sc, ch 3, leave remaining 2 sc unworked; finish off leaving a 1" end for tail. Unravel tail and trim ends as desired.

SHEEP (Make 2)
BODY
With White, ch 11 **loosely**, place marker in third ch from hook for Leg placement.
Row 1: Tr in second ch from hook, sc in next ch, (tr in next ch, sc in next ch) across: 10 sts.
Row 2 (Right side)**:** Ch 1, turn; sc in each st across.
Note: Mark Row 2 as **right** side.
Row 3: Ch 1, turn; sc in first sc, (tr in next sc, sc in next sc) across to last sc, (tr, slip st) in last sc: 11 sts.
Row 4: Ch 1, turn; skip first slip st, sc in each st across: 10 sts.
Row 5: Ch 1, turn; tr in first sc, sc in next sc, (tr in next sc, sc in next sc) across.
Row 6: Ch 2, turn; 2 sc in second ch from hook (tail), sc in each st across Body, ch 3, 2 sc in second ch from hook (ear), fold ear down over Body, slip st in last sc made on Body (sc **before** ch-3); finish off.

FACE
Row 1: With **right** side facing and working in end of rows, join Brown with sc in Row 6 at ear; 2 sc in next row, leave remaining 4 rows unworked: 3 sc.
Row 2: Ch 1, turn; pull up a loop in next 3 sc, YO and draw through all 4 loops on hook: one st.
Row 3: Ch 1, turn; sc in next st; finish off.

FIRST LEG
Row 1: With **right** side facing and working in free loops of beginning ch, join Brown with sc in marked ch; sc in next ch, leave remaining 7 chs unworked: 2 sc.
Rows 2 and 3: Ch 1, turn; sc in each sc across. Finish off.

NEXT LEG
Row 1: With **right** side facing and working in free loops of beginning ch, skip next 4 chs from First Leg and join Brown with sc in next ch; sc in next ch, leave remaining ch unworked: 2 sc.
Rows 2 and 3: Ch 1, turn; sc in each sc across. Finish off.

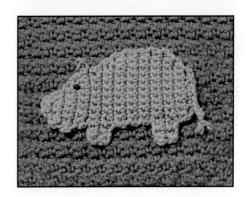

GIRAFFE (Make 2)

Row 1 (Right side): With Gold, ch 2, 3 sc in second ch from hook.

Note: Mark Row 1 as **right** side.

Row 2: Ch 1, turn; sc in first 2 sc, 2 sc in last sc: 4 sc.

Row 3: Ch 1, turn; sc in each sc across.

Row 4: Ch 1, turn; sc in each sc across to last sc, 2 sc in last sc: 5 sc.

Row 5: Ch 2, turn; sc in second ch from hook (ear) and in each sc across: 6 sc.

Row 6: Ch 25 **loosely**, turn; sc in second ch from hook and in each ch across, sc in next 3 sc, decrease, leave ear unworked: 28 sc.

Row 7: Ch 1, turn; work beginning decrease, sc in each sc across: 27 sc.

Row 8: Ch 1, turn; sc in first 16 sc, slip st in each sc across.

Row 9: Turn; working **around** slip sts on Row 8 and in sc on Row 7, slip st in first 2 sc, sc in next 9 sc, sc in next 8 sc on Row 8, leave remaining 8 sc unworked: 19 sts.

Row 10: Ch 1, turn; 2 sc in first sc, sc in next 5 sc, decrease, leave remaining 11 sts unworked: 8 sc.

Row 11: Ch 1, turn; work beginning decrease, sc in next 5 sc, 2 sc in last sc: 8 sc.

Row 12: Ch 1, turn; 2 sc in first sc, sc in next 5 sc, decrease: 8 sc.

Row 13: Ch 1, turn; work beginning decrease, sc in next 5 sc, 2 sc in last sc: 8 sc.

Row 14: Ch 7 **loosely**, turn; sc in second ch from hook and in next 5 chs, sc in next 6 sc, decrease: 13 sc.

Row 15: Ch 1, turn; work beginning decrease, sc in each sc across: 12 sc.

Row 16: Ch 1, turn; sc in each sc across to last 2 sc, decrease: 11 sc.

Row 17: Turn; slip st in first sc, ch 4, leave remaining 10 sc unworked; finish off leaving a 1" end for tail. Unravel tail and trim ends as desired.

HIPPO (Make 2)

With Grey and leaving a ½" end for tail, ch 9 **loosely**.

Row 1 (Right side): Sc in second ch from hook and in next 5 chs, leave remaining 2 chs unworked (tail): 6 sc.

Note: Mark Row 1 as **right** side.

Row 2: Ch 1, turn; 2 sc in first sc, sc in next 4 sc, 2 sc in last sc: 8 sc.

Row 3: Ch 1, turn; 2 sc in first sc, sc in each sc across: 9 sc.

Row 4: Ch 4 **loosely**, turn; sc in second ch from hook and in next 2 chs, sc in next 8 sc, 2 sc in last sc: 13 sc.

Rows 5 and 6: Ch 1, turn; sc in each sc across.

Row 7: Ch 1, turn; sc in first 10 sc, leave remaining 3 sc unworked.

Rows 8-12: Ch 1, turn; sc in each sc across.

Row 13: Ch 1, turn; work beginning decrease, sc in each sc across: 9 sc.

Row 14: Ch 4 **loosely**, turn; sc in second ch from hook and in next 2 chs, sc in next 7 sc, decrease: 11 sc.

Row 15: Ch 1, turn; sc in each sc across.

Row 16: Ch 1, turn; sc in each sc across to last 2 sc, decrease: 10 sc.

Row 17: Ch 3, turn; slip st in second ch from hook and in next ch (ear), sc in next 7 sc, leave remaining 3 sc unworked: 7 sc.

Row 18: Ch 1, turn; 2 sc in first sc, sc in next 6 sc, leave ear unworked: 8 sc.

Row 19: Ch 1, turn; work beginning decrease, sc in next 5 sc, 2 sc in last sc: 8 sc.

Row 20: Ch 1, turn; 2 sc in first sc, sc in each sc across: 9 sc.

Row 21: Ch 1, turn; work beginning decrease, sc in next 5 sc, decrease: 7 sc.

Row 22: Ch 1, turn; work beginning decrease, sc in each sc across: 6 sc.

Row 23: Ch 1, turn; work beginning decrease, sc in next 2 sc, decrease: 4 sc.

Row 24: Ch 1, turn; work beginning decrease, decrease; finish off: 2 sc.

Unravel tail and trim ends as desired.

Continued on page 14.

WORDS

LETTER "T" (Make 2)

Horizontal Line: With Rose, ch 10 **loosely**, (work Bobble, slip st) in second ch from hook, slip st in each ch across to last ch, (work Bobble, slip st) in last ch; finish off leaving a long end for sewing.

Vertical Line: With Rose, ch 20 **loosely**, (work Bobble, slip st) in second ch from hook, slip st in each ch across to last ch, (work Bobble, slip st) in last ch; finish off leaving a long end for sewing.

LETTER "W" (Make 2)

With Rose, ch 36 **loosely**, (work Bobble, slip st) in second ch from hook, ★ slip st in next 16 chs, (work Bobble, slip st) in next ch; repeat from ★ once **more**, finish off leaving a long end for sewing.

LETTER "O" (Make 2)

With Rose, ch 23 **loosely**, (work Bobble, slip st) in second ch from hook, slip st in each ch across; join with slip st to top of first Bobble, finish off leaving a long end for sewing.

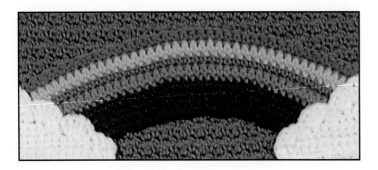

RAINBOW

COLOR SEQUENCE

Work 2 rows of **each** color: Purple, Dk Blue, Blue, Green, Gold, Rose.

With Purple, ch 30 **loosely**.

Row 1 (Right side)**:** Working in back ridges of beginning ch, sc in second ch from hook and in next 3 chs, (2 sc in next ch, sc in next 4 chs) across: 34 sc.

Note: Mark Row 1 as **right** side.

Row 2: Ch 1, turn; 2 sc in first sc, sc in each sc across to last sc, 2 sc in last sc changing to next color in last sc: 36 sc.

Row 3: Ch 1, turn; 2 sc in first sc, sc in each sc across to last sc, 2 sc in last sc: 38 sc.

Rows 4-11: Repeat Rows 2 and 3, 4 times: 54 sc.

Row 12: Ch 1, turn; 2 sc in first sc, sc in each sc across to last sc, 2 sc in last sc; finish off leaving a long end for sewing.

CLOUD (Make 2)

With White, ch 28 **loosely**.

Row 1: Sc in second ch from hook and in each ch across: 27 sc.

Row 2 (Right side)**:** Ch 1, turn; work beginning decrease, sc in each sc across to last 2 sc, decrease: 25 sc.

Note: Mark Row 2 as **right** side.

Rows 3-7: Ch 1, turn; skip first sc, decrease, sc in each sc across to last 3 sc, decrease, leave remaining sc unworked: 5 sc.

Row 8: Ch 1, turn; 2 sc in first sc, sc in next 3 sc, 2 sc in last sc: 7 sc.

Row 9: Ch 1, turn; work beginning decrease, sc in next 3 sc, decrease: 5 sc.

Row 10: Ch 1, turn; work beginning decrease, sc in next sc, decrease: 3 sc.

Edging: Ch 1, do **not** turn; working in end of rows, skip first row, sc in next 2 rows, (5 dc in next row, skip next row, sc in next row) twice, 3 dc in last row; working in free loops of beginning ch, 3 sc in ch at base of first sc, sc in each ch across to last ch, 3 sc in last ch; working in end of rows, 3 dc in first row, (sc in next row, skip next row, 5 dc in next row) twice, sc in next 2 rows, skip last row; working across sts on Row 10, sc in first sc, 3 dc in next sc, sc in last sc; join with slip st to first sc, finish off leaving a long end for sewing.

STAR (Make 4)
CENTER
Rnd 1 (Right side): With Gold, ch 2, 5 sc in second ch from hook; join with slip st to first sc.

Note: Mark Rnd 1 as **right** side.

Rnd 2: Ch 1, 2 sc in same st and in each sc around; join with slip st to first sc: 10 sc.

Rnd 3: Ch 1, sc in same st, 2 sc in next sc, (sc in next sc, 2 sc in next sc) around; join with slip st to first sc: 15 sc.

Rnd 4: Ch 1, 2 sc in same st and in each sc around; join with slip st to first sc, do **not** finish off: 30 sc.

FIRST POINT
Row 1: Ch 1, sc in same st and in next 5 sc, leave remaining 24 sc unworked: 6 sc.

Row 2: Ch 1, **turn**; work beginning decrease, sc in next 2 sc, decrease: 4 sc.

Row 3: Ch 1, turn; sc in each sc across.

Row 4: Ch 1, turn; work beginning decrease, decrease: 2 sc.

Row 5: Ch 1, turn; sc in each sc across.

Row 6: Ch 1, turn; work beginning decrease: one sc.

Row 7: Ch 1, turn; sc in next sc; finish off.

NEXT THREE POINTS
Row 1: With **right** side facing, join Gold with sc in next sc on Rnd 4 of Center from last Point made; sc in next 5 sc, leave remaining sc unworked: 6 sc.

Rows 2-7: Work same as First Point.

LAST POINT
Row 1: With **right** side facing, join Gold with sc in next sc on Rnd 4 of Center from last Point made; sc in last 5 sc: 6 sc.

Rows 2-7: Work same as First Point; at end of Row 7, do **not** finish off.

EDGING
Ch 1, do **not** turn; sc evenly around entire Star working 3 sc in end of each Point; join with slip st to first sc, finish off.

FINISHING
Use safety pins to hold crocheted pieces in place while sewing to Afghan Body.

Center and sew Rainbow and Clouds to Top Panel.

Using photos, pages 5-15, as a guide:

Sew eyes on animals and people.
For each spot on Giraffes, thread ends of a 5" length of Gold up from back of Giraffe through holes in button and knot ends to secure. Unravel ends and trim as desired.
Sew buttons to Stars in same manner as Giraffe spots.
Sew Ark pieces together attaching House to Bottom and Roof.
Sew Large Heart to House.
Sew Ark to Center Panel.
Sew Doves to Center Panel, lapping First Wing over Second Wing on Right Dove and lapping Second Wing over First Wing on Left Dove.
Sew Noah, Mrs. Noah, Small Heart, and Words to Bottom Panel.
Sew Elephants, Camels, Sheep, Giraffes, and Hippos to Side Panels.
Sew one Star to each Corner Panel.

second prize

Sarah Anne Phillips

While making curly crocheted toys, Sarah Anne Phillips was inspired to create "something pretty." She developed the eye-catching pattern of this winning blanket in honor of her newest grandchild, Alyssa Anne. A resident of Texas, Sarah has designed numerous toys and decor items, with afghans being her favorite.

BLUE & WHITE CHECKERBOARD

Finished Size: 53" x 65½"

MATERIALS
Worsted Weight Yarn:
  Ecru - 32 ounces, (910 grams, 1,810 yards)
  Blue - 32 ounces, (910 grams, 1,810 yards)
Crochet hook, size H (5.00 mm) **or** size needed for gauge
Safety pin

GAUGE: In pattern, 13 sts = 4"; 10 rows = 3¾"

Gauge Swatch: 4" square
Ch 14 **loosely**.
Row 1: Sc in second ch from hook and in each ch across: 13 sc.
Row 2: Ch 3 **(counts as first dc)**, turn; dc in next sc and in each sc across.
Row 3: Ch 1, turn; sc in each dc across.
Rows 4-11: Repeat Rows 2 and 3, 4 times.
Finish off.

Note: Each row is worked across length of Afghan.

STITCH GUIDE

> **FRONT POST TREBLE CROCHET**
> **(abbreviated FPtr)**
> YO twice, insert hook from **front** to **back** around post of st indicated **(Fig. 4, page 126)**, YO and pull up a loop (4 loops on hook), (YO and draw through 2 loops on hook) 3 times. Skip dc behind FPtr.

AFGHAN
With Ecru, ch 210 **loosely**.
Row 1 (Right side)**:** Sc in second ch from hook and in each ch across: 209 sc.
Note: Loop a short piece of yarn around any stitch to mark Row 1 as **right** side.
Row 2: Ch 3 **(counts as first dc, now and throughout)**, turn; dc in next sc and in each sc across; drop Ecru.

Note: Place dropped loop from hook onto safety pin to keep piece from unraveling as you work the next row. Hold safety pin and dropped yarn to **right** side, **now and throughout**.

Row 3: With **right** side facing, join Blue with sc in first dc **(see Joining With Sc, page 125)**; ★ work FPtr around sc one row **below** next dc, (sc in next dc, work FPtr around sc one row **below** next dc) 3 times, sc in next 9 dc; repeat from ★ across.
Row 4: Ch 3, turn; dc in next sc and in each st across; drop Blue.
Row 5: With **right** side facing, pick up Ecru; ch 4, working **behind** dropped loop, sc in first dc, ★ work FPtr around st one row **below** next dc, (sc in next dc, work FPtr around st one row **below** next dc) 3 times, sc in next 9 dc; repeat from ★ across.
Row 6: Ch 3, turn; dc in next sc and in each st across; drop Ecru.
Row 7: Repeat Row 5 picking up Blue.
Row 8: Ch 3, turn; dc in next st and in each st across; drop Blue.
Row 9: With **right** side facing, pick up Ecru; ch 4, working **behind** dropped loop, sc in first 9 dc,

★ work FPtr around st one row **below** next dc, (sc in next dc, work FPtr around st one row **below** next dc) 3 times, sc in next 9 dc; repeat from ★ across to last 8 dc, (work FPtr around st one row **below** next dc, sc in next dc) 4 times.

Row 10: Ch 3, turn; dc in next FPtr and in each st across; drop Ecru.

Row 11: Repeat Row 9 picking up Blue.
Rows 12-14: Repeat Rows 8-10.
Row 15: Repeat Row 5 picking up Blue.
Row 16: Ch 3, turn; dc in next sc and in each st across; do **not** finish off, drop Blue.

Continued on page 18.

Rows 17-140: Repeat Rows 5-16, 10 times; then repeat Rows 5-8 once **more**.

Trim: With **right** side facing, pick up Ecru; ch 4, working **behind** dropped loop, **now and throughout**, sc in first dc, drop Ecru, pick up Blue, ch 4, (skip next dc, sc in next dc, drop Blue, pick up Ecru, ch 4, skip next dc, sc in next dc, drop Ecru, pick up Blue, ch 4) across; working in end of rows, sc in same st as last sc, slip st in same row and in next sc row, drop Blue, pick up Ecru, ch 4, sc in top of next dc row, slip st in same row and in next sc row, drop Ecru, pick up Blue, ch 4,

★ sc in top of next dc row, slip st in same row and in next sc row, drop Blue, pick up Ecru, ch 4, sc in top of next dc row, slip st in same row and in next sc row, drop Ecru, pick up Blue, ch 4; repeat from ★ across; working in free loops of beginning ch *(Fig. 3b, page 126)*, sc in first ch, drop Blue, pick up Ecru, ch 4, † skip next ch, sc in next ch, drop Ecru, pick up Blue, ch 4, skip next ch, sc in next ch, drop Blue, pick up Ecru, ch 4 †, repeat from † to † across; working in end rows, slip st in first row, cut Ecru, pick up Blue, ch 4, skip next dc row, working **behind** next ch-4, slip st in next sc row; finish off.

third prize

Julene S. Watson

A fascination with plaid and a friend's challenge to "translate" Log Cabin quilt squares into crochet inspired Julene S. Watson to create this stunning winner. A resident of California, Julene proudly tells how she was taught the "womanly arts" of crochet and quilting at the age of 9 by her paternal grandmother, a descendant of Wyoming pioneer farmers.

WINDOWS OF HEAVEN

Finished Size: 43" x 64"

MATERIALS
Worsted Weight Yarn:
Navy - 20 ounces, (570 grams, 1,130 yards)
Dk Blue - 10 ounces, (280 grams, 565 yards)
Blue - 8½ ounces, (240 grams, 480 yards)
Periwinkle - 6 ounces, (170 grams, 340 yards)
Pale Blue - 4½ ounces, (130 grams, 255 yards)
Lt Blue - 4 ounces, (110 grams, 225 yards)
White - 3½ ounces, (100 grams, 200 yards)
Crochet hook, size H (5.00 mm) **or** size needed for gauge
Yarn needle

GAUGE: Each Square = 5¼"

Gauge Swatch: 1¼" square
Work same as Square through Rnd 2.

SQUARE (Make 96)
Rnd 1 (Right side)**:** With White, ch 2 **loosely**, 8 sc in second ch from hook; join with slip st to first sc.
Note: Loop a short piece of yarn around any stitch to mark Rnd 1 as **right** side.
Rnd 2: Ch 3, sc in same st, ch 1, skip next sc, ★ (sc, ch 2, sc) in next sc, ch 1, skip next sc; repeat from ★ 2 times **more**; join with slip st in first ch-3 sp: 7 sc and 8 sps.

Note: Begin working in rows.

Row 1: Ch 2, sc in same sp, ch 1, sc in next ch-1 sp, ch 1, (sc, ch 2, sc) in next ch-2 sp, (ch 1, sc in next sp) twice changing to Lt Blue in last sc *(Fig. 5, page 126)*, leave remaining sps unworked: 6 sc and 6 sps.

Rows 2-4: Ch 2, turn; (sc in next ch-1 sp, ch 1) across to next ch-2 sp, (sc, ch 2, sc) in ch-2 sp, (ch 1, sc in next sp) across, changing to Pale Blue in last sc on Row 4: 9 sps.

Rows 5-7: Ch 2, turn; (sc in next ch-1 sp, ch 1) across to next ch-2 sp, (sc, ch 2, sc) in ch-2 sp, (ch 1, sc in next sp) across, changing to Periwinkle in last sc on Row 7; do **not** finish off: 12 sps.

Continued on page 20.

Rows 8-10: Ch 2, turn; (sc in next ch-1 sp, ch 1) across to next ch-2 sp, (sc, ch 2, sc) in ch-2 sp, (ch 1, sc in next sp) across, changing to Blue in last sc on Row 10: 15 sps.

Rows 11-13: Ch 2, turn; (sc in next ch-1 sp, ch 1) across to next ch-2 sp, (sc, ch 2, sc) in ch-2 sp, (ch 1, sc in next sp) across, changing to Dk Blue in last sc on Row 13: 18 sps.

Rows 14-16: Ch 2, turn; (sc in next ch-1 sp, ch 1) across to next ch-2 sp, (sc, ch 2, sc) in ch-2 sp, (ch 1, sc in next sp) across, changing to Navy in last sc on Row 16: 21 sps.

Note: Begin working in rnds.

Rnd 1: Ch 2, turn; (sc in next ch-1 sp, ch 1) 10 times, (sc, ch 2, sc) in next ch-2 sp, ch 1, (sc in next ch-1 sp, ch 1) 9 times, (sc, ch 2, sc) in next ch-2 sp, ch 1; working in end of rows and in sps on Rnd 2, skip next row, (sc in next row, ch 1, skip next row) 7 times, (sc in next sp, ch 1) twice, (sc, ch 2, sc) in next ch-2 sp, ch 1, sc in next sp, ch 1, skip next slip st, (sc in next row, ch 1, skip next row) 8 times; join with slip st in first ch-2 sp: 44 sps.

Rnd 2: Ch 1, do **not** turn; (sc, ch 2, sc) in same sp, ch 1, (sc in next ch-1 sp, ch 1) 10 times, ★ (sc, ch 2, sc) in next corner ch-2 sp, ch 1, (sc in next ch-1 sp, ch 1) 10 times; repeat from ★ 2 times **more**; join with slip st to first sc, finish off: 48 sps.

ASSEMBLY

With Navy, using photo as guide for placement, page 19, and working through **inside** loops, whipstitch Squares together forming 8 vertical strips of 12 Squares each *(Fig. 6b, page 126)*, beginning in second ch of first corner ch-2 and ending in first ch of next corner ch-2; then whipstitch Strips together in same manner.

EDGING

Rnd 1: With **right** side facing, join Navy with sc in upper right corner ch-2 sp *(see Joining With Sc, page 125)*; ch 2, sc in same sp, ch 1, ★ (sc in next sp, ch 1) across to next corner ch-2 sp, (sc, ch 2, sc) in corner ch-2 sp, ch 1; repeat from ★ 2 times **more**, (sc in next sp, ch 1) across; join with slip st to first sc: 520 sps.

Rnd 2: Slip st in next corner ch-2 sp, ch 1, (sc, ch 2, sc) in same sp, ch 1, ★ (sc in next ch-1 sp, ch 1) across to next corner ch-2 sp, (sc, ch 2, sc) in corner ch-2 sp, ch 1; repeat from ★ 2 times **more**, (sc in next ch-1 sp, ch 1) across; join with slip st to first sc, finish off.

REVERSIBLE

Working with a size P hook, Ruthie Marks experimented until she found just the right light and airy stitch for this dramatic yet surprisingly simple afghan.

Finished Size: 45½" x 60"

MATERIALS
Worsted Weight Yarn:
    Black - 25½ ounces, (720 grams, 1,440 yards)
    Variegated - 21 ounces, (600 grams, 1,220 yards)
Crochet hook, size P (10.00 mm) **or** size needed for gauge
Yarn needle

GAUGE: In pattern, 7 exsc = 4"; 7 rows = 4¼"

Gauge Swatch: 4"w x 4¼"h
Ch 8 **loosely**.
Work same as Afghan Body for 7 rows.
Finish off.

STITCH GUIDE

EXTENDED SINGLE CROCHET
(abbreviated exsc)
Insert hook in st indicated, YO and pull up a loop, YO and draw through one loop on hook, YO and draw through both loops on hook.

AFGHAN BODY
FRONT
With Variegated, ch 76 **loosely**.

Row 1: Work exsc in second ch from hook and in each ch across: 75 exsc.

Row 2 (Right side)**:** Ch 1, turn; work exsc in each exsc across.

Note: Loop a short piece of yarn around any stitch to mark Row 2 as **right** side and bottom edge.

Rows 3-95: Ch 1, turn; work exsc in each exsc across.
Finish off.

BACK

With Black, work same as Front; at end of Row 95, do **not** finish off.

EDGING

Rnd 1: Ch 1, turn; holding **wrong** sides of Front and Back together, Front facing, bottom edges at same end, and working through **both** thicknesses, 2 sc in first st, sc evenly spaced around working 3 sc in each corner, sc in same st as first sc; join with slip st to first sc.

Rnds 2 and 3: Ch 2, turn; hdc in same st, ★ hdc in each st across to center st of next corner 3-st group, 3 hdc in center st; repeat from ★ 2 times **more**, hdc in each st across and in same st as beginning ch-2; join with slip st to top of beginning ch-2.
Finish off.

CHECKERBOARD

Designed by Carol Alexander and Brenda Stratton, this neutral floral throw has the perfect mix of elegance and sophistication!

Finished Size: 47" x 62½"

MATERIALS

Worsted Weight Yarn:
  Ecru - 25 ounces, (710 grams, 1,415 yards)
  Brown - 25 ounces, (710 grams, 1,415 yards)
Crochet hook, size H (5.00 mm) **or** size needed
  for gauge
Yarn needle

GAUGE: Each Square = 8¾"

Gauge Swatch: 3" diameter
Work same as Square A or B through Rnd 2.

STITCH GUIDE

TREBLE CROCHET *(abbreviated tr)*
YO twice, insert hook in st or sp indicated, YO and pull up a loop (4 loops on hook), (YO and draw through 2 loops on hook) 3 times.

CLUSTER *(uses one st)*
★ YO twice, insert hook in st indicated, YO and pull up a loop, (YO and draw through 2 loops on hook) twice; repeat from ★ once **more**, YO and draw through all 3 loops on hook.

LONG DOUBLE CROCHET
  (abbreviated LDC)
YO, insert hook in st indicated, YO and pull up a loop even with loop on hook, (YO and draw through 2 loops on hook) twice.

SQUARE

Referring to the table below, make the number of Squares specified in the colors indicated.

	Square A Make 18	Square B Make 17
Rnds 1-3	Ecru	Brown
Rnds 4 & 5	Brown	Ecru
Rnds 6 & 7	Ecru	Brown
Rnd 8	Brown	Ecru
Rnd 9	Ecru	Brown

Rnd 1 (Right side)**:** With color indicated, ch 2 **loosely**, 16 sc in second ch from hook; join with slip st to first sc.
Note: Loop a short piece of yarn around any stitch to mark Rnd 1 as **right** side.
Rnd 2: [(Ch 3, work Cluster, ch 4, slip st) in same st **(first Petal made)]**, slip st in next sc, ★ [(slip st, ch 3, work Cluster, ch 4, slip st) in next sc **(Petal made)]**, slip st in next sc; repeat from ★ around; join with slip st in slip st at base of beginning ch-3: 8 Petals.
Rnd 3: Working in Back Loops Only *(Fig. 2, page 125)*, slip st in next 3 chs and in top of next Cluster, ch 3, (slip st in top of next Petal, ch 3) around; join with slip st to **both** loops of slip st at top of first Petal, finish off: 8 ch-3 sps.
Rnd 4: With **right** side facing, join next color with sc in both loops of slip st at top of any Petal *(see Joining With Sc, page 125)*; 2 hdc in next ch-3 sp, working **around** same ch-3, work LDC in Back Loop Only of slip st **between** Petals on Rnd 2, 2 hdc in same ch-3 sp on Rnd 3, ★ sc in **both** loops of next slip st, 2 hdc in next ch-3 sp, working **around** same ch-3, work LDC in Back Loop Only of slip st **between** Petals on Rnd 2, 2 hdc in same ch-3 sp on Rnd 3; repeat from ★ around; join with slip st to first sc: 48 sts.
Rnd 5: Dc in next 2 hdc, 2 tr in next LDC, dc in next 2 hdc, ★ slip st in next sc, dc in next 2 hdc, 2 tr in next LDC, dc in next 2 hdc; repeat from ★ around; join with slip st in same st as joining slip st, finish off: 56 sts.
Rnd 6: Working in Back Loops Only, join next color with sc in second tr of any 2-tr group; ★ † hdc in next 2 dc, dc in next slip st, hdc in next 2 dc, sc in next tr †, 2 sc in next tr; repeat from ★ 6 times **more**, then repeat from † to † once, sc in same st as first sc; join with slip st to **both** loops of first sc: 64 sts.
Rnd 7: Ch 1, working in both loops, sc in same st and in next 8 sts, ★ † hdc in next hdc, dc in next hdc, tr in next dc, (2 tr, ch 2, 2 tr) in next hdc, tr in next hdc, dc in next sc, hdc in next sc †, sc in next 9 sts; repeat from ★ 2 times **more**, then repeat from † to † once; join with slip st to first sc, finish off: 76 sts and 4 ch-2 sps.
Rnd 8: With **right** side facing, join next color with slip st in any corner ch-2 sp; ch 3 **(counts as first dc, now and throughout)**, (3 dc, ch 2, 4 dc) in same sp, ★ † skip next 4 sts, [(2 dc, ch 2, 2 dc) in next st, skip next 4 sts] 3 times †, (4 dc, ch 2, 4 dc) in next corner ch-2 sp; repeat from ★ 2 times **more**, then repeat from † to † once; join with slip st to first dc, finish off: 80 dc and 16 ch-2 sps.

Continued on page 24.

Rnd 9: With **right** side facing and working in Back Loops Only, join next color with slip st in second ch of any corner ch-2; ch 3, (dc, ch 3, 2 dc) in same st, ★ † dc in next 4 dc, tr in sp **before** next dc, skip next dc, [dc in next dc, hdc in next 2 chs, dc in next dc, skip next dc, tr in sp **before** next dc, skip next dc] 3 times, dc in next 3 dc and in next ch †, (2 dc, ch 3, 2 dc) in next ch; repeat from ★ 2 times **more**, then repeat from † to † once; join with slip st to first dc, finish off: 112 sts and 4 ch-3 sps.

ASSEMBLY

With Ecru, using photo as a guide for placement, page 23, and working through **inside** loops, whipstitch Squares together forming 5 vertical strips of 7 Squares each *(Fig. 6b, page 126)*, beginning in center ch of first corner ch-3 and ending in center ch of next corner ch-3; then whipstitch strips together in same manner.

EDGING

Rnd 1: With **right** side facing and working in Back Loops Only, join Brown with slip st in center ch of any corner ch-3; ch 2 **(counts as first hdc, now and throughout)**, (hdc, ch 2, 2 hdc) in same st, ★ hdc in each st and each joining across to center ch of next corner ch-3, (2 hdc, ch 2, 2 hdc) in center ch; repeat from ★ 2 times **more**, hdc in each st and each joining across; join with slip st to first hdc, finish off.

Rnd 2: With **right** side facing and working in Back Loops Only, join Ecru with slip st in first ch of any corner ch-2; ch 2, hdc in same ch, ch 2, 2 hdc in next ch, ★ hdc in each hdc across to next corner ch-2, 2 hdc in next ch, ch 2, 2 hdc in next ch; repeat from ★ 2 times **more**, hdc in each hdc across; join with slip st to first hdc, finish off.

Rnd 3: With Brown, repeat Rnd 2.

TWO-WAY HEARTS

Shell and popcorn stitches make a lovely twosome in this dainty crochet wrap designed by Mary R. Lewis in honor of Red Heart® Yarns' 60th anniversary.

Finished Size: 52½" x 54"

MATERIALS

Worsted Weight Yarn:
43 ounces, (1,220 grams, 2,430 yards)
Crochet hook, size I (5.50 mm) **or** size needed for gauge

GAUGE: In pattern, 12 dc = 4"; 10 rows = 4¼"

Gauge Swatch: 4"w x 4¼"h
Ch 13 **loosely**.
Row 1: Sc in second ch from hook and in each ch across: 12 sc.
Row 2: Ch 3 **(counts as first dc)**, turn; dc in next sc and in each sc across.
Row 3: Ch 1, turn; sc in each dc across.
Rows 4-10: Repeat Rows 2 and 3, 3 times; then repeat Row 2 once **more**.
Finish off.

STITCH GUIDE

POPCORN
4 Dc in next sc, drop loop from hook, insert hook in first dc of 4-dc group, hook dropped loop and draw through, ch 1 to close.
SHELL
(2 Dc, ch 1, 2 dc) in next sc.

AFGHAN

Ch 159 **loosely**.
Row 1 (Right side): Dc in fourth ch from hook **(3 skipped chs count as first dc)** and in each ch across: 157 dc.
Note: Loop a short piece of yarn around any stitch to mark Row 1 as **right** side.
Row 2: Ch 1, turn; sc in each dc across.
Row 3: Ch 3 **(counts as first dc, now and throughout)**, turn; dc in next sc and in each sc across.
Rows 4-6: Repeat Rows 2 and 3 once, then repeat Row 2 once **more**.
Row 7: Ch 3, turn; dc in next sc, ch 1, ★ skip next sc, dc in next 18 sc, work Popcorn, dc in next 18 sc, ch 1; repeat from ★ across to last 3 sc, skip next sc, dc in last 2 sc; do **not** finish off: 4 Popcorns, 148 dc, and 5 ch-1 sps.

Continued on page 26.

Row 8: Ch 1, turn; sc in each st and in each ch-1 sp across: 157 sc.

Row 9: Ch 3, turn; (dc in next sc, ch 1, skip next sc) twice, dc in next 14 sc, work Popcorn, dc in next 3 sc, work Popcorn, ★ dc in next 15 sc, ch 1, skip next sc, dc in next sc, ch 1, skip next sc, dc in next 15 sc, work Popcorn, dc in next 3 sc, work Popcorn; repeat from ★ 2 times **more**, dc in next 14 sc, ch 1, skip next sc, dc in next sc, ch 1, skip next sc, dc in last 2 sc: 8 Popcorns, 139 dc, and 10 ch-1 sps.

Row 10: Ch 1, turn; sc in each st and in each ch-1 sp across: 157 sc.

Row 11: Ch 3, turn; dc in next sc, ch 1, ★ skip next sc, dc in next 14 sc, work Popcorn, dc in next 7 sc, work Popcorn, dc in next 14 sc, ch 1; repeat from ★ across to last 3 sc, skip next sc, dc in last 2 sc: 8 Popcorns, 144 dc, and 5 ch-1 sps.

Row 12: Ch 1, turn; sc in each st and in each ch-1 sp across: 157 sc.

Row 13: Ch 3, turn; dc in next sc, ch 1, ★ skip next sc, dc in next 12 sc, work Popcorn, dc in next 11 sc, work Popcorn, dc in next 12 sc, ch 1; repeat from ★ across to last 3 sc, skip next sc, dc in last 2 sc: 8 Popcorns, 144 dc, and 5 ch-1 sps.

Row 14: Ch 1, turn; sc in each st and in each ch-1 sp across: 157 sc.

Row 15: Ch 3, turn; dc in next sc, ch 1, ★ skip next sc, dc in next 10 sc, work Popcorn, dc in next 15 sc, work Popcorn, dc in next 10 sc, ch 1; repeat from ★ across to last 3 sc, skip next sc, dc in last 2 sc: 8 Popcorns, 144 dc, and 5 ch-1 sps.

Row 16: Ch 1, turn; sc in each st and in each ch-1 sp across: 157 sc.

Row 17: Ch 3, turn; dc in next sc, ch 1, ★ skip next sc, dc in next 8 sc, work Popcorn, dc in next 19 sc, work Popcorn, dc in next 8 sc, ch 1; repeat from ★ across to last 3 sc, skip next sc, dc in last 2 sc: 8 Popcorns, 144 dc, and 5 ch-1 sps.

Row 18: Ch 1, turn; sc in each st and in each ch-1 sp across: 157 sc.

Row 19: Ch 3, turn; dc in next sc, ch 1, ★ skip next sc, dc in next 6 sc, work Popcorn, (dc in next 11 sc, work Popcorn) twice, dc in next 6 sc, ch 1; repeat from ★ across to last 3 sc, skip next sc, dc in last 2 sc: 12 Popcorns, 140 dc, and 5 ch-1 sps.

Row 20: Ch 1, turn; sc in each st and in each ch-1 sp across: 157 sc.

Row 21: Ch 3, turn; (dc in next sc, ch 1, skip next sc) twice, dc in next 4 sc, work Popcorn, dc in next 9 sc, work Popcorn, dc in next 3 sc, work Popcorn, dc in next 9 sc, work Popcorn, ★ dc in next 5 sc, ch 1, skip next sc, dc in next sc, ch 1, skip next sc, dc in next 5 sc, work Popcorn, dc in next 9 sc, work Popcorn, dc in next 3 sc, work Popcorn, dc in next 9 sc, work Popcorn; repeat from ★ 2 times **more**, dc in next 4 sc, ch 1, skip next sc, dc in next sc, ch 1, skip next sc, dc in last 2 sc: 16 Popcorns, 131 dc, and 10 ch-1 sps.

Row 22: Ch 1, turn; sc in each st and in each ch-1 sp across: 157 sc.

Row 23: Ch 3, turn; dc in next sc, ch 1, ★ skip next sc, dc in next 8 sc, work Popcorn, dc in next 5 sc, work Popcorn, dc in next 7 sc, work Popcorn, dc in next 5 sc, work Popcorn, dc in next 8 sc, ch 1; repeat from ★ across to last 3 sc, skip next sc, dc in last 2 sc: 16 Popcorns, 136 dc, and 5 ch-1 sps.

Row 24: Ch 1, turn; sc in each st and in each ch-1 sp across: 157 sc.

Row 25: Ch 3, turn; dc in next sc and in each sc across.

Row 26: Ch 1, turn; sc in each dc across.

Row 27: Ch 3, turn; dc in next 8 sc, skip next 2 sc, work Shell, (skip next 2 sc, dc in next 5 sc, skip next 2 sc, work Shell) twice, ★ skip next 2 sc, dc in next 13 sc, skip next 2 sc, work Shell, (skip next 2 sc, dc in next 5 sc, skip next 2 sc, work Shell) twice; repeat from ★ 2 times **more**, skip next 2 sc, dc in last 9 sc: 145 dc and 12 ch-1 sps.

Rows 28-30: Repeat Rows 24-26.

Row 31: Ch 3, turn; dc in next sc, ch 1, † skip next sc, dc in next 6 sc, skip next 2 sc, work Shell, ★ skip next 2 sc, dc in next 5 sc, skip next 2 sc, work Shell; repeat from ★ once **more**, skip next 2 sc, dc in next 6 sc, ch 1 †, (skip next sc, dc in next 18 sc, ch 1) 4 times, repeat from † to † once, skip next sc, dc in last 2 sc: 144 dc and 13 ch-1 sps.

Row 32: Ch 1, turn; sc in each dc and in each ch-1 sp across: 157 sc.

Row 33: Ch 3, turn; (dc in next sc, ch 1, skip next sc) twice, dc in next 4 sc, (skip next 2 sc, work Shell, skip next 2 sc, dc in next 5 sc) 3 times, ch 1, skip next sc, dc in next sc, ch 1, ★ skip next sc, dc in next 15 sc, ch 1, skip next sc, dc in next 3 sc, ch 1, skip next sc, dc in next 15 sc, ch 1, skip next sc, dc in next sc, ch 1; repeat from ★ once **more**, skip next sc, (dc in next 5 sc, skip next 2 sc, work Shell, skip next 2 sc) 3 times, dc in next 4 sc, ch 1, skip next sc, dc in next sc, ch 1, skip next sc, dc in last 2 sc: 137 dc and 20 ch-1 sps.

Row 34: Ch 1, turn; sc in each dc and in each ch-1 sp across: 157 sc.

Row 35: Ch 3, turn; dc in next dc, ch 1, skip next sc, dc in next 37 sc, ch 1, ★ skip next sc, dc in next 14 sc, ch 1, skip next sc, dc in next 7 sc, ch 1, skip next sc, dc in next 14 sc, ch 1; repeat from ★ once **more**, skip next sc, dc in next 37 sc, ch 1, skip next sc, dc in last 2 sc: 148 dc and 9 ch-1 sps.

Row 36: Ch 1, turn; sc in each dc and in each ch-1 sp across: 157 sc.

Row 37: Ch 3, turn; dc in next sc, ch 1, skip next sc, dc in next 37 sc, ch 1, ★ skip next sc, dc in next 12 sc, ch 1, skip next sc, dc in next 11 sc, ch 1, skip next sc, dc in next 12 sc, ch 1; repeat from ★ once **more**, skip next sc, dc in next 37 sc, ch 1, skip next sc, dc in last 2 sc: 148 dc and 9 ch-1 sps.

Row 38: Ch 1, turn; sc in each dc and in each ch-1 sp across: 157 sc.

Row 39: Ch 3, turn; dc in next sc, ch 1, skip next sc, dc in next 37 sc, ch 1, ★ skip next sc, dc in next 10 sc, ch 1, skip next sc, dc in next 15 sc, ch 1, skip next sc, dc in next 10 sc, ch 1; repeat from ★ once **more**, skip next sc, dc in next 37 sc, ch 1, skip next sc, dc in last 2 sc: 148 dc and 9 ch-1 sps.

Row 40: Ch 1, turn; sc in each dc and in each ch-1 sp across: 157 sc.

Row 41: Ch 3, turn; dc in next sc, ch 1, skip next sc, dc in next 37 sc, ch 1, ★ skip next sc, dc in next 8 sc, ch 1, skip next sc, dc in next 19 sc, ch 1, skip next sc, dc in next 8 sc, ch 1; repeat from ★ once **more**, skip next sc, dc in next 37 sc, ch 1, skip next sc, dc in last 2 sc: 148 dc and 9 ch-1 sps.

Row 42: Ch 1, turn; sc in each dc and in each ch-1 sp across: 157 sc.

Row 43: Ch 3, turn; dc in next sc, ch 1, skip next sc, dc in next 37 sc, ch 1, ★ skip next sc, dc in next 6 sc, ch 1, skip next sc, (dc in next 11 sc, ch 1, skip next sc) twice, dc in next 6 sc, ch 1; repeat from ★ once **more**, skip next sc, dc in next 37 sc, ch 1, skip next sc, dc in last 2 sc: 146 dc and 11 ch-1 sps.

Row 44: Ch 1, turn; sc in each dc and in each ch-1 sp across: 157 sc.

Row 45: Ch 3, turn; (dc in next sc, ch 1, skip next sc) twice, dc in next 4 sc, (skip next 2 sc, work Shell, skip next 2 sc, dc in next 5 sc) 3 times, ch 1, skip next sc, dc in next sc, ch 1, skip next sc, dc in next 5 sc, ★ ch 1, skip next sc, dc in next 9 sc, ch 1, skip next sc, dc in next 3 sc, ch 1, skip next sc, dc in next 9 sc, ch 1, skip next sc, dc in next 5 sc, ch 1, skip next sc, dc in next sc, ch 1, skip next sc, dc in next 5 sc; repeat from ★ once **more**, skip next 2 sc, work Shell, (skip next 2 sc, dc in next 5 sc, skip next 2 sc, work Shell) twice, skip next 2 sc, dc in next 4 sc, ch 1, skip next sc, dc in next sc, ch 1, skip next sc, dc in last 2 sc: 133 dc and 24 ch-1 sps.

Row 46: Ch 1, turn; sc in each dc and in each ch-1 sp across: 157 sc.

Row 47: Ch 3, turn; dc in next sc, ch 1, † skip next sc, dc in next 6 sc, skip next 2 sc, work Shell, (skip next 2 sc, dc in next 5 sc, skip next 2 sc, work Shell) twice, skip next 2 sc, dc in next 6 sc, ch 1 †, ★ skip next sc, dc in next 8 sc, ch 1, skip next sc, dc in next 5 sc, ch 1, skip next sc, dc in next 7 sc, ch 1, skip next sc, dc in next 5 sc, ch 1, skip next sc, dc in next 8 sc, ch 1; repeat from ★ once **more**, then repeat from † to † once, skip next sc, dc in last 2 sc: 138 dc and 19 ch-1 sps.

Rows 48-54: Repeat Rows 24-27 once, then repeat Rows 24-26 once **more**.

Row 55: Ch 3, turn; dc in next 39 sc, ch 1, ★ skip next sc, dc in next 6 sc, skip next 2 sc, work Shell, (skip next 2 sc, dc in next 5 sc, skip next 2 sc, work Shell) twice, skip next 2 sc, dc in next 6 sc, ch 1; repeat from ★ once **more**, skip next sc, dc in last 40 sc: 148 dc and 9 ch-1 sps.

Row 56: Ch 1, turn; sc in each dc and in each ch-1 sp across.

Rows 57-69: Repeat Rows 55 and 56, 6 times; then repeat Row 55 once **more**.

Rows 70-76: Repeat Rows 24-27 once, then repeat Rows 24-26 once **more**.

Row 77: Repeat Row 47.

Row 78: Repeat Row 46.

Rows 79 and 80: Repeat Rows 45 and 46.

Rows 81 and 82: Repeat Rows 43 and 44.

Rows 83 and 84: Repeat Rows 41 and 42.

Rows 85 and 86: Repeat Rows 39 and 40.

Rows 87 and 88: Repeat Rows 37 and 38.

Rows 89 and 90: Repeat Rows 35 and 36.

Rows 91 and 92: Repeat Rows 33 and 34.

Row 93: Repeat Row 31.

Rows 94-100: Repeat Rows 24-27 once, then repeat Rows 24-26 once **more**.

Rows 101 and 102: Repeat Rows 23 and 24.

Rows 103 and 104: Repeat Rows 21 and 22.

Rows 105 and 106: Repeat Rows 19 and 20.

Rows 107 and 108: Repeat Rows 17 and 18.

Rows 109 and 110: Repeat Rows 15 and 16.

Rows 111 and 112: Repeat Rows 13 and 14.

Rows 113 and 114: Repeat Rows 11 and 12.

Rows 115 and 116: Repeat Rows 9 and 10.

Rows 117 and 118: Repeat Rows 7 and 8.

Rows 119-124: Repeat Rows 25 and 26, 3 times.

Row 125: Ch 3, turn; dc in next sc, ch 1, ★ skip next sc, dc in next sc, ch 1; repeat from ★ across to last 3 sc, skip next sc, dc in last 2 sc; finish off: 80 dc and 77 ch-1 sps.

TRIM
TOP
With **right** side facing, join yarn with slip st in first dc on Row 125; 2 sc in next dc, (slip st in next ch-1 sp, 2 sc in next dc) across to last dc, slip st in last dc; finish off.

BOTTOM
Row 1: With **right** side facing and working in free loops of beginning ch *(Fig. 3b, page 126)*, join yarn with sc in first ch *(see Joining With Sc, page 125)*; sc in each ch across: 157 sc.

Row 2: Ch 3, turn; dc in next sc, ch 1, ★ skip next sc, dc in next sc, ch 1; repeat from ★ across to last 3 sc, skip next sc, dc in last 2 sc: 80 dc and 77 ch-1 sps.

Row 3: Turn; slip st in first dc, 2 sc in next dc, (slip st in next ch-1 sp, 2 sc in next dc) across to last dc, slip st in last dc; finish off.

GEMS

*Scallop-like designs in square "settings" and a diamond-inspired border
make this jewel of a throw by Geneva Warren a real treasure.*

Finished Size: 44$\frac{1}{2}$" x 57$\frac{1}{2}$"

MATERIALS
Worsted Weight Yarn:
 Green - 19 ounces, (540 grams, 1,075 yards)
 Off-White - 14 ounces, (400 grams, 790 yards)
 Dk Green - 14 ounces, (400 grams, 790 yards)
Crochet hook, size I (5.50 mm) **or** size needed
 for gauge
Yarn needle

GAUGE: Each Square = 6$\frac{1}{2}$"

Gauge Swatch: 2$\frac{3}{4}$" diameter
Work same as Square through Rnd 2.

STITCH GUIDE

TREBLE CROCHET *(abbreviated tr)*
YO twice, insert hook in sc indicated, YO and pull
up a loop (4 loops on hook), (YO and draw through
2 loops on hook) 3 times.

SQUARE (Make 48)
With Green, ch 4; join with slip st to form a ring.
Rnd 1 (Right side)**:** Ch 4 **(counts as first dc plus
ch 1)**, dc in ring, ch 2, ★ (dc, ch 1, dc) in ring, ch 2;
repeat from ★ 2 times **more**; join with slip st to first dc,
finish off: 8 dc and 8 sps.
Note: Loop a short piece of yarn around any stitch to
mark Rnd 1 as **right** side.
Rnd 2: With **right** side facing, join Off-White with
slip st in any ch-2 sp; ch 3 **(counts as first dc, now
and throughout)**, 4 dc in same sp, (sc, ch 2, sc) in
next ch-1 sp, ★ 5 dc in next ch-2 sp, (sc, ch 2, sc) in
next ch-1 sp; repeat from ★ 2 times **more**; join with
slip st to first dc, finish off: 28 sts and 4 ch-2 sps.
Rnd 3: With **right** side facing, join Dk Green with
slip st in any ch-2 sp; ch 3, 4 dc in same sp, skip next
2 sts, working in Back Loops Only **(Fig. 2, page 125)**,
sc in next dc, ch 2, skip next dc, sc in next dc, skip next
2 sts, ★ 5 dc in next ch-2 sp, skip next 2 sts, working
in Back Loops Only, sc in next dc, ch 2, skip next dc,
sc in next dc, skip next 2 sts; repeat from ★ 2 times
more; join with slip st to first dc, finish off.

Rnd 4: With **right** side facing, join Green with sc in
any ch-2 sp **(see Joining With Sc, page 125)**; ch 2,
sc in same sp, ch 3, skip next 3 sts, (sc, ch 2, sc) in
Back Loop Only of next dc, ch 3, skip next 3 sts,
★ (sc, ch 2, sc) in next ch-2 sp, ch 3, skip next 3 sts,
(sc, ch 2, sc) in Back Loop Only of next dc, ch 3, skip
next 3 sts; repeat from ★ 2 times **more**; join with
slip st to first sc, finish off: 16 sps.
Rnd 5: With **right** side facing, join Off-White with
slip st in any ch-2 sp; ch 3, 4 dc in same sp, (sc, ch 2,
sc) in next ch-3 sp, ★ 5 dc in next ch-2 sp, (sc, ch 2,
sc) in next ch-3 sp; repeat from ★ around; join with
slip st to first dc, finish off: 56 sts and 8 ch-2 sps.
Rnd 6: With **right** side facing, join Dk Green with
slip st in any ch-2 sp; ch 3, 4 dc in same sp, ch 1, skip
next 3 sts, sc in Back Loop Only of next dc, ch 1, skip
next 3 sts, ★ 5 dc in next ch-2 sp, ch 1, skip next
3 sts, sc in Back Loop Only of next dc, ch 1, skip next
3 sts; repeat from ★ around; join with slip st to first dc,
finish off: 48 sts and 16 ch-1 sps.
Rnd 7: With **right** side facing, join Green with sc in
both loops of any sc; ★ † ch 3, skip next 2 dc, sc in
Back Loop Only of next dc, ch 3, skip next 2 dc, (2 tr,
ch 2, 2 tr) in **both** loops of next sc, ch 3, skip next
2 dc, sc in Back Loop Only of next dc, ch 3, skip next
2 dc †, sc in **both** loops of next sc; repeat from ★
2 times **more**, then repeat from † to † once; join with
slip st to **both** loops of first sc, do **not** finish off: 28 sts
and 20 sps.
Rnd 8: Ch 1, working in both loops, sc in same st,
3 sc in next ch-3 sp, sc in next sc, 3 sc in next ch-3 sp,
★ † sc in next 2 tr, (sc, ch 2, sc) in next ch-2 sp, sc in
next 2 tr, 3 sc in next ch-3 sp †, (sc in next sc, 3 sc in
next ch-3 sp) 3 times; repeat from ★ 2 times **more**,
then repeat from † to † once, sc in next sc, 3 sc in last
ch-3 sp; join with slip st to first sc, finish off: 84 sc and
4 ch-2 sps.

ASSEMBLY
With Green and working through **inside** loops,
whipstitch Squares together forming 6 vertical strips of
8 Squares each **(Fig. 6b, page 126)**, beginning in
second ch of first corner ch-2 and ending in first ch of
next corner ch-2; then whipstitch strips together in
same manner.

EDGING

Rnd 1: With **right** side facing and working in Back Loops Only, join Green with sc in second ch of upper right corner ch-2; † sc in next 21 sc and in next ch, (sc in next joining and in next ch, sc in next 21 sc and in next ch) 5 times, ch 1, sc in next ch, sc in next 21 sc and in next ch, (sc in next joining and in next ch, sc in next 21 sc and in next ch) 7 times, ch 1 †, sc in next ch, repeat from † to † once; join with slip st to first sc, finish off: 668 sc and 4 ch-1 sps.

Rnd 2: With **right** side facing and working in Back Loops Only, join Off-White with sc in any corner ch-1; skip next 2 sc, 5 dc in next sc, skip next 2 sc, ★ sc in next st, skip next 2 sc, 5 dc in next sc, skip next 2 sc; repeat from ★ around; join with slip st to **both** loops of first sc, finish off.

Continued on page 30.

Rnd 3: With **right** side facing and working in both loops, join Dk Green with slip st in any corner sc; ch 3, 4 dc in same st, skip next 2 dc, sc in next dc, skip next 2 dc, ★ 5 dc in next sc, skip next 2 dc, sc in next dc, skip next 2 dc; repeat from ★ around; join with slip st to first dc, finish off.

Rnd 4: With **right** side facing, join Off-White with sc in center dc of any corner 5-dc group; ★ † ch 1, skip next 2 dc, 5 dc in next sc, (skip next 2 dc, sc in next dc, skip next 2 dc, 5 dc in next sc) across to next corner 5-dc group, ch 1, skip next 2 dc †, sc in next dc; repeat from ★ 2 times **more**, then repeat from † to † once; join with slip st to first sc, finish off.

Rnd 5: With **right** side facing; join Dk Green with slip st in any corner sc; ch 3, 6 dc in same st, skip next 2 dc, sc in next dc, ★ (skip next 2 dc, 5 dc in next sc, skip next 2 dc, sc in next dc) across to within 2 dc of next corner sc, skip next 2 dc, 7 dc in corner sc, skip next 2 dc, sc in next dc; repeat from ★ 2 times **more**, skip next 2 dc, (5 dc in next sc, skip next 2 dc, sc in next dc, skip next 2 dc) across; join with slip st to first dc, finish off.

Rnd 6: With **right** side facing and working in Back Loops Only, join Green with sc in first dc of any corner 7-dc group; 2 sc in next dc, (sc in next dc, 2 sc in next dc) twice, ★ sc in each st across to next corner 7-dc group, (sc in next dc, 2 sc in next dc) 3 times; repeat from ★ 2 times **more**, sc in each st across; join with slip st to first sc, finish off.

SQUARE POSTS

Designed by Shirley Zebrowski, this distinctive coverlet features two-tone blocks created using a textured front post cluster stitch.

Finished Size: 49" x 61"

MATERIALS
Worsted Weight Yarn:
    Red - 29 ounces, (820 grams, 1,640 yards)
    Teal - 29 ounces, (820 grams, 1,640 yards)
Crochet hook, size J (6.00 mm) **or** size needed
    for gauge
Yarn needle

GAUGE: Each Square = 12"

Gauge Swatch: 3¼" square
Work same as Square A or B through Rnd 2.

STITCH GUIDE

FRONT POST CLUSTER
(abbreviated FP Cluster)
★ YO, insert hook from **front** to **back** around post of st indicated *(Fig. 4, page 126)*, YO and pull up a loop, YO and draw through 2 loops on hook; repeat from ★ once **more**, YO and draw through all 3 loops on hook. Skip st behind FP Cluster.

SQUARE
Referring to the table below, make the number of Squares specified in the colors indicated.

	Square A Make 10	Square B Make 10
Rnds 1-5	Red	Teal
Rnds 6-9	Teal	Red

With color indicated, ch 6; join with slip st to form a ring.

Rnd 1 (Right side): Ch 3 **(counts as first dc, now and throughout)**, 15 dc in ring; join with slip st to first dc: 16 dc.

Note: Loop a short piece of yarn around any stitch to mark Rnd 1 as **right** side.

Rnd 2: Ch 3, dc in same st and in next dc, work FP Cluster around next dc, dc in next dc, ★ (2 dc, ch 2, 2 dc) in next dc, dc in next dc, work FP Cluster around next dc, dc in next dc; repeat from ★ 2 times **more**, 2 dc in same st as first dc, ch 1, sc in first dc to form last ch-2 sp: 28 sts and 4 ch-2 sps.

Rnd 3: Ch 3, dc in same sp and in next 3 dc, work FP Cluster around next FP Cluster, dc in next 3 dc, ★ (2 dc, ch 2, 2 dc) in next ch-2 sp, dc in next 3 dc, work FP Cluster around next FP Cluster, dc in next 3 dc; repeat from ★ 2 times **more**, 2 dc in same sp as first dc, ch 1, sc in first dc to form last ch-2 sp: 44 sts and 4 ch-2 sps.

Rnd 4: Ch 3, dc in same sp and in next 5 dc, work FP Cluster around next FP Cluster, dc in next 5 dc, ★ (2 dc, ch 2, 2 dc) in next ch-2 sp, dc in next 5 dc, work FP Cluster around next FP Cluster, dc in next 5 dc; repeat from ★ 2 times **more**, 2 dc in same sp as first dc, ch 1, sc in first dc to form last ch-2 sp; do **not** finish off: 60 sts and 4 ch-2 sps.

Continued on page 32.

Rnd 5: Ch 3, dc in same sp and in next dc, ★ † work FP Cluster around next dc, dc in next 5 dc, work FP Cluster around next FP Cluster, dc in next 5 dc, work FP Cluster around next dc, dc in next dc †, (2 dc, ch 2, 2 dc) in next ch-2 sp, dc in next dc; repeat from ★ 2 times **more**, then repeat from † to † once, 2 dc in same sp as first dc, ch 2; join with slip st to first dc, finish off: 76 sts and 4 ch-2 sps.

Rnd 6: With **right** side facing, join next color indicated with slip st in any corner ch-2 sp; ch 3, dc in same sp and in next 3 dc, ★ † work FP Cluster around next FP Cluster, (dc in next 5 dc, work FP Cluster around next FP Cluster) twice, dc in next 3 dc †, (2 dc, ch 2, 2 dc) in next ch-2 sp, dc in next 3 dc; repeat from ★ 2 times **more**, then repeat from † to † once, 2 dc in same sp as first dc, ch 1, sc in first dc to form last ch-2 sp: 92 sts and 4 ch-2 sps.

Rnd 7: Ch 3, dc in same sp and in next 5 dc, (work FP Cluster around next FP Cluster, dc in next 5 dc) 3 times, ★ (2 dc, ch 2, 2 dc) in next ch-2 sp, dc in next 5 dc, (work FP Cluster around next FP Cluster, dc in next 5 dc) 3 times; repeat from ★ 2 times **more**, 2 dc in same sp as first dc, ch 1, sc in first dc to form last ch-2 sp: 108 sts and 4 ch-2 sps.

Rnd 8: Ch 3, dc in same sp and in next dc, ★ † work FP Cluster around next dc, dc in next 5 dc, (work FP Cluster around next FP Cluster, dc in next 5 dc) 3 times, work FP Cluster around next dc, dc in next dc †, (2 dc, ch 2, 2 dc) in next ch-2 sp, dc in next dc; repeat from ★ 2 times **more**, then repeat from † to † once, 2 dc in same sp as first dc, ch 1, sc in first dc to form last ch-2 sp: 124 sts and 4 ch-2 sps.

Rnd 9: Ch 3, dc in same sp and in next 3 dc, ★ † work FP Cluster around next FP Cluster, (dc in next 5 dc, work FP Cluster around next FP Cluster) 4 times, dc in next 3 dc †, (2 dc, ch 3, 2 dc) in next ch-2 sp, dc in next 3 dc; repeat from ★ 2 times **more**, then repeat from † to † once, 2 dc in same sp as first dc, ch 3; join with slip st to first dc, finish off: 140 sts and 4 ch-3 sps.

ASSEMBLY

With Teal, using photo as a guide for placement, page 31, and working through **inside** loops, whipstitch Squares together forming 4 vertical strips of 5 Squares each *(Fig. 6b, page 126)*, beginning in center ch of first corner ch-3 and ending in center ch of next corner ch-3; then whipstitch strips together in same manner.

EDGING

Rnd 1: With **right** side facing, join Teal with sc in any corner ch-3 sp *(see Joining With Sc, page 125)*; sc in same sp, ★ sc in each st and in each sp across to next corner ch-3 sp, 3 sc in corner ch-3 sp; repeat from ★ 2 times **more**, sc in each st and in each sp across, sc in same sp as first sc; join with slip st to first sc: 670 sc.

Rnd 2: Ch 1, 3 sc in same st, ★ sc in each sc across to center sc of next corner 3-sc group, 3 sc in center sc; repeat from ★ 2 times **more**, sc in each sc across; join with slip st to first sc, finish off.

FIESTA

As fun as a fall festival, Merry L. Daugherty's vibrant creation is stitched in panels that are joined together with a no-sew method.

Finished Size: 52" x 60½"

MATERIALS

Worsted Weight Yarn:
Black - 18 ounces, (510 grams, 1,015 yards)
Purple - 12 ounces, (340 grams, 680 yards)
Brown - 11 ounces, (310 grams, 620 yards)
Variegated - 5 ounces, (140 grams, 290 yards)
Crochet hook, size H (5.00 mm) **or** size needed for gauge
Afghan hook, size H (5.00 mm) **or** size needed for gauge

GAUGE: In pattern, Panel A or B, 21 sts = 6";
Rows 1-18 = 7½"
Panel C, 10 sts = 2½"; 8 rows = 6"

Gauge Swatch: 6"w x 7½"h
Work same as Panel A through Row 18.

Continued on page 34.

STITCH GUIDE

DOUBLE AFGHAN STITCH
(abbreviated double Afghan St)
YO, with yarn in **back**, insert hook from **right** to **left** under next vertical strand *(Fig. A)*, YO and pull up a loop, YO and draw through 2 loops on hook, YO and draw through one loop on hook.

Fig. A

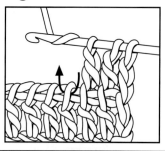

PANEL A (Make 3)
With crochet hook and Purple, ch 23 **loosely**, place marker in third ch from hook for st placement.
Row 1 (Wrong side)**:** Dc in fourth ch from hook **(3 skipped chs count as first dc)** and in each ch across: 21 dc.
Note: Loop a short piece of yarn around **back** of any stitch to mark **right** side and bottom edge.
Rows 2-12: Ch 3 **(counts as first dc, now and throughout)**, turn; dc in next dc and in each dc across changing to Black in last dc on Row 12 *(Fig. 5, page 126)*.
Rows 13-18: Ch 1, turn; sc in each st across changing to Brown in last sc on Row 18.
Rows 19-30: Ch 3, turn; dc in next st and in each st across changing to Black in last dc on Row 30.
Rows 31-36: Ch 1, turn; sc in each st across changing to Purple in last sc on Row 36.
Rows 37-48: Ch 3, turn; dc in next st and in each st across changing to Black in last dc on Row 48.
Rows 49-138: Repeat Rows 13-48 twice, then repeat Rows 13-30 once **more**; at end of Row 138, do **not** change colors.
Finish off.

PANEL B (Make 2)
With crochet hook and Brown, ch 23 **loosely**, place marker in third ch from hook for st placement.
Row 1 (Wrong side)**:** Dc in fourth ch from hook **(3 skipped chs count as first dc)** and in each ch across: 21 dc.
Note: Mark **back** of any stitch as **right** side and bottom edge.
Rows 2-12: Ch 3, turn; dc in next dc and in each dc across changing to Black in last dc on Row 12.
Rows 13-18: Ch 1, turn; sc in each st across changing to Purple in last sc on Row 18.

34

Rows 19-30: Ch 3, turn; dc in next st and in each st across changing to Black in last dc on Row 30.
Rows 31-36: Ch 1, turn; sc in each st across changing to Brown in last sc on Row 36.
Rows 37-48: Ch 3, turn; dc in next st and in each st across changing to Black in last dc on Row 48.
Rows 49-138: Repeat Rows 13-48 twice, then repeat Rows 13-30 once **more**; at end of Row 138, do **not** change colors.
Finish off.

TRIM
Using Placement Diagram as a guide, work Right Side and Left Side Trim on center Panel A and on each Panel B; work Right Side Trim on left Panel A and Left Side Trim on right Panel A.

RIGHT SIDE
With **wrong** side facing and working across end of rows, join Black with sc *(see Joining With Sc, page 125)* in free loop of ch at base of first dc on Row 1 *(Fig. 3b, page 126)*; ch 3, skip first row, sc in next row, (ch 4, skip next row, sc in next row) 5 times, ★ (ch 3, skip next 2 sc rows, sc in next sc row) twice, (ch 4, skip next row, sc in next row) 6 times; repeat from ★ 6 times **more**; finish off: 62 sps.

LEFT SIDE
With **wrong** side facing and working across end of rows, join Black with sc in Row 138; ★ (ch 4, skip next row, sc in next row) 6 times, (ch 3, skip next 2 rows, sc in next row) twice; repeat from ★ 6 times **more**, (ch 4, skip next row, sc in next row) 5 times, ch 3, skip last row, sc in marked ch; finish off: 62 sps.

PLACEMENT DIAGRAM

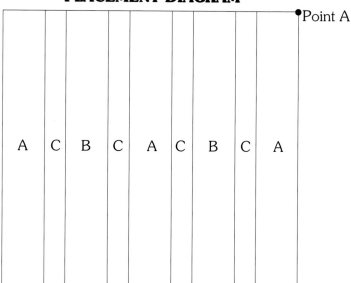

•Point A

A C B C A C B C A

PANEL C (Make 4)

With afghan hook and Black, ch 11 **loosely**, place marker in second ch from hook for st placement.

Note: Each double Afghan St row is worked in 2 steps, working to the **left** picking up loops and then working to the **right** completing each stitch.

Row 1 (Right side)**:** YO, working from **right** to **left**, insert hook in third ch from hook, YO and pull up a loop, YO and draw through 2 loops on hook, YO and draw through one loop on hook (2 loops on hook) *(Fig. B)*, ★ YO, insert hook in **next** ch, YO and pull up a loop, YO and draw through 2 loops on hook, YO and draw through one loop on hook; repeat from ★ across (10 loops on hook); working from **left** to **right**, [YO and draw through 2 loops on hook *(Fig. C)*] across until one loop remains on hook: 10 sts.

Fig. B

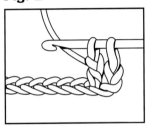

Fig. C

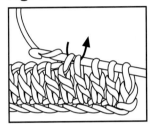

Note: Mark Row 1 as **right** side and bottom edge.

Rows 2-8: Ch 2, working from **right** to **left**, skip first vertical strand, work double Afghan Sts across (10 loops on hook); working from **left** to **right**, (YO and draw through 2 loops on hook) across changing to Variegated in last st on Row 8.

Rows 9 and 10: Ch 2, working from **right** to **left**, skip first vertical strand, work double Afghan Sts across (10 loops on hook); working from **left** to **right**, (YO and draw through 2 loops on hook) across changing to Black in last st on Row 10.

Rows 11-18: Ch 2, working from **right** to **left**, skip first vertical strand, work double Afghan Sts across (10 loops on hook); working from **left** to **right**, (YO and draw through 2 loops on hook) across changing to Variegated in last st on Row 18.

Rows 19-77: Repeat Rows 9-18, 5 times; then repeat Rows 9-17 once **more**; at end of Row 77, do **not** change colors and do **not** finish off.

Note: Change to crochet hook.

TRIM
RIGHT SIDE

Row 1: Ch 1, turn; working in end of rows, sc in top of Row 77, [(ch 3, sc in top of next row) twice, ch 4, skip next row, sc in top of next row] twice, ★ † (ch 3, sc in top of next row) 4 times, ch 4, skip next row, sc in top of next row, (ch 3, sc in top of next row) twice, ch 4 †, skip next row, sc in top of next row; repeat from ★ 5 times **more**, then repeat from † to † once, sc in marked ch: 62 sps.

Row 2 (Joining row)**:** Ch 2, turn; using Placement Diagram as guide, page 34, holding Panels with **wrong** sides together and bottom edges at **opposite** ends, sc in first sc of Right Side Trim on **previous** Panel, ch 2, sc in first ch-4 sp on **new Panel**, ch 2, sc in next sp on **previous Panel**, ch 2, ★ sc in next sp on **new Panel**, ch 2, sc in next sp on **previous Panel**, ch 2; repeat from ★ across, sc in last sc on **new Panel**, ch 2, slip st in last sc on **previous Panel**; finish off.

LEFT SIDE

Row 1: With **wrong** side facing and working in end of rows, join Black with sc in free loop of ch at base of Row 1; ch 4, sc in top of first row, (ch 3, sc in top of next row) twice, ch 4, skip next row, sc in top of next row, ★ (ch 3, sc in top of next row) 4 times, ch 4, skip next row, sc in top of next row, (ch 3, sc in top of next row) twice, ch 4, skip next row, sc in top of next row; repeat from ★ 6 times **more**, (ch 3, sc in top of next row) twice: 62 sps.

Row 2 (Joining row)**:** Ch 2, turn; using Placement Diagram as guide, holding Panels with **wrong** sides together and bottom edges at **opposite** ends, sc in first sc of Left Side Trim on **previous Panel**, ch 2, sc in first ch-3 sp on **new Panel**, ch 2, sc in next sp on **previous Panel**, ch 2, ★ sc in next sp on **new Panel**, ch 2, sc in next sp on **previous Panel**, ch 2; repeat from ★ across, sc in last sc on **new Panel**, ch 2, slip st in last sc on **previous Panel**; finish off.

EDGING

Rnd 1: With **right** side facing, join Variegated with slip st in first dc at Point A; ch 3, 2 dc in same st, work 190 dc evenly spaced across to next corner dc, 5 dc in corner dc; work 229 dc evenly spaced across end of rows; working in free loops of beginning ch, 5 dc in ch at base of first dc, work 190 dc evenly spaced across to last ch, 5 dc in last ch; work 229 dc evenly spaced across end of rows, 2 dc in same st as first dc; join with slip st to first dc: 858 dc.

Rnd 2: Ch 4, (dc, ch 1) 4 times in same st, ★ † [skip next 2 dc, (dc, ch 1) twice in next dc] across to next corner 5-dc group, skip next 2 dc †, (dc, ch 1) 5 times in next dc; repeat from ★ 2 times **more**, then repeat from † to † once; join with slip st to third ch of beginning ch-4, finish off.

BUNNY LOVE

"Hoppy" hares and hearts abound on a field of filet crochet in
this light 'n' lacy coverlet design by Patricia Zihala.

Finished Size: 66½" x 83"

MATERIALS
Worsted Weight Yarn:
    60 ounces, (1,700 grams, 3,390 yards)
Crochet hook, size I (5.50 mm) **or** size needed
    for gauge

GAUGE: In pattern, 12 dc = 4"; 7 rows = 4½"

Gauge Swatch: 4"w x 4½"h
Ch 14 **loosely.**
Row 1: Dc in fourth ch from hook **(3 skipped chs count as first dc)** and in each ch across: 12 dc.
Rows 2-7: Ch 3 **(counts as first dc)**, turn; dc in next dc and in each dc across.
Finish off.

AFGHAN
Ch 201 **loosely.**
Row 1 (Right side)**:** Dc in back ridge of fourth ch from hook *(Fig. 1, page 125)* and each ch across **(3 skipped chs count as first dc):** 199 dc.
Row 2: Ch 3 **(counts as first dc, now and throughout)**, turn; dc in next dc and in each dc across.
Row 3: Ch 3, turn; dc in next 4 dc, ch 1, (skip next dc, dc in next dc, ch 1) 10 times, ★ skip next dc, dc in next 3 dc, ch 1, (skip next dc, dc in next dc, ch 1) 10 times; repeat from ★ across to last 6 dc, skip next dc, dc in last 5 dc: 111 dc and 88 ch-1 sps.
Row 4: Ch 3, turn; dc in next 4 dc, ★ † ch 1, (dc in next dc, ch 1) 4 times, dc in next dc and in next ch-1 sp, (dc in next dc, ch 1) 5 times †, dc in next 3 dc; repeat from ★ 6 times **more**, then repeat from † to † once, dc in last 5 dc: 119 dc and 80 ch-1 sps.
Row 5: Ch 3, turn; dc in next 4 dc, ★ † (ch 1, dc in next dc) 4 times, dc in next ch-1 sp, dc in next 3 dc and in next ch-1 sp, (dc in next dc, ch 1) 4 times †, dc in next 3 dc; repeat from ★ 6 times **more**, then repeat from † to † once, dc in last 5 dc: 135 dc and 64 ch-1 sps.
Row 6: Ch 3, turn; dc in next 4 dc, ★ † (ch 1, dc in next dc) 3 times, dc in next ch-1 sp, dc in next 7 dc and in next ch-1 sp, (dc in next dc, ch 1) 3 times †, dc in next 3 dc; repeat from ★ 6 times **more**, then repeat from † to † once, dc in last 5 dc: 151 dc and 48 ch-1 sps.

Row 7: Ch 3, turn; dc in next 4 dc, ★ † (ch 1, dc in next dc) twice, dc in next ch-1 sp, dc in next 11 dc and in next ch-1 sp, (dc in next dc, ch 1) twice †, dc in next 3 dc; repeat from ★ 6 times **more**, then repeat from † to † once, dc in last 5 dc: 167 dc and 32 ch-1 sps.
Row 8: Ch 3, turn; dc in next 4 dc, ★ † ch 1, dc in next dc, dc in next ch-1 sp and in next 15 dc, dc in next ch-1 sp and in next dc, ch 1 †, dc in next 3 dc; repeat from ★ 6 times **more**, then repeat from † to † once, dc in last 5 dc: 183 dc and 16 ch-1 sps.
Rows 9 and 10: Ch 3, turn; dc in next 4 dc, ch 1, dc in next 19 dc, ch 1, ★ dc in next 3 dc, ch 1, dc in next 19 dc, ch 1; repeat from ★ across to last 5 dc, dc in last 5 dc.
Row 11: Ch 3, turn; dc in next 4 dc, ch 1, dc in next 9 dc, ch 1, skip next dc, dc in next 9 dc, ch 1, ★ dc in next 3 dc, ch 1, dc in next 9 dc, ch 1, skip next dc, dc in next 9 dc, ch 1; repeat from ★ across to last 5 dc, dc in last 5 dc: 175 dc and 24 ch-1 sps.
Row 12: Ch 3, turn; dc in next 4 dc, ★ † ch 1, dc in next dc, ch 1, skip next dc, dc in next 5 dc, ch 1, skip next dc, (dc in next dc, ch 1) twice, skip next dc, dc in next 5 dc, ch 1, skip next dc, dc in next dc, ch 1 †, dc in next 3 dc; repeat from ★ 6 times **more**, then repeat † to † once, dc in last 5 dc: 143 dc and 56 ch-1 sps.
Row 13: Ch 3, turn; dc in next 4 dc, ★ † ch 1, (dc in next dc, ch 1) twice, (skip next dc, dc in next dc, ch 1) twice, (dc in next dc, ch 1) 3 times, (skip next dc, dc in next dc, ch 1) twice, dc in next dc, ch 1 †, dc in next 3 dc; repeat from ★ 6 times **more**, then repeat † to † once, dc in last 5 dc: 111 dc and 88 ch-1 sps.
Row 14: Ch 3, turn; dc in next dc and in each dc and each ch-1 sp across: 199 dc.
Row 15: Ch 3, turn; dc in next 4 dc, ch 1, (skip next dc, dc in next dc, ch 1) 22 times, ★ skip next dc, dc in next 3 dc, ch 1, (skip next dc, dc in next dc, ch 1) 22 times; repeat from ★ 2 times **more**, skip next dc, dc in last 5 dc: 107 dc and 92 ch-1 sps.
Row 16: Ch 3, turn; dc in next 4 dc, † (ch 1, dc in next dc) 3 times, (dc in next ch-1 sp and in next dc) 18 times, ch 1, dc in next dc, ch 1, dc in next 3 dc, (ch 1, dc in next dc) twice, (dc in next ch-1 sp and in next dc) 18 times, ch 1, (dc in next dc, ch 1) twice †, dc in next 3 dc, repeat from † to † once, dc in last 5 dc; do **not** finish off: 179 dc and 20 ch-1 sps.

Continued on page 38.

Row 17: Ch 3, turn; dc in next 4 dc, † ch 1, (dc in next dc, ch 1) twice, dc in next 37 dc, ch 1, dc in next dc, ch 1, dc in next 3 dc, ch 1, dc in next dc, ch 1, dc in next 37 dc, ch 1, (dc in next dc, ch 1) twice †, dc in next 3 dc, repeat from † to † once, dc in last 5 dc.

Row 18: Ch 3, turn; dc in next 4 dc, † ch 1, (dc in next dc and in next ch-1 sp) twice, dc in next 37 dc, ch 1, dc in next dc, ch 1, dc in next 3 dc, ch 1, dc in next dc, ch 1, dc in next 37 dc, (dc in next ch-1 sp and in next dc) twice, ch 1 †, dc in next 3 dc, repeat from † to † once, dc in last 5 dc: 187 dc and 12 ch-1 sps.

Row 19: Ch 3, turn; dc in next 4 dc, † ch 1, dc in next 39 dc, ch 1, skip next dc, (dc in next dc, ch 1) twice, dc in next 3 dc, ch 1, (dc in next dc, ch 1) twice, skip next dc, dc in next 39 dc, ch 1 †, dc in next 3 dc, repeat from † to † once, dc in last 5 dc: 183 dc and 16 ch-1 sps.

Row 20: Ch 3, turn; dc in next 4 dc, † ch 1, dc in next 37 dc, ch 1, skip next dc, (dc in next dc, ch 1) 3 times, dc in next 3 dc, ch 1, (dc in next dc, ch 1) 3 times, skip next dc, dc in next 37 dc, ch 1 †, dc in next 3 dc, repeat from † to † once, dc in last 5 dc: 179 dc and 20 ch-1 sps.

Row 21: Ch 3, turn; dc in next 4 dc, † ch 1, dc in next dc, ch 1, skip next dc, dc in next 33 dc, ch 1, skip next dc, (dc in next dc, ch 1) 4 times, dc in next 3 dc, ch 1, (dc in next dc, ch 1) 4 times, skip next dc, dc in next 33 dc, ch 1, skip next dc, dc in next dc, ch 1 †, dc in next 3 dc, repeat from † to † once, dc in last 5 dc: 171 dc and 28 ch-1 sps.

Row 22: Ch 3, turn; dc in next 4 dc, † ch 1, (dc in next dc, ch 1) twice, skip next dc, dc in next 29 dc, ch 1, skip next dc, (dc in next dc, ch 1) 5 times, dc in next 3 dc, ch 1, (dc in next dc, ch 1) 5 times, skip next dc, dc in next 29 dc, ch 1, skip next dc, (dc in next dc, ch 1) twice †, dc in next 3 dc, repeat from † to † once, dc in last 5 dc: 163 dc and 36 ch-1 sps.

Row 23: Ch 3, turn; dc in next 4 dc, † ch 1, (dc in next dc, ch 1) twice, dc in next 29 dc and in next ch-1 sp, (dc in next dc, ch 1) 5 times, dc in next 3 dc, (ch 1, dc in next dc) 5 times, dc in next ch-1 sp and in next 29 dc, ch 1, (dc in next dc, ch 1) twice †, dc in next 3 dc, repeat from † to † once, dc in last 5 dc: 167 dc and 32 ch-1 sps.

Row 24: Ch 3, turn; dc in next 4 dc, † ch 1, (dc in next dc, ch 1) 3 times, skip next dc, dc in next 29 dc, (dc in next ch-1 sp and in next dc) 3 times, ch 1, dc in next dc, ch 1, dc in next 3 dc, ch 1, dc in next dc, ch 1, (dc in next dc and in next ch-1 sp) 3 times, dc in next 29 dc, ch 1, skip next dc, (dc in next dc, ch 1) 3 times †, dc in next 3 dc, repeat from † to † once, dc in last 5 dc: 175 dc and 24 ch-1 sps.

Row 25: Ch 3, turn; dc in next 4 dc, † ch 1, (dc in next dc, ch 1) 3 times, dc in next 35 dc, dc in next ch-1 sp and in next dc, ch 1, dc in next 3 dc, ch 1, dc in next dc, dc in next ch-1 sp and in next 35 dc, ch 1, (dc in next dc, ch 1) 3 times †, dc in next 3 dc, repeat from † to † once, dc in last 5 dc: 179 dc and 20 ch-1 sps.

Row 26: Ch 3, turn; dc in next 4 dc, † ch 1, (dc in next dc, ch 1) 4 times, skip next dc, dc in next 35 dc, ch 1, dc in next 3 dc, ch 1, dc in next 35 dc, ch 1, skip next dc, (dc in next dc, ch 1) 4 times †, dc in next 3 dc, repeat from † to † once, dc in last 5 dc: 175 dc and 24 ch-1 sps.

Row 27: Ch 3, turn; dc in next 4 dc, † ch 1, (dc in next dc, ch 1) 5 times, skip next dc, dc in next 33 dc, ch 1, dc in next 3 dc, ch 1, dc in next 33 dc, ch 1, skip next dc, (dc in next dc, ch 1) 5 times †, dc in next 3 dc, repeat from † to † once, dc in last 5 dc: 171 dc and 28 ch-1 sps.

Row 28: Ch 3, turn; dc in next 4 dc, † ch 1, (dc in next dc, ch 1) 6 times, skip next dc, dc in next 25 dc, ch 1, skip next dc, dc in next 5 dc, ch 1, dc in next 3 dc, ch 1, dc in next 5 dc, ch 1, skip next dc, dc in next 25 dc, ch 1, skip next dc, (dc in next dc, ch 1) 6 times †, dc in next 3 dc, repeat from † to † once, dc in last 5 dc: 163 dc and 36 ch-1 sps.

Row 29: Ch 3, turn; dc in next 4 dc, † ch 1, (dc in next dc, ch 1) 7 times, skip next dc, (dc in next dc, ch 1, skip next dc) 6 times, dc in next 11 dc, dc in next ch-1 sp and in next 5 dc, ch 1, dc in next 3 dc, ch 1, dc in next 5 dc, dc in next ch-1 sp and in next 11 dc, ch 1, (skip next dc, dc in next dc, ch 1) 7 times, (dc in next dc, ch 1) 6 times †, dc in next 3 dc, repeat from † to † once, dc in last 5 dc: 139 dc and 60 ch-1 sps.

Row 30: Ch 3, turn; dc in next 4 dc, † ch 1, (dc in next dc, ch 1) 13 times, dc in next 17 dc, ch 1, dc in next 3 dc, ch 1, dc in next 17 dc, ch 1, (dc in next dc, ch 1) 13 times †, dc in next 3 dc, repeat from † to † once, dc in last 5 dc.

Row 31: Ch 3, turn; dc in next 4 dc, † (ch 1, dc in next dc) 13 times, dc in next ch-1 sp and in next 15 dc, ch 1, skip next dc, dc in next dc, ch 1, dc in next 3 dc, ch 1, dc in next dc, ch 1, skip next dc, dc in next 15 dc and in next ch-1 sp, (dc in next dc, ch 1) 13 times †, dc in next 3 dc, repeat from † to † once, dc in last 5 dc.

Row 32: Ch 3, turn; dc in next 4 dc, † (ch 1, dc in next dc) 4 times, dc in next ch-1 sp and in next dc, (ch 1, dc in next dc) 7 times, dc in next ch-1 sp and in next 15 dc, ch 1, skip next dc, (dc in next dc, ch 1) twice, dc in next 3 dc, ch 1, (dc in next dc, ch 1) twice, skip next dc, dc in next 15 dc and in next ch-1 sp, (dc in next dc, ch 1) 7 times, dc in next dc and in next ch-1 sp, (dc in next dc, ch 1) 4 times †, dc in next 3 dc, repeat from † to † once, dc in last 5 dc: 143 dc and 56 ch-1 sps.

Row 33: Ch 3, turn; dc in next 4 dc, † (ch 1, dc in next dc) 3 times, dc in next ch-1 sp, dc in next 3 dc and in next ch-1 sp, (dc in next dc, ch 1) 5 times, dc in next dc and in next ch-1 sp, (dc in next 7 dc, ch 1, skip next dc) twice, (dc in next dc, ch 1) 3 times, dc in next 3 dc, (ch 1, dc in next dc) 3 times, (ch 1, skip next dc, dc in next 7 dc) twice, dc in next ch-1 sp, (dc in next dc, ch 1) 5 times, dc in next dc and in next ch-1 sp, dc in next 3 dc and in next ch-1 sp, (dc in next dc, ch 1) 3 times †, dc in next 3 dc, repeat from † to † once, dc in last 5 dc: 147 dc and 52 ch-1 sps.

Row 34: Ch 3, turn; dc in next 4 dc, † (ch 1, dc in next dc) twice, dc in next ch-1 sp and in next 7 dc, dc in next ch-1 sp and in next dc, (ch 1, dc in next dc) 3 times, dc in next ch-1 sp and in next 7 dc, ch 1, skip next dc, dc in next dc, dc in next ch-1 sp and in next 7 dc, ch 1, (dc in next dc, ch 1) 3 times, dc in next 3 dc, ch 1, (dc in next dc, ch 1) 3 times, dc in next 7 dc, dc in next ch-1 sp and in next dc, ch 1, skip next dc, dc in next 7 dc and in next ch-1 sp, (dc in next dc, ch 1) 3 times, dc in next dc and in next ch-1 sp, dc in next 7 dc and in next ch-1 sp, (dc in next dc, ch 1) twice †, dc in next 3 dc, repeat from † to † once, dc in last 5 dc: 159 dc and 40 ch-1 sps.

Row 35: Ch 3, turn; dc in next 4 dc, † ch 1, dc in next dc and in next ch-1 sp, dc in next 11 dc and in next ch-1 sp, (dc in next dc, ch 1) twice, dc in next 7 dc, ch 1, skip next dc, dc in next dc, dc in next ch-1 sp and in next 7 dc, ch 1, skip next dc, (dc in next dc, ch 1) 4 times, dc in next 3 dc, ch 1, (dc in next dc, ch 1) 4 times, skip next dc, dc in next 7 dc, dc in next ch-1 sp and in next dc, ch 1, skip next dc, dc in next 7 dc, (ch 1, dc in next dc) twice, dc in next ch-1 sp and in next 11 dc, dc in next ch-1 sp and in next dc, ch 1 †, dc in next 3 dc, repeat from † to † once, dc in last 5 dc: 163 dc and 36 ch-1 sps.

Row 36: Ch 3, turn; dc in next 4 dc, † ch 1, dc in next 15 dc, ch 1, dc in next dc, ch 1, dc in next 5 dc, ch 1, skip next dc, dc in next dc, dc in next ch-1 sp and in next 7 dc, ch 1, skip next dc, (dc in next dc, ch 1) 5 times, dc in next 3 dc, ch 1, (dc in next dc, ch 1) 5 times, skip next dc, dc in next 7 dc, dc in next ch-1 sp and in next dc, ch 1, skip next dc, dc in next 5 dc, ch 1, dc in next dc, ch 1, dc in next 15 dc, ch 1 †, dc in next 3 dc, repeat from † to † once, dc in last 5 dc: 159 dc and 40 ch-1 sps.

Row 37: Ch 3, turn; dc in next 4 dc, † ch 1, dc in next 15 dc, (ch 1, dc in next dc) twice, (ch 1, skip next dc, dc in next dc) twice, dc in next ch-1 sp and in next 7 dc, ch 1, skip next dc, (dc in next dc, ch 1) 6 times, dc in next 3 dc, ch 1, (dc in next dc, ch 1) 6 times, skip next dc, dc in next 7 dc, dc in next ch-1 sp and in next dc, ch 1, (skip next dc, dc in next dc, ch 1) twice, dc in next dc, ch 1, dc in next 15 dc, ch 1 †, dc in next 3 dc, repeat from † to † once, dc in last 5 dc: 151 dc and 48 ch-1 sps.

Row 38: Ch 3, turn; dc in next 4 dc, † ch 1, dc in next 7 dc, ch 1, skip next dc, dc in next 7 dc, ch 1, (dc in next dc, ch 1) 3 times, dc in next 7 dc, ch 1, skip next dc, (dc in next dc, ch 1) 7 times, dc in next 3 dc, ch 1, (dc in next dc, ch 1) 7 times, skip next dc, dc in next 7 dc, ch 1, (dc in next dc, ch 1) 3 times, dc in next 7 dc, ch 1, skip next dc, dc in next 7 dc, ch 1 †, dc in next 3 dc, repeat from † to † once, dc in last 5 dc: 143 dc and 56 ch-1 sps.

Row 39: Ch 3, turn; dc in next 4 dc, † ch 1, [dc in next dc, ch 1, (skip next dc, dc in next dc, ch 1) 3 times] twice, (dc in next dc, ch 1) 4 times, (skip next dc, dc in next dc, ch 1) 3 times, (dc in next dc, ch 1) 7 times, dc in next 3 dc, ch 1, (dc in next dc, ch 1) 8 times, (skip next dc, dc in next dc, ch 1) 3 times, (dc in next dc, ch 1) 4 times, (skip next dc, dc in next dc, ch 1) 3 times, dc in next dc, ch 1, (skip next dc, dc in next dc, ch 1) 3 times †, dc in next 3 dc, repeat from † to † once, dc in last 5 dc: 107 dc and 92 ch-1 sps.

Row 40: Ch 3, turn; dc in next dc and in each dc and each ch-1 sp across: 199 dc.

Rows 41-128: Repeat Rows 3-40 twice, then repeat Rows 3-14 once **more**.

Row 129: Ch 3, turn; dc in next dc and in each dc across; finish off.

LOTS OF BLOCKS

*Cascading cubes of color square beautifully with one another
in this clever op-art wrap created by C.A. Riley.*

Finished Size: 47½" x 61½"

MATERIALS
Worsted Weight Yarn:
    Purple - 13 ounces, (370 grams, 735 yards)
    Blue - 9 ounces, (260 grams, 510 yards)
    Green - 6 ounces, (170 grams, 340 yards)
    Brown - 6 ounces, (170 grams, 340 yards)
    Rust - 6 ounces, (170 grams, 340 yards)
    Red - 6 ounces, (170 grams, 340 yards)
Crochet hook, size I (5.50 mm) **or** size needed
    for gauge

Note: Each row is worked across length of Afghan. Afghan is worked using two strands of yarn, forming stitches with first color and working over one strand of second color, carrying yarn with normal tension across top of previous row. Do **not** cut yarn unless instructed.

GAUGE: In pattern, 12 sts and 10 rows = 4"

Gauge Swatch: 4" square
With Blue, ch 13 **loosely**.
Row 1: With Blue and working over Purple, sc in second ch from hook, hdc in next ch, (sc in next ch, hdc in next ch) across: 12 sts.
Rows 2-10: With Blue, ch 1, turn; working over Purple, sc in first hdc, hdc in next sc, (sc in next hdc, hdc in next sc) across.
Finish off.

AFGHAN BODY
With Blue, ch 177 **loosely**.
Row 1 (Right side)**:** With Blue and working over Purple, sc in second ch from hook, hdc in next ch, (sc in next ch, hdc in next ch) 7 times changing to Purple in last hdc *(Fig. 5, page 126)*, working over Blue, (sc in next ch, hdc in next ch) 8 times changing to Blue in last hdc, ★ working over Purple, (sc in next ch, hdc in next ch) 8 times changing to Purple in last hdc, working over Blue, (sc in next ch, hdc in next ch) 8 times changing to Blue in last hdc; repeat from ★ 3 times **more**, working over Purple, (sc in next ch, hdc in next ch) across: 176 sts.

Note: Continue changing colors in same manner throughout.

Rows 2-4: With Blue, ch 1, turn; working over Purple, sc in first hdc, hdc in next sc, (sc in next hdc, hdc in next sc) 7 times, ★ with Purple and working over Blue, (sc in next hdc, hdc in next sc) 8 times, with Blue and working over Purple, (sc in next hdc, hdc in next sc) 8 times; repeat from ★ across.

Rows 5-12: With Blue, ch 1, turn; working over Purple, sc in first hdc, hdc in next sc, sc in next hdc, hdc in next sc, ★ † with Purple and working over Blue, (sc in next hdc, hdc in next sc) 4 times, with Blue and working over Purple, (sc in next hdc, hdc in next sc) twice †, with Purple and working over Blue, (sc in next hdc, hdc in next sc) twice, with Blue and working over Purple, (sc in next hdc, hdc in next sc) 4 times, with Purple and working over Blue, (sc in next hdc, hdc in next sc) twice, with Blue and working over Purple, (sc in next hdc, hdc in next sc) twice; repeat from ★ 4 times **more**, then repeat from † to † once.

Rows 13-16: Repeat Rows 2-4 once, then repeat Row 2 once **more**, changing to Green in last hdc made on Row 16; cut Purple.

Row 17: With Green, ch 1, turn; working over Blue, sc in first hdc, hdc in next sc, (sc in next hdc, hdc in next sc) 7 times, ★ with Blue and working over Green, (sc in next hdc, hdc in next sc) 8 times, with Green and working over Blue, (sc in next hdc, hdc in next sc) 8 times; repeat from ★ across.

Rows 18-32: Replacing Blue with Green and Purple with Blue, repeat Rows 2-16, changing to Brown in last hdc made on Row 32; cut Blue.

Row 33: Replacing Green with Brown and Blue with Green, repeat Row 17.

Rows 34-48: Replacing Blue with Brown and Purple with Green, repeat Rows 2-16, changing to Rust in last hdc on Row 48; cut Green.

Row 49: Replacing Green with Rust and Blue with Brown, repeat Row 17.

Rows 50-64: Replacing Blue with Rust and Purple with Brown, repeat Rows 2-16, changing to Red in last hdc made on Row 64; cut Brown.

Row 65: Replacing Green with Red and Blue with Rust, repeat Row 17.

Rows 66-80: Replacing Blue with Red and Purple with Rust, repeat Rows 2-16, changing to Purple in last hdc made on Row 80; cut Rust.

Row 81: Replacing Green with Purple and Blue with Red, repeat Row 17; do **not** finish off.

Continued on page 42.

41

Rows 82-96: Replacing Blue with Purple and Purple with Red, repeat Rows 2-16, changing to Blue in last hdc made on Row 96; cut Red.

Row 97: Replacing Green with Blue and Blue with Purple, repeat Row 17.

Rows 98-112: Repeat Rows 2-16; at end of Row 112, cut Blue; do **not** finish off.

EDGING

Rnd 1: With Purple, ch 2 **(counts as first hdc)**, turn; hdc in same st and in each st across to last sc, 3 hdc in last sc; hdc in end of each row across; working in free loops of beginning ch **(Fig. 3b, page 126)**, 3 hdc in first ch, hdc in each ch across to ch at base of last sc, 3 hdc in ch at base of last sc; hdc in end of each row across, hdc in same st as first hdc; join with slip st to first hdc: 584 hdc.

Rnd 2: Ch 1, do **not** turn; 2 sc in same st, working in Back Loops Only **(Fig. 2, page 125)**, ★ sc in each hdc across to center hdc of next corner 3-hdc group, 3 sc in center hdc; repeat from ★ 2 times **more**, sc in each hdc across and in same st as first sc; join with slip st to Back Loop Only of first sc: 592 sc.

Rnd 3: Ch 1, working in Back Loops Only, 2 sc in same st, ★ sc in each sc across to center sc of next corner 3-sc group, 3 sc in center sc; repeat from ★ 2 times **more**, sc in each sc across and in same st as first sc; join with slip st to Back Loop Only of first sc: 600 sc.

Rnd 4: Ch 1, working in Back Loops Only, (sc, ch 1, sc) in same st, skip next sc, ★ (sc, ch 1, sc) in next sc, skip next sc; repeat from ★ around; join with slip st to **both** loops of first sc, finish off.

BLUE DIAMONDS

Stunning in appearance, Nanette M. Seale's brilliant throw features dozens of triangles in two shades of blue accented with off-white clusters.

Finished Size: 52" x 65"

MATERIALS

Worsted Weight Yarn:
  Off-White - 34 ounces, (970 grams, 1,920 yards)
  Blue - 15 ounces, (430 grams, 850 yards)
  Dk Blue - 15 ounces, (430 grams, 850 yards)
Crochet hook, size H (5.00 mm) **or** size needed for gauge
Yarn needle

GAUGE: Each Square = 12½"

Gauge Swatch: 3¼" square
Work same as Square through Rnd 2.

STITCH GUIDE

2-DC CLUSTER (uses one st or sp)
★ YO, insert hook in st or sp indicated, YO and pull up a loop, YO and draw through 2 loops on hook; repeat from ★ once **more**, YO and draw through all 3 loops on hook.

3-DC CLUSTER (uses one st or sp)
★ YO, insert hook in st or sp indicated, YO and pull up a loop, YO and draw through 2 loops on hook; repeat from ★ 2 times **more**, YO and draw through all 4 loops on hook.

4-DC CLUSTER (uses one sp)
★ YO, insert hook in sp indicated, YO and pull up a loop, YO and draw through 2 loops on hook; repeat from ★ 3 times **more**, YO and draw through all 5 loops on hook.

5-DC CLUSTER (uses one sp)
★ YO, insert hook in sp indicated, YO and pull up a loop, YO and draw through 2 loops on hook; repeat from ★ 4 times **more**, YO and draw through all 6 loops on hook.

Continued on page 44.

SQUARE (Make 20)

Rnd 1 (Right side)**:** With Off-White, ch 3, work (2-dc Cluster, ch 3, 3-dc Cluster) in third ch from hook, ch 1, ★ work (3-dc Cluster, ch 3, 3-dc Cluster) in same ch, ch 1; repeat from ★ 2 times **more**; join with slip st to top of first 2-dc Cluster: 8 Clusters and 8 sps.

Note #1: Loop a short piece of yarn around any stitch to mark Rnd 1 as **right** side.

Note #2: When changing colors *(Fig. 5, page 126)*, keep unused color on **wrong** side of work; do **not** cut yarn until color is no longer needed. Use a separate skein or ball for each color change.

Rnd 2: Slip st in first ch-3 sp, ch 2, work (2-dc Cluster, ch 3, 3-dc Cluster) in same sp changing to Blue in last Cluster, † 5 dc in next ch-1 sp changing to Off-White in last dc, work (3-dc Cluster, ch 3, 3-dc Cluster) in next ch-3 sp changing to Dk Blue in last Cluster †, 5 dc in next ch-1 sp changing to Off-White in last dc, work (3-dc Cluster, ch 3, 3-dc Cluster) in next ch-3 sp changing to Blue in last Cluster, repeat from † to † once, 5 dc in last ch-1 sp; join with slip st to top of first 2-dc Cluster: 20 dc and 4 ch-3 sps.

Note: Continue to change colors in same manner throughout.

Rnd 3: Turn; slip st in first dc, ch 3 **(counts as first dc, now and throughout)**, dc in same st, † dc in next 3 dc, 2 dc in next dc, with Off-White, work (3-dc Cluster, ch 3, 3-dc Cluster) in next ch-3 sp, with Blue, skip next 3-dc Cluster, 2 dc in next dc, dc in next 3 dc, 2 dc in next dc, with Off-White, work (3-dc Cluster, ch 3, 3-dc Cluster) in next ch-3 sp †, with Dk Blue, skip next 3-dc Cluster, 2 dc in next dc, repeat from † to † once; join with slip st to first dc: 28 dc and 4 ch-3 sps.

Rnd 4: Turn; slip st in first 3-dc Cluster and in next ch-3 sp, ch 2, work (3-dc Cluster, ch 4, 4-dc Cluster) in same sp, † with Blue, skip next 3-dc Cluster, 2 dc in next dc, dc in next 5 dc, 2 dc in next dc, with Off-White, work (4-dc Cluster, ch 4, 4-dc Cluster) in next ch-3 sp, with Dk Blue, skip next 3-dc Cluster, 2 dc in next dc, dc in next 5 dc, 2 dc in next dc †, with Off-White, work (4-dc Cluster, ch 4, 4-dc Cluster) in next ch-3 sp, repeat from † to † once; join with slip st to top of first 3-dc Cluster: 36 dc and 4 ch-4 sps.

Rnd 5: Turn; slip st in first dc, ch 3, dc in same st, † dc in next 7 dc, 2 dc in next dc, with Off-White, work (4-dc Cluster, ch 5, 4-dc Cluster) in next ch-4 sp, with Blue, skip next 4-dc Cluster, 2 dc in next dc, dc in next 7 dc, 2 dc in next dc, with Off-White, work (4-dc Cluster, ch 5, 4-dc Cluster) in next ch-4 sp †, with Dk Blue, skip next 4-dc Cluster, 2 dc in next dc, repeat from † to † once; join with slip st to first dc: 44 dc and 4 ch-5 sps.

Rnd 6: Turn; slip st in first 4-dc Cluster and in next ch-5 sp, ch 2, work (3-dc Cluster, ch 5, 4-dc Cluster) in same sp, † with Blue, skip next 4-dc Cluster, dc in sp **before** next dc, 2 dc in next dc, dc in next 9 dc, 2 dc in next dc, dc in sp **before** next Cluster, with Off-White, work (4-dc Cluster, ch 5, 4-dc Cluster) in next ch-5 sp, with Dk Blue, skip next 4-dc Cluster, dc in sp **before** next dc, 2 dc in next dc, dc in next 9 dc, 2 dc in next dc, dc in sp **before** next Cluster †, with Off-White, work (4-dc Cluster, ch 5, 4-dc Cluster) in next ch-5 sp, repeat from † to † once; join with slip st to top of first 3-dc Cluster: 60 dc and 4 ch-5 sps.

Rnd 7: Turn; slip st in sp **before** first dc, ch 3, 2 dc in first dc, † dc in next 13 dc, 2 dc in next dc, dc in sp **before** next Cluster, with Off-White, work (5-dc Cluster, ch 5, 5-dc Cluster) in next ch-5 sp, with Blue, skip next 4-dc Cluster, dc in sp **before** next dc, 2 dc in next dc, dc in next 13 dc, 2 dc in next dc, dc in sp **before** next Cluster, with Off-White, work (5-dc Cluster, ch 5, 5-dc Cluster) in next ch-5 sp †, with Dk Blue, skip next 4-dc Cluster, dc in sp **before** next dc, 2 dc in next dc, repeat from † to † once; join with slip st to first dc: 76 dc and 4 ch-5 sps.

Rnd 8: Turn; slip st in first 5-dc Cluster and in next ch-5 sp, ch 2, work (4-dc Cluster, ch 6, 5-dc Cluster) in same sp, † with Blue, skip next 5-dc Cluster, dc in sp **before** next dc, 2 dc in next dc, dc in next 17 dc, 2 dc in next dc, dc in sp **before** next Cluster, with Off-White, work (5-dc Cluster, ch 6, 5-dc Cluster) in next ch-5 sp, with Dk Blue, skip next 5-dc Cluster, dc in sp **before** next dc, 2 dc in next dc, dc in next 17 dc, 2 dc in next dc, dc in sp **before** next Cluster †, with Off-White, work (5-dc Cluster, ch 6, 5-dc Cluster) in next ch-5 sp, repeat from † to † once; join with slip st to top of first 4-dc Cluster: 92 dc and 4 ch-6 sps.

Rnd 9: Turn; slip st in sp **before** first dc, ch 3, 2 dc in first dc, † dc in next 21 dc, 2 dc in next dc, dc in sp **before** next Cluster, cut Dk Blue; with Off-White, work (5-dc Cluster, ch 6, 5-dc Cluster) in next ch-6 sp, cut Off-White; with Blue, skip next 5-dc Cluster, dc in sp **before** next dc, 2 dc in next dc, dc in next 21 dc, 2 dc in next dc, dc in sp **before** next Cluster, cut Blue; with Off-White, work (5-dc Cluster, ch 6, 5-dc Cluster) in next ch-6 sp †, cut Off-White; with Dk Blue, skip next 5-dc Cluster, dc in sp **before** next dc, 2 dc in next dc, repeat from † to † once; join with slip st to first dc; do **not** cut last Off-White: 108 dc and 4 ch-6 sps.

Rnd 10: Ch 2, turn; work 2-dc Cluster in sp **before** first 5-dc Cluster, ch 1, ★ † work (5-dc Cluster, ch 6, 5-dc Cluster) in next ch-6 sp, ch 1, skip next 5-dc Cluster, work 3-dc Cluster in sp **before** next dc, ch 1, skip next dc, (work 3-dc Cluster in next dc, ch 1, skip next dc) 13 times †, work 3-dc Cluster in sp **before** next Cluster, ch 1; repeat from ★ 2 times **more**, then repeat from † to † once; join with slip st to top of first 2-dc Cluster: 68 Clusters and 68 sps.

Rnd 11: Ch 1, do **not** turn; sc in same st, sc in next ch-1 sp and next 5-dc Cluster, 9 sc in next corner ch-6 sp, ★ sc in each Cluster and in each ch-1 sp across to next corner ch-6 sp, 9 sc in corner ch-6 sp; repeat from ★ 2 times **more**, sc in each Cluster and in each ch-1 sp across; join with slip st to first sc, finish off: 168 sc.

ASSEMBLY

With Off-White, using photo as a guide for placement, page 43, and working through **inside** loops, whipstitch Squares together forming 4 vertical strips of 5 Squares each *(Fig. 6b, page 126)*, beginning in center sc of first corner 9-sc group and ending in center sc of next corner 9-sc group; then whipstitch strips together in same manner.

EDGING

Rnd 1: With **right** side facing and working in Back Loops Only *(Fig. 2, page 125)*, join Dk Blue with sc in center sc of lower right corner 9-sc group *(see Joining With Sc, page 125)*; 2 sc in same st, † sc in next 41 sc, (sc in same st as joining on same Square and same st as joining on next Square, sc in next 41 sc) across to center sc of next corner 9-sc group, 3 sc in center sc, 2 sc in next sc, sc in next 40 sc, (sc in same st as joining on same Square and same st as joining on next Square, sc in next 41 sc) across to center sc of next corner 9-sc group †, 3 sc in center sc, repeat from † to † once; join with slip st to **both** loops of first sc, finish off: 780 sc.

Rnd 2: With **right** side facing and working in both loops, join Blue with sc in center sc of any corner 3-sc group; 2 sc in same st, sc in each sc around working 3 sc in center sc of each corner 3-sc group; join with slip st to first sc, finish off: 788 sc.

Rnd 3: With **right** side facing, join Off-White with slip st in center sc of any corner 3-sc group; ch 2, work (2-dc Cluster, ch 3, 3-dc Cluster) in same st, ch 1, ★ skip next sc, (work 3-dc Cluster in next sc, ch 1, skip next sc) across to center sc of next corner 3-sc group, work (3-dc Cluster, ch 3, 3-dc Cluster) in center sc, ch 1; repeat from ★ 2 times **more**, skip next sc, (work 3-dc Cluster in next sc, ch 1, skip next sc) across; join with slip st to top of first 2-dc Cluster, finish off: 398 Clusters and 398 sps.

Rnd 4: With **right** side facing, join Blue with sc in any corner ch-3 sp; 2 sc in same sp, ★ sc in each Cluster and in each ch-1 sp across to next corner ch-3 sp, 3 sc in corner ch-3 sp; repeat from ★ 2 times **more**, sc in each Cluster and in each ch-1 sp across; join with slip st to first sc, finish off.

PAINTBRUSH

Framed and fringed in black with "strokes" of variegated stripes, this dynamic afghan by Rubie Critchlow was stitched all in double crochet.

Finished Size: 43½" x 63"

MATERIALS
Worsted Weight Yarn:
  Black - 20 ounces, (570 grams, 1,130 yards)
  Gold - 6½ ounces, (180 grams, 370 yards)
  Red - 6½ ounces, (180 grams, 370 yards)
  Variegated - 5 ounces, (140 grams, 290 yards)
  Blue - 4 ounces, (110 grams, 225 yards)
  Green - 4 ounces, (110 grams, 225 yards)
  Rust - 4 ounces, (110 grams, 225 yards)
  Purple - 4 ounces, (110 grams, 225 yards)
  Dk Red - 4 ounces, (110 grams, 225 yards)
Crochet hook, size F (3.75 mm) **or** size needed
  for gauge

GAUGE: In pattern, 11 dc = 3"; 8 rows = 3¾"

Gauge Swatch: 3"w x 3¾"h
With Black, ch 14 **loosely**.
Work same as Afghan for 8 rows.
Finish off.

AFGHAN

With Black, ch 160 **loosely**, place marker in third ch from hook for st placement.
Row 1: Dc in fourth ch from hook **(3 skipped chs count as first dc)** and in each ch across: 158 dc.
Row 2 (Right side)**:** Ch 3 **(counts as first dc, now and throughout)**, turn; dc in next dc and in each dc across.
Note: Loop a short piece of yarn around any stitch to mark Row 2 as **right** side.
Row 3: Ch 3, turn; dc in next dc and in each dc across; finish off.
Row 4: With **right** side facing, join Gold with slip st in first dc; ch 3, dc in next dc and in each dc across.
Rows 5 and 6: Ch 3, turn; dc in next dc and in each dc across; at end of Row 6, finish off.
Row 7: With **wrong** side facing, join Variegated with slip st in first dc; ch 3, dc in next dc and in each dc across; finish off.
Rows 8-10: Repeat Rows 4-6.

Row 11: With **wrong** side facing, join Black with slip st in first dc; ch 3, dc in next dc and in each dc across; finish off.
Rows 12-14: With Red, repeat Rows 4-6.
Row 15: Repeat Row 7.
Rows 16-18: With Red, repeat Rows 4-6.
Row 19: Repeat Row 11.
Rows 20-22: With Blue, repeat Rows 4-6.
Row 23: Repeat Row 7.
Rows 24-26: With Blue, repeat Rows 4-6.
Row 27: Repeat Row 11.
Rows 28-30: With Green, repeat Rows 4-6.
Row 31: Repeat Row 7.
Rows 32-34: With Green, repeat Rows 4-6.
Row 35: Repeat Row 11.
Rows 36-38: With Rust, repeat Rows 4-6.
Row 39: Repeat Row 7.
Rows 40-42: With Rust, repeat Rows 4-6.
Row 43: Repeat Row 11.
Rows 44-46: With Purple, repeat Rows 4-6.
Row 47: Repeat Row 7.
Rows 48-50: With Purple, repeat Rows 4-6.
Row 51: Repeat Row 11.
Rows 52-54: With Dk Red, repeat Rows 4-6.
Row 55: Repeat Row 7.
Rows 56-58: With Dk Red, repeat Rows 4-6.
Row 59: Repeat Row 11.
Rows 60-130: Repeat Rows 4-59 once, then repeat Rows 4-18 once **more**.
Row 131: With **wrong** side facing, join Black with slip st in first dc; ch 3, dc in next dc and in each dc across.
Rows 132 and 133: Ch 3, turn; dc in next dc and in each dc across; at end of Row 133, do **not** finish off.
Edging: Ch 1, turn; 2 sc in first dc, sc in each dc across to last dc, 3 sc in last dc; 2 sc in end of each row across; working in free loops of beginning ch *(Fig. 3b, page 126)*, 3 sc in marked ch, sc in each ch across to last ch, 3 sc in last ch; 2 sc in end of each row across, sc in same st as first sc; join with slip st to first sc, finish off.

Holding 6 strands of Black together, each 17" long, add fringe in every other sc across short edges of Afghan *(Figs. 9c & d, page 127)*.

SNOWMAN

*Using worsted and sport weight yarns, Carol Ann Marks set this frosty fellow in
a grey landscape reminiscent of a winter's day in the neighborhood.*

Finished Size: 48" x 60½"

MATERIALS

Worsted Weight Yarn:
    Lt Grey - 38½ ounces,
      (1,090 grams, 2,175 yards)
    Variegated - 6 ounces, (170 grams, 350 yards)
    Red - 3 ounces, (90 grams, 170 yards)
    White - 3 ounces, (90 grams, 170 yards)
    Green - 1½ ounces, (40 grams, 85 yards)
    Brown - 1 ounce, (30 grams, 55 yards)
    Grey - ½ ounce, (20 grams, 30 yards)
Sport Weight Yarn:
    Orange - small amount
    Black - small amount
Crochet hook, size H (5.00 mm) **or** size needed
    for gauge
½" Buttons - 2 (for eyes)
Sewing needle and thread
Yarn needle

GAUGE: In pattern, 12 sc and 14 rows = 4"

Gauge Swatch: 4" square
Ch 13 **loosely**.
Row 1: Sc in second ch from hook and in each ch
across: 12 sc.
Rows 2-14: Ch 1, turn; sc in each sc across.
Finish off.

STITCH GUIDE

BEGINNING DECREASE (uses first 2 sc)
Pull up a loop in first 2 sc, YO and draw through all
3 loops on hook **(counts as one sc)**.
DECREASE (uses last 2 sc)
Pull up a loop in last 2 sc, YO and draw through all
3 loops on hook **(counts as one sc)**.
PICOT
Ch 3, sc in third ch from hook.

AFGHAN BODY

With Lt Grey, ch 131 **loosely**.
Row 1 (Right side)**:** Sc in second ch from hook and in
each ch across: 130 sc.
Note: Loop a short piece of yarn around any stitch to
mark Row 1 as **right** side.
Rows 2-64: Ch 1, turn; sc in each sc across.
Row 65: Ch 1, turn; sc in first 41 sc changing to Grey
in last sc made **(Fig. 5, page 126)**, sc in next 40 sc
changing to Lt Grey in last sc made, sc in each sc
across.

Note: Continue changing colors in same manner
throughout.

Row 66: Ch 1, turn; sc in first 51 sc, with Grey sc in
next 37 sc, with Lt Grey sc in each sc across.
Row 67: Ch 1, turn; sc in first 43 sc, with Grey sc in
next 21 sc, with Lt Grey sc in each sc across.
Row 68: Ch 1, turn; sc in first 68 sc, with Grey sc in
next 18 sc, with Lt Grey sc in each sc across.
Row 69: Ch 1, turn; sc in first 46 sc, with Grey sc in
next 15 sc, cut Grey, with Lt Grey sc in each sc across.
Rows 70-76: Ch 1, turn; sc in each sc across.
Row 77: Ch 1, turn; sc in first 68 sc, with Grey sc in
next 21 sc, with Lt Grey sc in each sc across.
Row 78: Ch 1, turn; sc in first 40 sc, with Grey sc in
next 20 sc, with Lt Grey sc in each sc across.
Row 79: Ch 1, turn; sc in first 71 sc, with Grey sc in
next 22 sc, with Lt Grey sc in each sc across.
Row 80: Ch 1, turn; sc in first 35 sc, with Grey sc in
next 26 sc, with Lt Grey sc in each sc across.
Row 81: Ch 1, turn; sc in first 67 sc, with Grey sc in
next 27 sc, cut Grey, with Lt Grey sc in each sc across.
Rows 82-194: Ch 1, turn; sc in each sc across.
Finish off.

Continued on page 50.

EDGING

Rnd 1: With **right** side facing, join Red with sc in first sc on Row 194 *(see Joining With Sc, page 125)*; sc in same st and in each sc across to last sc, 3 sc in last sc; sc evenly spaced across end of rows; working in free loops of beginning ch *(Fig. 3b, page 126)*, 3 sc in first ch, sc in each ch across to ch at base of last sc, 3 sc in ch at base of last sc; sc evenly spaced across end of rows, sc in same st as first sc; join with slip st to first sc.

Rnd 2: Ch 1, 3 sc in same st, ★ sc in each sc across to center sc of next corner 3-sc group, 3 sc in center sc; repeat from ★ 2 times **more**, sc in each sc across; join with slip st to first sc, finish off.

Rnd 3: With **right** side facing, join Variegated with sc in center sc of any corner 3-sc group; ★ sc in same st and in each sc across to center sc of next corner 3-sc group, 3 sc in center sc; repeat from ★ 2 times **more**, sc in each sc across and in same st as first sc; join with slip st to first sc.

Rnds 4-8: Ch 1, 2 sc in same st, ★ sc in next sc and in each sc across to center sc of next corner 3-sc group, 3 sc in center sc; repeat from ★ 2 times **more**, sc in each sc across and in same st as first sc; join with slip st to first sc.
Finish off.

Rnd 9: With **right** side facing, join Red with slip st in any sc; ch 1, working from **left** to **right**, work reverse sc in each sc around *(Figs. 8a-d, page 127)*; join with slip st to first st, finish off.

ADDITIONAL PIECES
SNOWMAN
BODY

With White, ch 16 **loosely**.
Row 1: Sc in second ch from hook and in each ch across: 15 sc.
Row 2 (Right side): Ch 1, turn; 2 sc in first sc, sc in each sc across to last sc, 2 sc in last sc: 17 sc.
Note: Loop a short piece of yarn around any stitch to mark Row 2 as **right** side.
Row 3: Ch 1, turn; sc in each sc across.
Row 4 (Increase row): Ch 1, turn; 2 sc in first sc, sc in each sc across to last sc, 2 sc in last sc: 19 sc.
Rows 5-8: Repeat Rows 3 and 4 twice: 23 sc.
Rows 9-16: Ch 1, turn; sc in each sc across.
Rows 17 (Decrease row): Ch 1, turn; work beginning decrease, sc in each sc across to last 2 sc, decrease: 21 sc.
Row 18: Ch 1, turn; sc in each sc across.
Rows 19-26: Repeat Rows 17 and 18, 4 times: 13 sc.
Row 27 (Increase row): Ch 1, turn; 2 sc in first sc, sc in each sc across to last sc, 2 sc in last sc: 15 sc.
Row 28: Ch 1, turn; sc in each sc across.
Rows 29-31: Repeat Rows 27 and 28 once, then repeat Row 27 once **more**: 19 sc.
Rows 32-36: Ch 1, turn; sc in each sc across.

Row 37 (Decrease row): Ch 1, turn; work beginning decrease, sc in each sc across to last 2 sc, decrease: 17 sc.
Row 38: Ch 1, turn; sc in each sc across.
Rows 39-41: Repeat Rows 37 and 38 once, then repeat Row 37 once **more**: 13 sc.
Row 42: Ch 1, turn; sc in each sc across changing to Variegated in last sc; do **not** finish off.

SCARF

Row 1 (Decrease row): Ch 1, turn; working in Back Loops Only *(Fig. 2, page 125)*, work beginning decrease, sc in each sc across to last 2 sc, decrease: 11 sc.
Row 2: Ch 1, turn; sc in Back Loop Only of each sc across.
Rows 3 and 4: Repeat Rows 1 and 2: 9 sc.
Row 5: Ch 1, turn; working in Back Loops Only, 2 sc in first sc, sc in each sc across to last sc, 2 sc in last sc changing to White in last sc; do **not** finish off: 11 sc.

HEAD

Row 1: Ch 1, turn; sc in Back Loop Only of each sc across.
Row 2: Ch 1, turn; working in both loops, 2 sc in first sc, sc in each sc across to last sc, 2 sc in last sc: 13 sc.
Row 3: Ch 1, turn; sc in each sc across.
Row 4: Ch 1, turn; 2 sc in first sc, sc in each sc across to last sc, 2 sc in last sc: 15 sc.
Rows 5-9: Ch 1, turn; sc in each sc across, changing to Red in last sc at end of Row 9; do **not** finish off.

HAT

Row 1: Ch 1, turn; sc in Front Loop Only of each sc across.
Row 2: Ch 1, turn; working in both loops, work beginning decrease, sc in each sc across to last 2 sc, decrease: 13 sc.
Row 3: Ch 1, turn; sc in each sc across.
Row 4 (Decrease row): Ch 1, turn; work beginning decrease, sc in each sc across to last 2 sc, decrease: 11 sc.
Rows 5-13: Repeat Rows 3 and 4, 4 times; then repeat Row 3 once **more**: 3 sc.
Row 14: Ch 11, turn; slip st in first sc, ch 11, (slip st in next sc, ch 11) twice, slip st in end of Row 13; finish off.
Brim: With **right** side facing and working in free loops of sts on Row 9 of Head *(Fig. 3a, page 126)*, join Red with sc in end of Row 9; (ch 1, sc in next sc) across; finish off.

ARM (Make 2)

With White, ch 3 **loosely**.
Row 1: 2 Sc in second ch from hook, sc in last ch: 3 sc.
Row 2: Ch 1, turn; sc in each sc across.
Row 3: Ch 1, turn; 2 sc in first sc, decrease.
Rows 4 and 5: Repeat Rows 2 and 3.
Rows 6-10: Ch 1, turn; sc in each sc across.
Row 11: Ch 1, turn; work beginning decrease, 2 sc in last sc.
Row 12: Ch 1, turn; sc in each sc across.
Rows 13-16: Repeat Rows 11 and 12 twice.
Finish off.

SCARF TIE (Make 2)
With Variegated, ch 4 **loosely**.
Row 1: Sc in second ch from hook and in each ch across: 3 sc.
Rows 2-20: Ch 1, turn; sc in each sc across. Finish off.

Using 2 strands of Variegated, each 4" long, add fringe in each sc across Row 20 *(Figs. 9c & d, page 127)*.

SIGN
CENTER
With White, ch 16 **loosely**.
Row 1 (Right side): Sc in second ch from hook and in each ch across: 15 sc.
Note: Loop a short piece of yarn around any stitch to mark Row 1 as **right** side.
Rows 2-6: Ch 1, turn; sc in each sc across. Finish off.

EDGING
Rnd 1: With **right** side facing, join Brown with sc in first sc on Row 6; 2 sc in same st, sc in each sc across to last sc, 3 sc in last sc; sc in end of each row across; working in free loops of beginning ch, 3 sc in first ch, sc in each sc across to ch at base of last sc, 3 sc in ch at base of last sc; sc in end of each row across; join with slip st to first sc: 50 sc.
Rnd 2: Ch 1, working from **left** to **right**, work reverse sc in each sc around; join with slip st to first st, finish off.

POST
With Brown, ch 3 **loosely**.
Row 1: Sc in second ch from hook and in next ch: 2 sc.
Rows 2-20: Ch 1, turn; sc in each sc across. Finish off.

TREE
Row 1: With Green, ch 2, 3 sc in second ch from hook: 3 sc.
Row 2: Ch 1, turn; sc in each sc across.
Row 3: Ch 1, turn; 2 sc in first sc, sc in next sc, 2 sc in last sc: 5 sc.
Row 4: Ch 1, turn; sc in each sc across.
Row 5 (Increase row): Ch 1, turn; 2 sc in first sc, sc in each sc across to last sc, 2 sc in last sc: 7 sc.
Rows 6-8: Repeat Rows 4 and 5 once, then repeat Row 4 once **more**: 9 sc.
Row 9: Turn; slip st in first 3 sc, ch 1, sc in same st and in next 4 sc, leave remaining 2 sc unworked: 5 sc.
Row 10: Ch 1, turn; 2 sc in first sc, sc in next 3 sc, 2 sc in next sc, leave remaining sts unworked: 7 sc.
Rows 11 and 12: Ch 1, turn; 2 sc in first sc, sc in each sc across to last sc, 2 sc in last sc: 11 sc.
Rows 13-17: Repeat Rows 4 and 5 twice, then repeat Row 4 once **more**: 15 sc.
Row 18: Turn; slip st in first 4 sc, ch 1, sc in same st and in next 8 sc, leave remaining 3 sc unworked: 9 sc.

Row 19: Ch 1, turn; 2 sc in first sc, sc in next 7 sc, 2 sc in next sc, leave remaining sts unworked: 11 sc.
Rows 20 and 21: Ch 1, turn; 2 sc in first sc, sc in each sc across to last sc, 2 sc in last sc: 15 sc.
Rows 22-24: Repeat Rows 4 and 5 once, then repeat Row 4 once **more**: 17 sc.
Row 25: Turn; slip st in first 5 sc, ch 1, sc in same st and in next 8 sc, leave remaining 4 sc unworked: 9 sc.
Row 26: Ch 1, turn; 2 sc in first sc, sc in next 7 sc, 2 sc in next sc, leave remaining sts unworked: 11 sc.
Rows 27-29: Ch 1, turn; 2 sc in first sc, sc in each sc across to last sc, 2 sc in last sc: 17 sc.
Rows 30-34: Repeat Rows 4 and 5 twice, then repeat Row 4 once **more**: 21 sc.
Row 35: Turn; slip st in first 6 sc, ch 1, sc in same st and in next 10 sc, leave remaining 5 sc unworked: 11 sc.
Row 36 (Increase row): Ch 1, turn; 2 sc in first sc, sc in next 9 sc, 2 sc in next sc, leave remaining sts unworked: 13 sc.
Rows 37-41 (Increase rows): Ch 1, turn; 2 sc in first sc, sc in each sc across to last sc, 2 sc in last sc: 23 sc.
Row 42: Turn; slip st in first 7 sc, ch 1, sc in same st and in next 10 sc, leave remaining 6 sc unworked: 11 sc.
Rows 43-55: Repeat Rows 36-42 once, then repeat Rows 36-41 once **more**: 23 sc.
Rows 56 and 57: Ch 1, turn; sc in each sc across. Finish off.

SNOWFLAKES
#1 (Make 8)
With White, ch 3; join with slip st to form a ring.
Rnd 1 (Right side): Ch 1, (sc in ring, ch 5) 5 times; join with slip st to first sc, finish off.

#2 (Make 7)
With White, ch 2, (sc, work Picot) 5 times in second ch from hook; join with slip st to first sc, finish off.

FINISHING
Using photo as a guide for placement, page 49:

Sew Buttons to Head for eyes.
With Orange, add Straight Sts for nose *(Fig. 10, page 127)*.
With Black, add Straight Sts for mouth.
With Variegated, sew Ties to Scarf.
With White, sew Arms along Body, leaving a space to put Ties through.
With White, sew Snowman to Afghan.
With Black, add Straight Sts to center of Sign to form words "LET IT SNOW".
With Brown, sew Sign to Snowman Body.
With Brown, sew Post to Sign.
With Green, sew Tree to Afghan.
With White, sew Snowflakes to Afghan.

LOG CABIN GRANNY

Carole G. Wilder produced this heartwarming cover-up by combining classic design elements from favorite family heirlooms — hand-stitched quilts and crocheted afghans.

Finished Size: 49½" x 64½"

MATERIALS

Worsted Weight Yarn:
  Dk Blue - 17½ ounces, (500 grams, 990 yards)
  Variegated - 11½ ounces, (330 grams, 665 yards)
  Blue - 10½ ounces, (300 grams, 595 yards)
  Lt Blue - 7 ounces, (200 grams, 395 yards)
  Brown - 6½ ounces, (180 grams, 370 yards)
  Lt Brown - 3½ ounces, (100 grams, 200 yards)
  Red - 2 ounces, (60 grams, 115 yards)
Crochet hook, size H (5.00 mm) **or** size needed for gauge

GAUGE: Each Square = 7½"

Gauge Swatch: 1½" diameter
Work same as Foundation Rnd.

SQUARE (Make 48)

Foundation Rnd (Right side)**:** With Red, ch 4, 2 dc in fourth ch from hook, ch 2, (3 dc in same ch, ch 2) 3 times; join with slip st to top of beginning ch, finish off: 4 ch-2 sps.

Note #1: Loop a short piece of yarn around any stitch to mark Foundation Rnd as **right** side.

Note #2: Remainder of Square will be worked in rows.

Row 1: With **wrong** side facing, join Lt Brown with slip st in any ch-2 sp; ch 3 **(counts as first dc, now and throughout)**, 2 dc in same sp, ch 1, (3 dc, ch 2, 3 dc) in next ch-2 sp, ch 1, 3 dc in next ch-2 sp, leave remaining sp unworked: 3 sps.

Row 2: Ch 2, turn; 3 dc in next ch-1 sp, ch 1, (3 dc, ch 2, 3 dc) in next ch-2 sp, ch 1, 3 dc in next ch-1 sp, ch 2, skip next 2 dc, slip st in last dc; finish off: 5 sps.

Row 3: With **wrong** side facing, join Lt Blue with slip st in first ch-2 sp made on Row 2; ch 3, 2 dc in same sp, ch 1, 3 dc in next sp on Foundation Rnd (same sp as last 3 dc worked on Row 1), ch 1, (3 dc, ch 2, 3 dc) in next ch-2 sp, ch 1, 3 dc in next sp (same sp as first 3 dc worked on Row 1), ch 1, 3 dc in last ch-2 sp on Row 2.

Row 4: Ch 2, turn; (3 dc in next ch-1 sp, ch 1) twice, (3 dc, ch 2, 3 dc) in next ch-2 sp, (ch 1, 3 dc in next ch-1 sp) twice, ch 2, skip next 2 dc, slip st in last dc; finish off: 7 sps.

Row 5: With **wrong** side facing, join Brown with slip st in first ch-2 sp made on Row 4; ch 3, 2 dc in same sp, ch 1, (3 dc in next sp, ch 1) twice, (3 dc, ch 2, 3 dc) in next corner ch-2 sp, (ch 1, 3 dc in next sp) 3 times.

Row 6: Ch 2, turn; (3 dc in next ch-1 sp, ch 1) 3 times, (3 dc, ch 2, 3 dc) in next corner ch-2 sp, (ch 1, 3 dc in next ch-1 sp) 3 times, ch 2, skip next 2 dc, slip st in last dc; finish off: 9 sps.

Row 7: With **wrong** side facing, join Blue with slip st in first ch-2 sp made on Row 6; ch 3, 2 dc in same sp, ch 1, (3 dc in next sp, ch 1) 3 times, (3 dc, ch 2, 3 dc) in next corner ch-2 sp, (ch 1, 3 dc in next sp) 4 times.

Row 8: Ch 2, turn; (3 dc in next ch-1 sp, ch 1) 4 times, (3 dc, ch 2, 3 dc) in next corner ch-2 sp, (ch 1, 3 dc in next ch-1 sp) 4 times, ch 2, skip next 2 dc, slip st in last dc; finish off: 11 sps.

Row 9: With **wrong** side facing, join Variegated with slip st in first ch-2 sp made on Row 8; ch 3, 2 dc in same sp, ch 1, (3 dc in next sp, ch 1) 4 times, (3 dc, ch 2, 3 dc) in next corner ch-2 sp, (ch 1, 3 dc in next sp) 5 times.

Row 10: Ch 2, turn; (3 dc in next ch-1 sp, ch 1) 5 times, (3 dc, ch 2, 3 dc) in next corner ch-2 sp, (ch 1, 3 dc in next ch-1 sp) 5 times, ch 2, skip next 2 dc, slip st in last dc; finish off: 13 sps.

Row 11: With **wrong** side facing, join Dk Blue with slip st in first ch-2 sp made on Row 10; ch 3, 2 dc in same sp, ch 1, (3 dc in next sp, ch 1) 5 times, (3 dc, ch 2, 3 dc) in next corner ch-2 sp, (ch 1, 3 dc in next sp) 6 times.

Row 12: Ch 2, turn; (3 dc in next ch-1 sp, ch 1) 6 times, (3 dc, ch 2, 3 dc) in next corner ch-2 sp, (ch 1, 3 dc in next ch-1 sp) 6 times, ch 2, skip next 2 dc, slip st in last dc; finish off: 15 sps.

Continued on page 54.

ASSEMBLY

Using Placement Diagram as a guide, join Squares together forming 6 vertical strips of 8 Squares each as follows:

Holding 2 Squares with **right** sides together, working through **both** thicknesses and matching colors, join yarn with sc in first corner ch-2 sp *(see Joining With Sc, page 125)*; ch 3 **loosely**, (sc in next ch-1 sp, ch 3 **loosely**) across to next corner ch-2 sp, sc in corner ch-2 sp; finish off.

Join strips together in same manner.

PLACEMENT DIAGRAM

KEY

■ - Red

◣ - Browns

◣ - Blues

EDGING

Rnd 1: With **right** side facing, join Dk Blue with slip st in top right corner ch-2 sp at end of Row 12; ch 3, dc in same sp, † work 171 dc evenly spaced across to next corner ch-2 sp; (2 dc, ch 2, 2 dc) in corner ch-2 sp, work 225 dc evenly spaced across to next corner ch-2 sp †, (2 dc, ch 2, 2 dc) in corner ch-2 sp, repeat from † to † once, 2 dc in same sp as first dc, ch 2; join with slip st to first dc: 808 dc and 4 ch-2 sps.

Rnd 2: Ch 3, ★ dc in next dc and in each dc across to next corner ch-2 sp, (2 dc, ch 2, 2 dc) in corner sp; repeat from ★ around; join with slip st to first dc, finish off: 824 dc and 4 ch-2 sps.

Rnd 3: With **right** side facing, join Blue with sc in any corner ch-2 sp; ★ † skip next 2 dc, 5 dc in next dc, skip next 2 dc, (sc in next dc, skip next 2 dc, 5 dc in next dc, skip next 2 dc) across to next corner ch-2 sp †, sc in corner ch-2 sp; repeat from ★ 2 times **more**, then repeat from † to † once; join with slip st to first sc, finish off: 138 5-dc groups and 138 sc.

Rnd 4: With **right** side facing, join Lt Blue with slip st in any corner sc; ch 3, 6 dc in same st, skip next 2 dc, sc in next dc, ★ skip next 2 dc, (5 dc in next sc, skip next 2 dc, sc in next dc, skip next 2 dc) across to next corner sc, 7 dc in corner sc, skip next 2 dc, sc in next dc; repeat from ★ 2 times **more**, skip next 2 dc, (5 dc in next sc, skip next 2 dc, sc in next dc, skip next 2 dc) across; join with slip st to first dc, finish off.

BERRIES IN CREAM

Unusual twisted single crochets and lots of clusters pair up for this sweet treat of a wrap designed by Karen M. Robison.

Finished Size: 41" x 55½"

MATERIALS

Worsted Weight Yarn:
  Rose - 14 ounces, (400 grams, 790 yards)
  Blue - 13 ounces, (370 grams, 735 yards)
  Ecru - 9 ounces, (260 grams, 510 yards)
Crochet hook, size H (5.00 mm) **or** size needed for gauge

GAUGE: Each Square = 7¼"

Gauge Swatch: 2¾" diameter
Work same as First Square through Rnd 2.

Continued on page 56.

STITCH GUIDE

TWISTED SC
Holding yarn **behind** hook, insert hook from **back** to **front** in st or sp indicated, YO and pull up a loop, YO and draw through both loops on hook.

BEGINNING CLUSTER (uses one st)
Ch 2, ★ YO, insert hook in st indicated, YO and pull up a loop, YO and draw through 2 loops on hook; repeat from ★ 3 times **more**, YO and draw through all 5 loops on hook.

CLUSTER (uses one st)
★ YO, insert hook in st indicated, YO and pull up a loop, YO and draw through 2 loops on hook; repeat from ★ 4 times **more**, YO and draw through all 6 loops on hook.

PICOT
Ch 5, slip st in top of Cluster just made.

FIRST SQUARE

With Blue, ch 4; join with slip st to form a ring.

Rnd 1 (Right side): Ch 1, work 8 Twisted sc in ring; join with slip st to first sc.

Note: Loop a short piece of yarn around any stitch to mark Rnd 1 as **right** side.

Rnd 2: Work Beginning Cluster in same st, ch 3, (work Cluster in next sc, ch 3) around; join with slip st to top of Beginning Cluster: 8 Clusters and 24 chs.

Rnd 3: Slip st in next ch, work Beginning Cluster in same st, ch 3, skip next ch, work Cluster in next ch, ch 3, skip next Cluster, ★ work Cluster in next ch, ch 3, skip next ch, work Cluster in next ch, ch 3, skip next Cluster; repeat from ★ around; join with slip st to top of Beginning Cluster, finish off: 16 Clusters and 48 chs.

Rnd 4: With **right** side facing, join Ecru with slip st in first ch to left of any Cluster; ch 1, work Twisted sc in same st, ch 1, skip next ch, work Twisted sc in next ch, ch 1, skip next Cluster, ★ work Twisted sc in next ch, ch 1, skip next ch, work Twisted sc in next ch, ch 1, skip next Cluster; repeat from ★ around; join with slip st to first sc: 32 chs.

Rnd 5: Slip st in next ch, ch 1, work Twisted sc in same st, ch 3, skip next sc, work Twisted sc in next ch, ch 1, skip next sc, ★ work Twisted sc in next ch, ch 3, skip next sc, work Twisted sc in next ch, ch 1, skip next sc; repeat from ★ around; join with slip st to first sc, finish off.

Rnd 6: With **right** side facing, join Rose with slip st in center ch of any ch-3; ch 1, (work Twisted sc in same st, ch 3) twice, skip next 2 sc, [(work Twisted sc, ch 3) twice in center ch of next ch-3, skip next 2 sc] twice, work Cluster in next ch, ch 3, work Cluster in next ch, work Picot, ch 3, work Cluster in next ch, ch 3, skip next 2 sc, ★ [(work Twisted sc, ch 3) twice in center ch of next ch-3, skip next 2 sc] 3 times, work Cluster in next ch, ch 3, work Cluster in next ch, work Picot, ch 3, work Cluster in next ch, ch 3, skip next 2 sc; repeat from ★ 2 times **more**; join with slip st to first sc, finish off.

ADDITIONAL 34 SQUARES

Work same as First Square through Rnd 5.

Rnd 6 (Joining rnd)**:** Work One or Two Side Joining, arranging Squares into 5 rows of 7 Squares each.

Note: When joining to a Square that has been previously joined, work slip st in joining slip st.

ONE SIDE JOINING

Rnd 6 (Joining rnd)**:** With **right** side facing, join Rose with slip st in center ch of any ch-3; ch 1, (work Twisted sc in same st, ch 3) twice, skip next 2 sc, [(work Twisted sc, ch 3) twice in center ch of next ch-3, skip next 2 sc] twice, work Cluster in next ch, ch 3, work Cluster in next ch, ★ work Picot, ch 3, work Cluster in next ch, ch 3, skip next 2 sc, [(work Twisted sc, ch 3) twice in center ch of next ch-3, skip next 2 sc] 3 times, work Cluster in next ch, ch 3, work Cluster in next ch; repeat from ★ once **more**, ch 2, holding Squares with **wrong** sides together, slip st in corresponding corner Picot on **previous Square**, ch 2, slip st in top of last Cluster made on **new Square**, ch 1, slip st in center ch of next ch-3 on **previous Square**, ch 1, work Cluster in next ch on **new Square**, ch 1, slip st in center ch of next ch-3 on **previous Square**, ch 1, skip next 2 sc on **new Square**, † work Twisted sc in center ch of next ch-3, ch 1, slip st in center ch of next ch-3 on **previous Square**, ch 1, work Twisted sc in same ch on **new Square**, ch 1, slip st in center ch of next ch-3 on **previous Square**, ch 1, skip next 2 sc on **new Square** †, repeat from † to † 2 times **more**, work Cluster in next ch, ch 1, slip st in center ch of next ch-3 on **previous Square**, ch 1, work Cluster in next ch on **new Square**, ch 2, slip st in next corner Picot on **previous Square**, ch 2, slip st in top of last Cluster made on **new Square**, ch 3, work Cluster in next ch, ch 3, skip last 2 sc; join with slip st to first sc, finish off.

TWO SIDE JOINING

Rnd 6 (Joining rnd)**:** With **right** side facing, join Rose with slip st in center ch of any ch-3; ch 1, (work Twisted sc in same st, ch 3) twice, skip next 2 sc, [(work Twisted sc, ch 3) twice in center ch of next ch-3, skip next 2 sc] twice, work Cluster in next ch, ch 3, work Cluster in next ch, work Picot, ch 3, work Cluster in next ch, ch 3, skip next 2 sc, [(work Twisted sc, ch 3) twice in center ch of next ch-3, skip next 2 sc] 3 times, work Cluster in next ch, ch 3, work Cluster in next ch, ch 2, holding Squares with **wrong** sides together, slip st in corresponding corner Picot on **previous Square**, ch 2, slip st in top of last Cluster made on **new Square**, † ch 1, slip st in center ch of next ch-3 on **previous Square**, ch 1, work Cluster in next ch on **new Square**, ch 1, slip st in center ch of next ch-3 on **previous Square**, ch 1, skip next 2 sc on **new Square**, ★ work Twisted sc in center ch of next ch-3, ch 1, slip st in center ch of next ch-3 on **previous Square**, ch 1, work Twisted sc in same ch on **new Square**, ch 1, slip st in center ch of next ch-3 on **previous Square**, ch 1, skip next 2 sc on **new Square**; repeat from ★ 2 times **more**, work Cluster in next ch, ch 1, slip st in center ch of next ch-3 on **previous Square**, ch 1, work Cluster in next ch on **new Square**, ch 2 †, slip st in next joining slip st on **previous Square**, ch 2, slip st in top of last Cluster made on **new Square**, repeat from † to † once, slip st in next corner Picot on **previous Square**, ch 2, slip st in top of last Cluster made on **new Square**, ch 3, work Cluster in next ch, ch 3, skip last 2 sc; join with slip st to first sc, finish off.

EDGING

Rnd 1: With **right** side facing, join Rose with slip st in top right corner Picot; ch 1, (work Twisted sc in same sp, ch 3) 4 times, skip next 2 ch-3 sps, (work Twisted sc, ch 3) twice in center ch of next ch-3, [skip next ch-3 sp, (work Twisted sc, ch 3) twice in center ch of next ch-3] twice, skip next 2 ch-3 sps, ★ † (work Twisted sc, ch 3) twice in top of next Cluster, skip next joining, (work Twisted sc, ch 3) twice in slip st of next Picot, skip next 2 ch-3 sps, (work Twisted sc, ch 3) twice in center ch of next ch-3, [skip next ch-3 sp, (work Twisted sc, ch 3) twice in center ch of next ch-3] twice, skip next 2 ch-3 sps †, repeat from † to † across to next corner Picot, (work Twisted sc in corner Picot, ch 3) 4 times, skip next 2 ch-3 sps, (work Twisted sc, ch 3) twice in center ch of next ch-3, [skip next ch-3 sp, (work Twisted sc, ch 3) twice in center ch of next ch-3] twice; repeat from ★ 2 times **more**, then repeat from † to † across; join with slip st to first sc: 240 ch-3 sps.

Rnd 2: Slip st in next ch, work Beginning Cluster in same st, ch 3, (work Cluster in next ch, ch 3) twice, work Cluster in center ch of next ch-3, ch 3, † skip next sc, [work Cluster in next ch, (ch 3, work Cluster in next ch) twice, ch 1, skip next ch-3 sp, work Twisted sc in center ch of next ch-3, ch 1, skip next ch-3 sp] 12 times, (work Cluster in next ch, ch 3) 3 times, work Cluster in center ch of next ch-3, ch 3, skip next sc, [work Cluster in next ch, (ch 3, work Cluster in next ch) twice, ch 1, skip next ch-3 sp, work Twisted sc in center ch of next ch-3, ch 1, skip next ch-3 sp] 17 times †, (work Cluster in next ch, ch 3) 3 times, work Cluster in center ch of next ch-3, ch 3, repeat from † to † once; join with slip st to top of Beginning Cluster, finish off: 248 sps.

Rnd 3: With **right** side facing, join Ecru with slip st in first ch of first ch-3 to left of joining; ch 1, work Twisted sc in same st and in next 2 chs, ch 3, (skip next Cluster, work Twisted sc in next 3 chs, ch 3) 5 times, ★ † skip next 2 ch-1 sps, [(skip next Cluster, work Twisted sc in next 3 chs, ch 3) twice, skip next 2 ch-1 sps] across to next corner 7-Cluster group †, (skip next Cluster, work Twisted sc in next 3 chs, ch 3) 6 times; repeat from ★ 2 times **more**, then repeat from † to † once; join with slip st to first sc: 396 sc and 132 ch-3 sps.

Rnd 4: Slip st in next sc, ch 3, hdc in same st, (hdc, ch 1, hdc) in center ch of next ch-3, ★ (hdc, ch 1, hdc) in center sc of next 3-sc group, (hdc, ch 1, hdc) in center ch of next ch-3; repeat from ★ around; join with slip st to second ch of beginning ch-3, finish off.

WOVEN SCRAPS

To create this pretty coverlet, Cathy Grivnow wove short lattice strips together to make squares and then joined them in a distinctive arrangement.

Finished Size: 51" x 67½"

MATERIALS
Worsted Weight Yarn:
    Ecru - 53 ounces, (1,510 grams, 2,995 yards)
    Pink - 9½ ounces, (270 grams, 535 yards)
    Blue - 9½ ounces, (270 grams, 535 yards)
    Green - 9½ ounces, (270 grams, 535 yards)
Crochet hook, size H (5.00 mm) **or** size needed
    for gauge
Safety pins
Yarn needle

GAUGE: Each Square = 5¾"

Gauge Swatch: 1"w x 4½"h
Work same as Lattice Strip.

STITCH GUIDE

> **DECREASE** (uses 2 chs and 2 joinings)
> Insert hook in next ch, YO and pull up a loop, (insert hook in **next** joining, YO and pull up a loop) twice, insert hook in next unworked ch on next Square, YO and pull up a loop, YO and draw through all 5 loops on hook.

LATTICE STRIP
Note: Make the following number of Lattice Strips in the color indicated: Pink - 112, Blue - 112, Green - 108, and Ecru - 332.

With color indicated, ch 4 **loosely**.
Row 1 (Right side)**:** Sc in second ch from hook and in last 2 chs: 3 sc.
Note: Loop a short piece of yarn around any stitch to mark Row 1 as **right** side.
Rows 2-14: Ch 1, turn; sc in each sc across.
Finish off.

SQUARE
Note: Each Square consists of 8 Lattice Strips - 4 Ecru and 4 of Pink, Blue, **or** Green.

With **right** sides facing, using photo as a guide for placement, page 59, and using safety pins to hold Strips in place, weave Lattice Strips together to form Square.

BORDER
Note: Rnd 1 of Border is worked across short edges of Lattice Strips; be careful not to catch stitches on long edges of Strips as you work.

Rnd 1: With **right** side facing, join Ecru with sc in first st on Strip at top right corner **(see Joining With Sc, page 125)**; sc in next 2 sts, 3 sc in each of next 3 Strips, (ch 2, 3 sc in each of next 4 Strips) 3 times, hdc in first sc to form last ch-2 sp: 48 sc and 4 ch-2 sps.
Rnd 2: Ch 3 **(counts as first dc)**, (dc, ch 2, 2 dc) in same sp, ★ dc in each sc across to next corner ch-2 sp, (2 dc, ch 2, 2 dc) in corner ch-2 sp; repeat from ★ 2 times **more**, dc in each sc across; join with slip st to first dc, finish off: 64 dc and 4 ch-2 sps.

ASSEMBLY
With Ecru, using Placement Diagram as a guide, and working through **inside** loops, whipstitch Squares together **(Fig. 6b, page 126)**, beginning in second ch of first corner ch-2 and ending in first ch of next corner ch-2.

PLACEMENT DIAGRAM

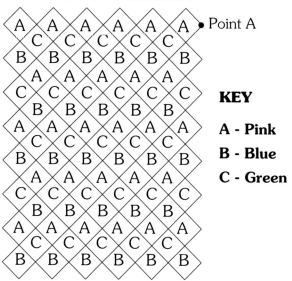

KEY

A - Pink

B - Blue

C - Green

Continued on page 60.

EDGING

Rnd 1: With **right** side facing and working in Back Loops Only *(Fig. 2, page 125)*, join Ecru with sc in first ch of corner ch-2 at Point A, page 58; sc in same ch and in next 17 sts, 2 sc in next ch, sc in next 17 sts, † decrease, sc in next 16 dc, (2 sc in next ch, sc in next 17 sts, decrease, sc in next 16 dc) 4 times, (2 sc in next ch, sc in next 17 sts) twice, decrease, sc in next 16 dc, (2 sc in next ch, sc in next 17 sts, decrease, sc in next 16 dc) 6 times †, (2 sc in next ch, sc in next 17 sts) twice, repeat from † to † once; join with slip st to first sc: 940 sts.

Rnd 2: Slip st in next sc, ch 4, dc in same st, (ch 1, dc in same st) 3 times, skip next 2 sc, sc in next sc, skip next 2 sc, dc in next sc, (ch 1, dc in same st) 4 times, † skip next 3 sc, sc in sp **before** next sc, skip next 3 sc, [dc in next sc, (ch 1, dc in same st) 4 times, skip next 2 sc, sc in next sc, skip next 2 sc] 4 times, 3 dc in next decrease, ★ skip next 2 sc, sc in next sc, skip next 2 sc, [dc in next sc, (ch 1, dc in same st) 4 times, skip next 2 sc, sc in next sc, skip next 2 sc] 5 times, 3 dc in next decrease; repeat from ★ 3 times **more**, [skip next 2 sc, sc in next sc, skip next 2 sc, dc in next sc, (ch 1, dc in same st) 4 times] 4 times, skip next 3 sc, sc in sp **before** next sc, skip next 3 sc, [dc in next sc, (ch 1, dc in same st) 4 times, skip next 2 sc, sc in next sc, skip next 2 sc] 4 times, 3 dc in next decrease, ♥ skip next 2 sc, sc in next sc, skip next 2 sc, [dc in next dc, (ch 1, dc in same st) 4 times, skip next 2 sc, sc in next sc, skip next 2 sc] 5 times, 3 dc in next decrease ♥; repeat from ♥ to ♥ 5 times **more** †, [skip next 2 sc, sc in next sc, skip next 2 sc, dc in next sc, (ch 1, dc in same st) 4 times] 4 times, repeat from † to † once, skip next 2 sc, sc in next sc, skip next 2 sc, [dc in next sc, (ch 1, dc in same st) 4 times, skip next 2 sc, sc in next sc, skip next 2 sc] twice; join with slip st to third ch of beginning ch-4, finish off.

ANGELS

Worked in one piece, this heavenly afghan by Nancy D. Luebke is highlighted by winged beauties with textured popcorn stitch halos.

Finished Size: 48" x 67½"

MATERIALS
Worsted Weight Yarn:
   52 ounces, (1,480 grams, 2,940 yards)
   Crochet hook, size I (5.50 mm) **or** size needed
      for gauge

GAUGE: In pattern, 13 dc and 8 rows = 4"

Gauge Swatch: 4" square
Ch 15 **loosely**.
Row 1: Dc in fourth ch from hook **(3 skipped chs count as first dc)** and in each ch across: 13 dc.
Rows 2-8: Ch 3 **(counts as first dc)**, turn; dc in next dc and in each dc across.
Finish off.

STITCH GUIDE

DOUBLE TREBLE CROCHET
   (abbreviated dtr)
YO 3 times, insert hook in st or sp indicated, YO and pull up a loop (5 loops on hook), (YO and draw through 2 loops on hook) 4 times. Push dtr to **right** side.

FRONT POST TREBLE CROCHET
   (abbreviated FPtr)
YO twice, insert hook from **front** to **back** around post of st indicated *(Fig. 4, page 126)*, YO and pull up a loop (4 loops on hook), (YO and draw through 2 loops on hook) 3 times. Skip st behind FPtr.

BACK POST TREBLE CROCHET
   (abbreviated BPtr)
YO twice, insert hook from **back** to **front** around post of st indicated *(Fig. 4, page 126)*, YO and pull up a loop (4 loops on hook), (YO and draw through 2 loops on hook) 3 times. Skip st in front of BPtr.

POPCORN
5 Dc in dc or sp indicated, drop loop from hook, insert hook in first dc of 5-dc group, hook dropped loop and draw through. Push Popcorn to **right** side.

DECREASE (uses next 2 dc)
★ YO, insert hook in **next** dc, YO and pull up a loop, YO and draw through 2 loops on hook; repeat from ★ once **more**, YO and draw through all 3 loops on hook **(counts as one dc)**.

CLUSTER (uses next 3 dc)
★ YO, insert hook in **next** dc, YO and pull up a loop, YO and draw through 2 loops on hook; repeat from ★ 2 times **more**, YO and draw through all 4 loops on hook.

Continued on page 62.

AFGHAN

Ch 156 **loosely**.

Row 1 (Right side)**:** Sc in second ch from hook and in each ch across: 155 sc.

Row 2: Ch 3 **(counts as first dc, now and throughout)**, turn; dc in next sc and in each sc across.

Row 3: Ch 3, turn; dc in next dc, ★ † work FPtr around next st, dc in next 2 dc, work Popcorn in next dc, dc in next 2 dc, work FPtr around next st, dc in next 2 dc †, ch 1, skip next dc, (dc in next dc, ch 1, skip next dc) 18 times, dc in next 2 dc; repeat from ★ 2 times **more**, then repeat from † to † once: 98 sts and 57 ch-1 sps.

Row 4: Ch 3, turn, dc in next dc, ★ † work BPtr around next FPtr, dc in next 5 sts, work BPtr around next FPtr, dc in next 2 dc †, dc in next ch-1 sp, (dc in next dc and in next ch-1 sp) 18 times, dc in next 2 dc; repeat from ★ 2 times **more**, then repeat from † to † once: 155 sts.

Row 5: Ch 3, turn; dc in next dc, ★ † work FPtr around next BPtr, dc in next 2 dc, work Popcorn in next dc, dc in next 2 dc, work FPtr around next BPtr, dc in next 2 dc †, (ch 1, skip next dc, dc in next dc) 4 times, ch 2, skip next dc, decrease, dc in next 15 dc, decrease, ch 2, skip next dc, (dc in next dc, ch 1, skip next dc) 4 times, dc in next 2 dc; repeat from ★ 2 times **more**, then repeat from † to † once: 119 sts and 30 sps.

Row 6: Ch 3, turn; dc in next dc, ★ † work BPtr around next FPtr, dc in next 5 sts, work BPtr around next FPtr, dc in next 2 dc †, (ch 1, dc in next dc) 4 times, ch 2, dc in next 17 dc, ch 2, (dc in next dc, ch 1) 4 times, dc in next 2 dc; repeat from ★ 2 times **more**, then repeat from † to † once.

Row 7: Ch 3, turn; dc in next dc, ★ † work FPtr around next BPtr, dc in next 2 dc, work Popcorn in next dc, dc in next 2 dc, work FPtr around next BPtr, dc in next 2 dc †, (ch 1, dc in next dc) 4 times, ch 3, decrease, dc in next 13 dc, decrease, ch 3, (dc in next dc, ch 1) 4 times, dc in next 2 dc; repeat from ★ 2 times **more**, then repeat from † to † once: 113 sts and 30 sps.

Row 8: Ch 3, turn; dc in next dc, ★ † work BPtr around next FPtr, dc in next 5 sts, work BPtr around next FPtr, dc in next 2 dc †, ch 1, (dc in next dc, ch 1) 4 times, skip next ch, dc in next ch, ch 1, dc in next 15 dc, ch 1, skip next ch, dc in next ch, ch 1, (dc in next dc, ch 1) 4 times, dc in next 2 dc; repeat from ★ 2 times **more**, then repeat from † to † once: 119 sts and 36 ch-1 sps.

Row 9: Ch 3, turn; dc in next dc, ★ † work FPtr around next BPtr, dc in next 2 dc, work Popcorn in next dc, dc in next 2 dc, work FPtr around next BPtr, dc in next 2 dc †, (ch 1, dc in next dc) 5 times, ch 2, decrease, dc in next 11 dc, decrease, ch 2, (dc in next dc, ch 1) 5 times, dc in next 2 dc; repeat from ★ 2 times **more**, then repeat from † to † once: 113 sts and 36 sps.

Row 10: Ch 3, turn; dc in next dc, ★ † work BPtr around next FPtr, dc in next 5 sts, work BPtr around next FPtr, dc in next 2 dc †, (ch 1, dc in next dc) 5 times, ch 2, dc in next 13 dc, ch 2, (dc in next dc, ch 1) 5 times, dc in next 2 dc; repeat from ★ 2 times **more**, then repeat from † to † once.

Row 11: Ch 3, turn; dc in next dc, ★ † work FPtr around next BPtr, dc in next 2 dc, work Popcorn in next dc, dc in next 2 dc, work FPtr around next BPtr, dc in next 2 dc †, (ch 1, dc in next dc) twice, ch 3, skip next dc, dc in next dc and in next ch-1 sp, ch 4, skip next ch-2 sp, decrease, dc in next 9 dc, decrease, ch 4, skip next dc, dc in next ch-1 sp and in next dc, ch 3, skip next dc, (dc in next dc, ch 1) twice, dc in next 2 dc; repeat from ★ 2 times **more**, then repeat from † to † once: 101 sts and 24 sps.

Row 12: Ch 3, turn; dc in next dc, ★ † work BPtr around next FPtr, dc in next 5 sts, work BPtr around next FPtr, dc in next 2 dc †, ch 1, dc in next dc, ch 3, skip next dc and next 2 chs, dc in next ch, 2 dc in each of next 2 dc, dc in next ch, ch 2, dc in next 11 dc, ch 2, skip next 3 chs, dc in next ch, 2 dc in each of next 2 dc, dc in next ch, ch 3, skip next dc, dc in next dc, ch 1, dc in next 2 dc; repeat from ★ 2 times **more**, then repeat from † to † once: 119 sts and 18 sps.

Row 13: Ch 3, turn; dc in next dc, ★ † work FPtr around next BPtr, dc in next 2 dc, work Popcorn in next dc, dc in next 2 dc, work FPtr around next BPtr, dc in next 2 dc †, ch 1, dc in next dc, ch 2, 2 dc in next dc, dc in next 4 dc, 2 dc in next dc, ch 2, decrease, dc in next 7 dc, decrease, ch 2, 2 dc in next dc, dc in next 4 dc, 2 dc in next dc, ch 2, dc in next dc, ch 1, dc in next 2 dc; repeat from ★ 2 times **more**, then repeat from † to † once: 125 sts and 18 sps.

Row 14: Ch 3, turn; dc in next dc, ★ † work BPtr around next FPtr, dc in next 5 sts, work BPtr around next FPtr, dc in next 2 dc †, ch 1, dc in next dc, ch 1, 2 dc in next dc, dc in next 6 dc, 2 dc in next dc, ch 2, decrease, dc in next 5 dc, decrease, ch 2, 2 dc in next dc, dc in next 6 dc, 2 dc in next dc, ch 1, dc in next dc, ch 1, dc in next 2 dc; repeat from ★ 2 times **more**, then repeat from † to † once: 131 sts and 18 sps.

Row 15: Ch 3, turn; dc in next dc, ★ † work FPtr around next BPtr, dc in next 2 dc, work Popcorn in next dc, dc in next 2 dc, work FPtr around next BPtr, dc in next 2 dc †, ch 1, dc in next dc, ch 1, dc in next 9 dc, 2 dc in next dc, ch 1, dc in next 7 dc, ch 1, 2 dc in next dc, dc in next 9 dc, ch 1, dc in next dc, ch 1, dc in next 2 dc; repeat from ★ 2 times **more**, then repeat from † to † once: 137 sts and 18 ch-1 sps.

Row 16: Ch 3, turn; dc in next dc, ★ † work BPtr around next FPtr, dc in next 5 sts, work BPtr around next FPtr, dc in next 2 dc †, ch 1, dc in next dc, ch 1, dc in next 11 dc, dc in next ch and in next 7 dc, dc in next ch and in next 11 dc, ch 1, dc in next dc, ch 1, dc in next 2 dc; repeat from ★ 2 times **more**, then repeat from † to † once: 143 sts and 12 ch-1 sps.

Row 17: Ch 3, turn; dc in next dc, ★ † work FPtr around next BPtr, dc in next 2 dc, work Popcorn in next dc, dc in next 2 dc, work FPtr around next BPtr, dc in next 2 dc †, ch 1, dc in next dc, ch 1, dc in next 31 dc, ch 1, dc in next dc, ch 1, dc in next 2 dc; repeat from ★ 2 times **more**, then repeat from † to † once.

Row 18: Ch 3, turn; dc in next dc, ★ † work BPtr around next FPtr, dc in next 5 sts, work BPtr around next FPtr, dc in next 2 dc †, ch 1, dc in next dc, ch 1, dc in next 31 dc, ch 1, dc in next dc, ch 1, dc in next 2 dc; repeat from ★ 2 times **more**, then repeat from † to † once.

Row 19: Repeat Row 17.

Row 20: Ch 3, turn; dc in next dc, ★ † work BPtr around next FPtr, dc in next 5 sts, work BPtr around next FPtr, dc in next 2 dc †, ch 1, dc in next dc, ch 2, decrease, dc in next 8 dc, decrease, ch 3, skip next dc, dc in next dc, work Cluster, dc in next dc, ch 3, skip next dc, decrease, dc in next 8 dc, decrease, ch 2, dc in next dc, ch 1, dc in next 2 dc; repeat from ★ 2 times **more**, then repeat from † to † once: 119 sts and 18 sps.

Row 21: Ch 3, turn; dc in next dc, ★ † work FPtr around next BPtr, dc in next 2 dc, work Popcorn in next dc, dc in next 2 dc, work FPtr around next BPtr, dc in next 2 dc †, ch 1, dc in next dc, ch 3, decrease, dc in next 6 dc, decrease, ch 2, skip next ch-3 sp, 2 dc in each of next 3 sts, ch 2, decrease, dc in next 6 dc, decrease, ch 3, dc in next dc, ch 1, dc in next 2 dc; repeat from ★ 2 times **more**, then repeat from † to † once: 116 sts and 18 sps.

Row 22: Ch 3, turn; dc in next dc, ★ † work BPtr around next FPtr, dc in next 5 sts, work BPtr around next FPtr, dc in next 2 dc †, ch 1, dc in next dc, ch 1, skip next ch, dc in next ch, ch 2, decrease, dc in next 4 dc, decrease, ch 3, dc in next 6 dc, ch 3, decrease, dc in next 4 dc, decrease, ch 2, skip next ch, dc in next ch, ch 1, dc in next dc, ch 1, dc in next 2 dc; repeat from ★ 2 times **more**, then repeat from † to † once: 110 sts and 24 sps.

Row 23: Ch 3, turn; dc in next dc, ★ † work FPtr around next BPtr, dc in next 2 dc, work Popcorn in next dc, dc in next 2 dc, work FPtr around next BPtr, dc in next 2 dc †, (ch 1, dc in next dc) twice, ch 3, decrease, dc in next 2 dc, decrease, ch 2, skip next ch, dc in next ch, ch 1, dc in next 6 dc, ch 1, skip next ch, dc in next ch, ch 2, decrease, dc in next 2 dc, decrease, ch 3, (dc in next dc, ch 1) twice, dc in next 2 dc; repeat from ★ 2 times **more**, then repeat from † to † once: 104 sts and 30 sps.

Row 24: Ch 3, turn; dc in next dc, ★ † work BPtr around next FPtr, dc in next 5 sts, work BPtr around next FPtr, dc in next 2 dc †, ch 1, (dc in next dc, ch 1) twice, skip next ch, dc in next ch, ch 5, skip next 4 dc, dc in next ch, ch 1, dc in next dc, ch 2, decrease, dc in next 2 dc, decrease, ch 2, dc in next dc, ch 1, skip next ch, dc in next ch, ch 5, skip next 4 dc and next ch, dc in next ch, ch 1, (dc in next dc, ch 1) twice, dc in next 2 dc; repeat from ★ 2 times **more**, then repeat from † to † once: 86 sts and 36 sps.

Row 25: Ch 3, turn; dc in next dc, ★ † work FPtr around next BPtr, dc in next 2 dc, work Popcorn in next dc, dc in next 2 dc, work FPtr around next BPtr, dc in next 2 dc †, ch 1, (dc in next dc, ch 1) 3 times, (skip next ch, dc in next ch, ch 1) twice, (dc in next dc, ch 1) twice, skip next ch, dc in next ch, ch 2, skip next 2 dc, dc in sp **before** next dc, ch 2, skip next 2 dc, dc in next ch, ch 1, (dc in next dc, ch 1) twice, (skip next ch, dc in next ch, ch 1) twice, (dc in next dc, ch 1) 3 times, dc in next 2 dc; repeat from ★ 2 times **more**, then repeat from † to † once: 95 sts and 54 sps.

Row 26: Ch 3, turn; dc in next dc, ★ † work BPtr around next FPtr, dc in next 5 sts, work BPtr around next FPtr, dc in next 2 dc †, ch 1, (dc in next dc, ch 1) 7 times, (work Popcorn in next sp, ch 1) 4 times, (dc in next dc, ch 1) 7 times, dc in next 2 dc; repeat from ★ 2 times **more**, then repeat from † to † once: 98 sts and 57 ch-1 sps.

Row 27: Ch 3, turn; dc in next dc, ★ † work FPtr around next BPtr, dc in next 2 dc, work Popcorn in next dc, dc in next 2 dc, work FPtr around next BPtr, dc in next 2 dc †, ch 1, (skip next ch-1 sp, dc in next st, ch 1) 18 times, dc in next 2 dc; repeat from ★ 2 times **more**, then repeat from † to † once.

Row 28: Repeat Row 4: 155 sts.

Rows 29-134: Repeat Rows 3-28, 4 times; then repeat Rows 3 and 4 once **more**: 155 sts.

Row 135: Ch 1, turn; sc in each st across; do **not** finish off.

Edging: Ch 1, do **not** turn; working in end of rows, skip first row, (sc in top of next dc, dtr around post of same dc) across to last row, sc in last row; working in free loops of beginning ch *(Fig. 3b, page 126)*, (dtr, sc) in first ch, dtr in next ch, (sc in next ch, dtr in next ch) across to ch at base of last sc, (sc, dtr) in ch at base of last sc; working in end of rows, sc in first row, (dtr around post of next dc, sc in top of same dc) across to last row, skip last row; working across sts on Row 135, (dtr, sc) in first sc, dtr in next sc, (sc in next sc, dtr in next sc) across to last sc, (sc, dtr) in last sc; join with slip st to first sc, finish off.

VIVA

Rosalie DeVries crocheted her quick-to-make motif in several color schemes before coming up with this eye-pleasing afghan.

Finished Size: 55" x 74½"

MATERIALS

Worsted Weight Yarn:
Purple - 24½ ounces, (700 grams, 1,385 yards)
Ecru - 16 ounces, (450 grams, 905 yards)
Lt Purple - 12½ ounces, (350 grams, 710 yards)
Green - 10½ ounces, (300 grams, 595 yards)
Crochet hook, size I (5.50 mm) **or** size needed
for gauge
Yarn needle

GAUGE: Each Square = 14"
Each Strip = 18" wide

Gauge Swatch: 5¼" diameter
(at widest point across Center)
Work same as Square A through Rnd 4.

STITCH GUIDE

TREBLE CROCHET *(abbreviated tr)*
YO twice, insert hook in st indicated, YO and pull
up a loop (4 loops on hook), (YO and draw through
2 loops on hook) 3 times.
DOUBLE TREBLE CROCHET
(abbreviated dtr)
YO 3 times, insert hook in st indicated, YO and
pull up a loop (5 loops on hook), (YO and draw
through 2 loops on hook) 4 times.

SQUARE A (Make 8)

With Ecru, ch 3 **loosely**.
Rnd 1 (Right side): 11 Hdc in third ch from hook; join
with slip st to top of beginning ch-3, finish off: 12 sts.
Note: Loop a short piece of yarn around any stitch to
mark Rnd 1 as **right** side.
Rnd 2: With **right** side facing, join Green with slip st
in same st as joining; ch 3, place marker in last ch
made for st placement, (dc, ch 3, slip st) in same st,
ch 2, skip next 2 hdc, ★ (slip st, ch 3, dc, ch 3, slip st)
in next hdc, ch 2, skip next 2 hdc; repeat from ★
2 times **more**; join with slip st to joining slip st,
finish off: 4 dc.

Rnd 3: With **right** side facing, join Purple with slip st
in marked ch; ch 3, remove marker and place in last ch
made for st placement, ★ † 3 dc in next dc, ch 3, slip st
in next ch, ch 3, skip next 2 chs and next slip st, slip st
in next ch-2 sp, ch 3, skip next slip st and next 2 chs †,
slip st in next ch, ch 3; repeat from ★ 2 times **more**,
then repeat from † to † once; join with slip st to joining
slip st, finish off: 12 dc.
Rnd 4: With **right** side facing, join Lt Purple with
slip st in marked ch; ch 3, remove marker and place in
last ch made for st placement, ★ † dc in next dc, 3 dc in
next dc, dc in next dc, ch 3, slip st in next ch, ch 3, skip
next 2 chs and next slip st, slip st in next ch, skip next
2 chs, dc in Back Loop Only of next slip st *(Fig. 2,
page 125)*, skip next 2 chs, slip st in next ch, ch 3,
skip next slip st and next 2 chs †, slip st in next ch,
ch 3, working in **both** loops; repeat from ★ 2 times
more, then repeat from † to † once; join with slip st to
joining slip st, finish off: 24 dc.
Rnd 5: With **right** side facing, join Ecru with slip st in
marked ch; ch 3, remove marker and place in last ch
made for st placement, ★ † dc in next 2 dc, 3 dc in next
dc, dc in next 2 dc, ch 3, slip st in next ch, ch 3, skip
next 2 chs and next slip st, slip st in next ch, skip next
2 chs and next slip st, 3 dc in Back Loop Only of next
dc †, (skip next slip st and next 2 chs, slip st in next ch,
ch 3) twice, working in **both** loops; repeat from ★
2 times **more**, then repeat from † to † once, skip next
slip st and next 2 chs, slip st in next ch, ch 3, skip next
slip st and next 2 chs; join with slip st to joining slip st,
finish off: 40 dc.
Rnd 6: With **right** side facing, join Purple with slip st
in marked ch; ch 3, remove marker and place in last ch
made for st placement, ★ † dc in next 3 dc, 3 tr in next
dc, dc in next 3 dc, ch 3, slip st in next ch, ch 3, skip
next 2 chs and next slip st, slip st in next ch, skip next
2 chs and next slip st, dc in next dc, 3 dc in next dc, dc
in next dc †, (skip next slip st and next 2 chs, slip st in
next ch, ch 3) twice; repeat from ★ 2 times **more**, then
repeat from † to † once, skip next slip st and next
2 chs, slip st in next ch, ch 3, skip next slip st and next
2 chs; join with slip st to joining slip st, finish off: 44 dc
and 12 tr.

Continued on page 66.

Rnd 7: With **right** side facing, join Lt Purple with sc in marked ch *(see Joining With Sc, page 125)*; sc in next 3 dc, ★ † hdc in next tr, 5 hdc in next tr, hdc in next tr, sc in next 4 sts, ch 3, skip next 2 chs and next slip st, slip st in next ch, skip next 2 chs and next slip st, 2 dc in next dc, dc in next 3 dc, 2 dc in next dc, skip next slip st and next 2 chs, slip st in next ch, ch 3, skip next slip st and next 2 chs †, sc in next 4 sts; repeat from ★ 2 times **more**, then repeat from † to † once; join with slip st to first sc, finish off: 28 dc, 28 hdc, and 32 sc.

Rnd 8: With **right** side facing, join Green with sc in center hdc of any corner 5-hdc group; (hdc, sc) in same st, ★ † sc in next 8 sts, skip next 2 chs and next slip st, dc in next 7 dc, skip next slip st and next 2 chs, sc in next 8 sts †, (sc, hdc, sc) in next hdc; repeat from ★ 2 times **more**, then repeat from † to † once; join slip st to first sc, finish off: 104 sts.

Rnd 9: With **right** side facing, join Purple with slip st in center hdc of any corner 3-st group; ★ † ch 5, dc in fourth ch from hook and in last ch **(Block made)**, skip next sc, (slip st in next st, slip st in Back Loop Only of next 3 sts, slip st in **both** loops of next st, ch 5, dc in fourth ch from hook and in last ch, skip next st) 4 times †, slip st in next hdc; repeat from ★ 2 times **more**, then repeat from † to † once; join with slip st to first slip st, finish off: 20 Blocks.

Rnd 10: With **right** side facing, join Ecru with slip st in Back Loop Only of same st as joining; ch 4 **(counts as first tr, now and throughout)**, (tr, dtr, 2 tr) in same st, ★ † skip next 2 chs, sc in next 3 chs, (skip next 2 dc and next slip st, tr in Back Loop Only of next 3 slip sts, skip next slip st and next 2 chs, sc in next 3 chs) across to within 2 dc of next corner slip st, skip next 2 dc †, (2 tr, dtr, 2 tr) in Back Loop Only of corner slip st; repeat from ★ 2 times **more**, then repeat from † to † once; join with slip st to first tr, finish off: 128 sts.

Rnd 11: With **right** side facing, join Purple with slip st in center dtr of any corner 5-st group; ★ † ch 5, dc in fourth ch from hook and in last ch, skip next tr, (slip st in next tr, slip in Back Loop Only of next 3 sc, slip st in **both** loops of next tr, ch 5, dc in fourth ch from hook and in last ch, skip next tr) across to center dtr of next corner 5-st group †, slip st in center dtr; repeat from ★ 2 times **more**, then repeat from † to † once; join with slip st to first slip st, finish off: 24 Blocks.

Rnd 12: With Lt Purple, repeat Rnd 10: 152 sts.

Rnd 13: Repeat Rnd 11: 28 Blocks.

Rnd 14: Repeat Rnd 10: 176 sts.

SQUARE B (Make 7)

Make same as Square A through Rnd 11: 24 Blocks.

Rnd 12: With Green, repeat Rnd 10: 128 sts.

Rnd 13: Repeat Rnd 11: 28 Blocks.

Rnd 14: Repeat Rnd 10: 176 sts.

SQUARE ASSEMBLY

With Ecru, using Placement Diagram as a guide, and working through **both** loops, whipstitch Squares together forming 3 vertical strips of 5 Squares each *(Fig. 6a, page 126)*, beginning in center dtr of first corner 5-st group and ending in center dtr of next corner 5-st group.

PLACEMENT DIAGRAM

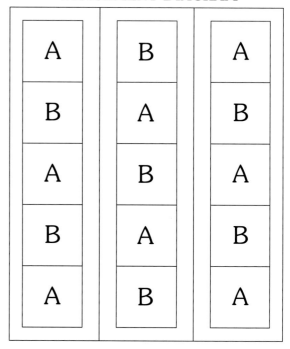

A	B	A
B	A	B
A	B	A
B	A	B
A	B	A

STRIP BORDER

Rnd 1: With **right** side facing and working across short edge of Strip, join Purple with slip st in center dtr of first corner 5-st group; † ch 5, dc in fourth ch from hook and in last ch, skip next tr, (slip st in next tr, slip st in Back Loop Only of next 3 sc, slip st in **both** loops of next tr, ch 5, dc in fourth ch from hook and in last ch, skip next tr) 7 times, slip st in next dtr, ch 5, dc in fourth ch from hook and in last ch, skip next tr, (slip st in next tr, slip st in Back Loop Only of next 3 sc, slip st in **both** loops of next tr, ch 5, dc in fourth ch from hook and in last ch, skip next tr) 7 times, ★ slip st in same st as joining on same Square and in same st as joining on next Square, ch 5, place marker in third ch from hook for st placement, dc in fourth ch from hook and in last ch, skip next tr, (slip st in next tr, slip st in Back Loop Only of next 3 sc, slip st in **both** loops of next tr, ch 5, dc in fourth ch from hook and in last ch, skip next tr) 7 times; repeat from ★ across to center dtr of next corner 5-st group †, slip st in center dtr, repeat from † to † once; join with slip st to first slip st, finish off: 96 Blocks.

Rnd 2: With **right** side facing, join Green with slip st in Back Loop Only of same st as joining; ch 4, (tr, dtr, 2 tr) in same st, † skip next 2 chs, sc in next 3 chs, (skip next 2 dc and next slip st, tr in Back Loop Only in next 3 slip sts, skip next slip st and next 2 chs, sc in next 3 chs) 7 times, skip next 2 dc, (2 tr, dtr, 2 tr) in Back Loop Only of next slip st, skip next 2 chs, sc in next 3 chs, (skip next 2 dc and next slip st, tr in Back Loop Only of next 3 slip sts, skip next slip st and next 2 chs, sc in next 3 chs) 7 times, ★ sc in next marked ch and next 2 chs, (skip next 2 dc and next slip st, tr in Back Loop Only of next 3 slip sts, skip next slip st and next 2 chs, sc in next 3 chs) 7 times; repeat from ★ across to within 2 dc of next corner slip st, skip next 2 dc †, (2 tr, dtr, 2 tr) in Back Loop Only of corner slip st, repeat from † to † once; join with slip st to first tr, finish off: 560 sts.

Rnd 3: With **right** side facing, join Purple with slip st in center dtr to left of joining; † ch 5, dc in fourth ch from hook and in last ch, skip next tr, (slip st in next tr, slip st in Back Loop Only of next 3 sc, slip st in **both** loops of next tr, ch 5, dc in fourth ch from hook and in last ch, skip next tr) 8 times, slip st in next dtr, ch 5, dc in fourth ch from hook and in last ch, skip next tr, slip st in next tr, (slip st in Back Loop Only of next 3 sc, slip st in **both** loops of next tr, ch 5, dc in fourth ch from hook and in last ch, skip next tr) 7 times, slip st in Back Loop Only of next 6 sc, slip st in **both** loops of next tr, ch 5, dc in fourth ch from hook and in last ch, skip next tr, ★ (slip st in next tr, slip st in Back Loop Only of next 3 sc, slip st in **both** loops of next tr, ch 5, dc in fourth ch from hook and in last ch, skip next tr) 6 times, slip st in next tr, slip st in Back Loop Only of next 6 sc, slip st in **both** loops of next tr, ch 5, dc in fourth ch from hook and in last ch, skip next tr; repeat from ★ 2 times **more**, (slip st in next tr, slip st in Back Loop Only of next 3 sc, slip st in **both** loops of next tr, ch 5, dc in fourth ch from hook and in last ch, skip next tr) 7 times †, slip st in next dtr, repeat from † to † once; join with slip st to first slip st, finish off: 92 Blocks.

Rnd 4: With **right** side facing, join Lt Purple with slip st in Back Loop Only of same st as joining; ch 4, (tr, dtr, 2 tr) in same st, † skip next 2 chs, sc in next 3 chs, (skip next 2 dc and next slip st, tr in Back Loop Only of next 3 slip sts, skip next slip st and next 2 chs, sc in next 3 chs) 8 times, skip next 2 dc, (2 tr, dtr, 2 tr) in Back Loop Only of next slip st, skip next 2 chs, sc in next 3 chs, (skip next 2 dc and next slip st, tr in Back Loop Only of next 3 slip sts, skip next slip st and next 2 chs, sc in next 3 chs) 7 times, skip next 2 dc and next slip st, tr in Back Loop Only of next 6 slip sts, skip next slip st and next 2 chs, sc in next 3 chs, ★ (skip next 2 dc and next slip st, tr in Back Loop Only of next 3 slip sts, skip next slip st and next 2 chs, sc in next 3 chs) 6 times, skip next 2 dc and next slip st, tr in Back Loop Only of next 6 slip sts, skip next slip st and next 2 chs, sc in next 3 chs; repeat from ★ 2 times **more**, (skip next 2 dc and next slip st, tr in Back Loop Only of next 3 slip sts, skip next slip st and next 2 chs, sc in next 3 chs) 7 times †, skip next 2 dc, (2 tr, dtr, 2 tr) in Back Loop Only of next slip st, repeat from † to † once; join with slip st to first tr, finish off: 584 sts.

Repeat on remaining 2 strips.

STRIP ASSEMBLY
With Lt Purple, using Placement Diagram as a guide, and working through **both** loops, whipstitch strips together beginning in center dtr of first corner 5-st group and ending in center dtr of next corner 5-st group.

EDGING
With **wrong** side facing, join Ecru with slip st in center dtr of any corner 5-st group; dc in next st, (slip st in next st, dc in next st) around; join with slip st to first slip st, finish off.

RIBBONS OF COLOR

*Long double crochet stitches and red cluster accents band together
beautifully in this striking fringed throw by Della Bieber.*

Finished Size: 43½" x 61"

MATERIALS

Worsted Weight Yarn:
Grey - 33 ounces, (940 grams, 1,865 yards)
Dk Grey - 12 ounces, (340 grams, 680 yards)
Red - 11 ounces, (310 grams, 620 yards)
Crochet hook, size H (5.00 mm) **or** size needed
for gauge

GAUGE: In pattern, 14 sc = 4½"; Rows 8-27 = 5¼"

Gauge Swatch: 4½" square
Ch 15 **loosely**.
Row 1: Sc in second ch from hook and each ch
across.
Rows 2-15: Ch 1, turn; sc in each sc across.
Finish off.

Note: Each row is worked across length of Afghan.

STITCH GUIDE

LONG DOUBLE CROCHET
(abbreviated LDC)
YO, insert hook in st indicated, YO and pull up a
loop even with loop on hook, (YO and draw
through 2 loops on hook) twice.
CLUSTER (uses one sc)
★ YO, insert hook in sc indicated, YO and pull up
a loop even with loop on hook; repeat from ★
2 times **more** (7 loops on hook), (YO and draw
through 2 loops on hook) twice, YO and draw
through remaining 5 loops on hook.

AFGHAN

With Grey, ch 190 **loosely**.
Row 1: Sc in second ch from hook and in each ch
across: 189 sc.
Row 2 (Right side): Ch 1, turn; sc in each sc across
changing to Dk Grey in last sc *(Fig. 5, page 126)*.
*Note: Loop a short piece of yarn around any stitch to
mark Row 2 as **right** side.*
Row 3: Ch 1, turn; sc in each sc across.
Row 4: Ch 1, turn; sc in each sc across changing to
Grey in last sc.

Rows 5 and 6: Ch 1, turn; sc in each sc across.
Row 7: Ch 1, turn; sc in each sc across changing to
Red in last sc.
Row 8: Ch 1, turn; sc in each sc across changing to
Dk Grey in last sc.
Row 9: Ch 1, turn; sc in each st across changing to
Grey in last sc.
Row 10: Ch 1, turn; sc in each sc across changing to
Red in last sc.
Row 11: Ch 1, turn; sc in each sc across changing to
Dk Grey in last sc.
Row 12: Ch 1, turn; sc in first 4 sc, ★ working
around previous rows, work LDC in sc 2 rows **below**
next sc, sc in next 4 sc on last row made; repeat from
★ across changing to Grey in last sc: 37 LDC and
152 sc.
Row 13: Ch 1, turn; sc in each st across changing to
Red in last sc: 189 sc.
Row 14: Ch 1, turn; sc in first 4 sc, (work Cluster in
next sc, sc in next 4 sc) across changing to Dk Grey in
last sc: 37 Clusters and 152 sc.
Rows 15-18: Repeat Rows 9-12.
Row 19: Ch 1, turn; sc in each st across.
Rows 20-26: Ch 1, turn; sc in Back Loop Only of
each sc across *(Fig. 2, page 125)*.
Row 27: Ch 1, turn; sc in both loops of each sc
across changing to Red in last sc.
Rows 28-158: Repeat Rows 8-27, 6 times; then
repeat Rows 8-18 once **more**.
Rows 159 and 160: Ch 1, turn; sc in each st
across.
Row 161: Ch 1, turn; sc in each sc across changing
to Dk Grey in last sc.
Row 162: Ch 1, turn; sc in each sc across.
Row 163: Ch 1, turn; sc in each sc across changing
to Grey in last sc.
Rows 164-166: Ch 1, turn; sc in each sc across; do
not finish off.
Edging: Ch 1, do **not** turn; sc in end of each row
across; working in free loops of beginning ch *(Fig. 3b,
page 126)*, slip st in ch at base of first sc and in each
ch across, ch 1; sc in end of each row across; slip st in
each sc across Row 166; finish off.

Holding 6 strands of Grey together, each 18" long, add
fringe evenly spaced across short edges of Afghan
(Figs. 9a & b, page 127).

HEARTS UNITED

Ideal for newlyweds, this afghan by Colleen Gilbert showcases the symbol of love surrounded by alternating circles of rose-colored hues.

Finished Size: 47½" x 63"

MATERIALS

Worsted Weight Yarn:
Ecru - 27 ounces, (770 grams, 1,525 yards)
Green - 15 ounces, (430 grams, 850 yards)
Lt Rose - 11 ounces, (310 grams, 620 yards)
Rose - 11 ounces, (310 grams, 620 yards)
Crochet hook, size H (5.00 mm) **or** size needed for gauge
Yarn needle

GAUGE: Each Square = 7¾"

Gauge Swatch: 3½" diameter
Work same as Square A or B through Rnd 3.

STITCH GUIDE

TREBLE CROCHET *(abbreviated tr)*
YO twice, insert hook in st indicated, YO and pull up a loop (4 loops on hook), (YO and draw through 2 loops on hook) 3 times.

FRONT POST DOUBLE CROCHET
    (abbreviated FPdc)
YO, insert hook from **front** to **back** around post of dc indicated *(Fig. 4, page 126)*, YO and pull up a loop (3 loops on hook), (YO and draw through 2 loops on hook) twice.

FRONT POST TREBLE CROCHET
    (abbreviated FPtr)
YO twice, insert hook from **front** to **back** around post of dc indicated *(Fig. 4, page 126)*, YO and pull up a loop (4 loops on hook), (YO and draw through 2 loops on hook) 3 times.

SQUARE A & B

Referring to the table below, make the number of Squares specified in the colors indicated.

	Square A Make 24	Square B Make 24
Rnds 1-3	Ecru	Ecru
Rnds 4-6	Rose	Lt Rose
Rnds 7-9	Ecru	Ecru
Rnds 10 & 11	Green	Green

With Ecru, ch 6; join with slip st to form a ring.
Rnd 1 (Right side)**:** Ch 1, 12 sc in ring; join with slip st to first sc.
Note: Loop a short piece of yarn around any stitch to mark Rnd 1 as **right** side.
Rnd 2: Ch 3 **(counts as first dc, now and throughout)**, dc in same st, 2 dc in each sc around; join with slip st to first dc: 24 dc.
Rnd 3: Ch 3, dc in same st and in next dc, (2 dc in next dc, dc in next dc) around; join with slip st to first dc, finish off: 36 dc.
Rnd 4: With **right** side facing, join next color indicated with sc in any dc *(see Joining With Sc, page 125)*; ★ † (2 sc in next dc, sc in next dc) twice, work FPdc around next dc, work 2 FPtr around dc one rnd **below** next dc, skip next 3 dc from last sc made, work FPdc around next dc on Rnd 3, skip dc **behind** FPdc just made †, sc in next dc; repeat from ★ 2 times **more**, then repeat from † to † once; join with slip st to first sc: 44 sts.
Rnd 5: Ch 1, sc in same st and in next 6 sc, ★ † working in Back Loops Only of next 4 sts **and** in Front Loops Only of skipped dc on Rnd 3 *(Fig. 2, page 125)*, sc in next st, (hdc, dc) in next st, hdc in next st, sc in next st †, sc in **both** loops of next 7 sc on Rnd 4; repeat from ★ 2 times **more**, then repeat from † to † once; join with slip st to **both** loops of first sc, do **not** finish off: 48 sts.

Continued on page 72.

Rnd 6: Slip st in next sc, ch 1, sc in same st and in next 4 sc, ★ † working in free loops of sts on Rnd 4 *(Fig. 3a, page 126)*, (dc, tr) in next FPdc, (tr, dc) in next FPtr, ch 1, skip next 3 sts from last sc made, slip st in **both** loops of next dc on Rnd 5, ch 1, working in free loops of sts on Rnd 4, (dc, tr) in next FPtr, (tr, dc) in next FPdc, skip next 3 sts from last slip st made †, sc in **both** loops of next 5 sc on Rnd 5; repeat from ★ 2 times **more**, then repeat from † to † once; join with slip st to first sc, finish off: 56 sts and 8 ch-1 sps.

Rnd 7: With **right** side facing, join Ecru with sc in same st as joining; sc in next 4 sc, ★ † working **behind** Rnd 6 and in skipped sts on Rnd 5, dc in first skipped sc, 2 dc in next sc, dc in next hdc, skip next slip st, dc in next hdc, 2 dc in next sc, dc in next sc †, sc in next 5 sc on Rnd 6; repeat from ★ 2 times **more**, then repeat from † to † once; join with slip st to first sc: 52 sts.

Rnd 8: Ch 2 **(counts as first hdc)**, hdc in next sc, ★ † sc in next 2 sc, hdc in next 2 sts, dc in next dc, 2 dc in next dc, (dc, tr) in next dc, (tr, ch 3, tr) in next dc, (tr, dc) in next dc, 2 dc in next dc, dc in next dc †, hdc in next 2 sc; repeat from ★ 2 times **more**, then repeat from † to † once; join with slip st to first hdc: 72 sts and 4 ch-3 sps.

Rnd 9: Ch 1, sc in same st and in each st across to next corner ch-3 sp, 5 sc in corner ch-3 sp, ★ sc in each st across to next corner ch-3 sp, 5 sc in corner ch-3 sp; repeat from ★ 2 times **more**, sc in each st across; join with slip st to first sc, finish off: 92 sc.

Rnd 10: With **right** side facing, join Green with slip st in first sc of any corner 5-sc group; ch 3, dc in next sc, ch 3, ★ skip next sc, dc in next 22 sc, ch 3; repeat from ★ 2 times **more**, skip next sc, dc in last 20 sc; join with slip st to first dc: 88 dc and 4 ch-3 sps.

Rnd 11: Ch 1, sc in same st and in next dc, 5 sc in next corner ch-3 sp, ★ sc in each dc across to next corner ch-3 sp, 5 sc in corner ch-3 sp; repeat from ★ 2 times **more**, sc in each dc across; join with slip st to first sc, finish off: 108 sc.

ASSEMBLY

With Green, using photo as a guide for placement, and working through **inside** loops, whipstitch Squares together forming 6 vertical strips of 8 Squares each *(Fig. 6b, page 126)*, beginning in center sc of first corner 5-sc group and ending in center sc of next corner 5-sc group; then whipstitch strips together in same manner.

EDGING

Rnd 1: With **right** side facing, join Ecru with sc in center sc of any corner 5-sc group; sc in same st and in next 26 sc, ★ † (sc in same st as joining on same Square, sc in same st as joining on next Square and in next 26 sc) across to center sc of next corner 5-sc group †, 3 sc in center sc, sc in next 26 sc; repeat from ★ 2 times **more**, then repeat from † to † once, sc in same st as first sc; join with slip st to first sc: 788 sc.

Rnd 2: Ch 1, 3 sc in same st, sc in each sc around working 3 sc in center sc of each corner 3-sc group; join with slip st to first sc, finish off.

STARLIGHT

Like a bagful of peppermints from a candy store, this playful afghan by
Carole G. Wilder is sure to bring seasonal whimsy to any room!

Finished Size: 56" (straight edge to straight edge)

MATERIALS
Worsted Weight Yarn:
Off-White - 24½ ounces,
(700 grams, 1,385 yards)
Red - 19½ ounces, (550 grams, 1,100 yards)
Crochet hook, size H (5.00 mm) **or** size needed
for gauge

GAUGE: Each Motif = 7" diameter

Gauge Swatch: 6½" diameter
Work same as First Motif through Row 25.

Continued on page 74.

STITCH GUIDE

TREBLE CROCHET (*abbreviated tr*)
YO twice, insert hook in st indicated, YO and pull up a loop (4 loops on hook), (YO and draw through 2 loops on hook) 3 times.

CLUSTER (*uses last 3 sts*)
† YO twice, insert hook in **next** st, YO and pull up a loop †, (YO and draw through 2 loops on hook) twice (2 loops on hook), repeat from † to † once, YO and draw through 2 loops on hook (4 loops on hook), YO **once**, insert hook in last st, YO and pull up a loop (6 loops on hook), (YO and draw through 2 loops on hook) 5 times.

FIRST MOTIF

With Red, ch 14 **loosely**.

Row 1 (Right side)**:** Sc in fifth ch from hook **(ring made)**, hdc in next ch, dc in next ch, 2 dc in next ch, dc in next ch, 2 tr in next ch, tr in next ch, work Cluster: 10 sts and one ring.

Note: Loop a short piece of yarn around any stitch to mark Row 1 as **right** side.

Row 2: Ch 1, turn; sc in each st across and in ring changing to Off-White in last sc *(Fig. 5, page 126)*; do **not** cut Red.

Note: Hold unused color to **wrong** side, **now and throughout**.

Row 3: Ch 1, turn; working in Back Loops Only *(Fig. 2, page 125)*, skip first sc, sc in next sc, hdc in next sc, dc in next sc, 2 dc in next sc, dc in next sc, 2 tr in next sc, tr in next sc, work Cluster.

Row 4: Ch 1, turn; sc in both loops of each st across, sc in ring changing to Red; do **not** cut Off-White.

Row 5: Ch 1, turn; working in Back Loops Only, skip first sc, sc in next sc, hdc in next sc, dc in next sc, 2 dc in next sc, dc in next sc, 2 tr in next sc, tr in next sc, work Cluster.

Row 6: Ch 1, turn; sc in both loops of each st across, sc in ring changing to Off-White; do **not** cut Red.

Rows 7-23: Repeat Rows 3-6, 4 times; then repeat Row 3 once **more**; at the end of Row 23, cut Red.

Row 24: Ch 1, turn; sc in both loops of each st across, sc in ring.

Row 25 (Joining row)**:** Turn; holding **right** side together, working in free loops of beginning ch *(Fig. 3b, page 126)* and in Back Loops Only of sts on Row 24, skip first sc on Row 24, slip st **loosely** in each st across.

Trim: Ch 2, with **right** side facing and working in ends of rows, slip st in Row 24, ch 3, slip st in second loop of next row *(Fig. A)*, ch 3, slip st in fourth loop of same row, ch 3, slip st in next sc row, ch 3, slip st in second loop of next row, ch 3, slip st in fourth loop of same row, ch 3, place marker around ch-3 just made for joining placement, ★ slip st in next sc row, ch 3, slip st in second loop of next row, ch 3, slip st in fourth loop of same row, ch 3; repeat from ★ around; join with slip st to first slip st, finish off: 36 ch-3 sps.

Fig. A

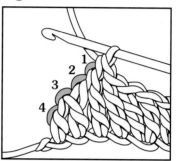

SECOND MOTIF

Work same as First Motif through Row 25.

Trim (Joining rnd)**:** Ch 2, with **right** side facing and working in end of rows, slip st in Row 24, ch 3, slip st in second loop of next row, ch 3, slip st in fourth loop of same row, ch 3, slip st in next sc row, ch 3, slip st in second loop of next row, ch 3, slip st in fourth loop of same row, ch 3, place marker around ch-3 just made for joining placement, slip st in next sc row, ★ ch 3, slip st in second loop of next row, ch 3, slip st in fourth loop of same row, ch 3, slip st in next sc row; repeat from ★ 7 times **more**, ch 1, holding Motifs with **wrong** sides together, slip st in marked ch-3 sp on **previous** Motif, † ch 1, slip st in second loop of next row on **new Motif**, ch 1, slip st in next ch-3 sp on **previous** Motif, ch 1, slip st in fourth loop of same row on **new Motif**, ch 1, slip st in next ch-3 sp on **previous** Motif, ch 1 †, slip st in next sc row on **new Motif**, ch 1, slip st in next ch-3 sp on **previous** Motif, repeat from † to † once; join with slip st to first slip st on **new Motif**, finish off.

ADDITIONAL 59 MOTIFS

Work same as First Motif through Row 25.

Trim (Joining rnd)**:** Following numerical order on Placement Diagram, work Two or Three Side Joining.

TWO SIDE JOINING

Ch 2, with **right** side facing and working in end of rows, slip st in Row 24, † ch 3, slip st in second loop of next row, ch 3, slip st in fourth loop of same row, ch 3, slip st in next sc row †, ch 3, slip st in second loop of next row, ch 3, slip st in fourth loop of same row, ch 3, place marker around ch-3 just made for joining placement, slip st in next sc row, repeat from † to † 6 times, ch 1, holding Motifs with **wrong** sides together, slip st in marked ch-3 sp on **previous Motif**, ch 1, slip st in second loop of next row on **new Motif**, ch 1, slip st in next ch-3 sp on **previous Motif**, ch 1, slip st in fourth loop of same row on **new Motif**, ch 1, slip st in next ch-3 sp on **previous Motif**, ch 1, ★ slip st in next sc row on **new Motif**, ch 1, slip st in next unworked ch-3 sp on **previous Motif**, ch 1, slip st in second loop of next row on **new Motif**, ch 1, slip st in next unworked ch-3 sp on **previous Motif**, ch 1, slip st in fourth loop of same row on **new Motif**, ch 1, slip st in next unworked ch-3 sp on **previous Motif**, ch 1; repeat from ★ 2 times **more**; join with slip st to first slip st on **new Motif**, finish off.

THREE SIDE JOINING

Ch 2, with **right** side facing and working in end of rows, slip st in Row 24, † ch 3, slip st in second loop of next row, ch 3, slip st in fourth loop of same row, ch 3, slip st in next sc row †, ch 3, slip st in second loop of next row, ch 3, slip st in fourth loop of same row, ch 3, place marker around ch-3 just made for joining placement, slip st in next sc row, repeat from † to † 4 times, ch 1, holding Motifs with **wrong** sides together, slip st in marked ch-3 sp on **previous Motif**, ch 1, slip st in second loop of next row on **new Motif**, ch 1, slip st in next ch-3 sp on **previous Motif**, ch 1, slip st in fourth loop of same row on **new Motif**, ch 1, slip st in next ch-3 sp on **previous Motif**, ch 1, ★ slip st in next sc row on **new Motif**, ch 1, slip st in next unworked ch-3 sp on **previous Motif**, ch 1, slip st in second loop of next row on **new Motif**, ch 1, slip st in next unworked ch-3 sp on **previous Motif**, ch 1, slip st in fourth loop of same row on **new Motif**, ch 1, slip st in next unworked ch-3 sp on **previous Motif**, ch 1; repeat from ★ 4 times **more**; join with slip st to first slip st on **new Motif**, finish off.

PLACEMENT DIAGRAM

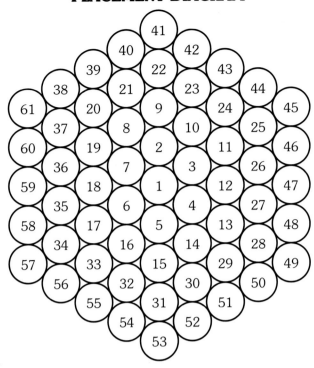

EDGING

Rnd 1: With **right** side facing, join Red with slip st in any joining slip st; ch 4, (slip st in next unworked ch-3 sp, ch 4) around to next joining slip st, ★ slip st in joining slip st, ch 4, (slip st in next unworked ch-3 sp, ch 4) around to next joining slip st; repeat from ★ around; join with slip st to first slip st, finish off.

Rnd 2: With **right** side facing, join Off-White with slip st in any ch-4 sp; ch 4, ★ drop loop from hook, insert hook from **front** to **back** in next ch-4 sp, hook dropped loop and draw through ch-4 sp, ch 4; repeat from ★ around; join with slip st to first slip st, finish off.

WHEELS IN A SQUARE

The waterwheel design of Anita Wandtke's country wrap will warm heart and home.

Finished Size: 40" x 61"

MATERIALS

Worsted Weight Yarn:
Blue - 22 ounces, (620 grams, 1,245 yards)
Red - 10 ounces, (280 grams, 565 yards)
Tan - 10 ounces, (280 grams, 565 yards)
Crochet hook, size G (4.00 mm) **or** size needed for gauge
Yarn needle

GAUGE: Each Square = 7"

Gauge Swatch: 4" diameter
Work same as Square through Rnd 3.

SQUARE (Make 40)

With Red, ch 6; join with slip st to form a ring.
Rnd 1 (Right side): Ch 3 **(counts as first dc, now and throughout)**, 15 dc in ring; join with slip st to first dc: 16 dc.
Note: Loop a short piece of yarn around any stitch to mark Rnd 1 as **right** side.
Rnd 2: Slip st in sp **before** next dc, ch 5, (dc in sp **before** next dc, ch 2) around; join with slip st to third ch of beginning ch-5: 16 ch-2 sps.
Rnd 3: Slip st in first ch-2 sp, ch 3, 2 dc in same sp, ch 1, (3 dc in next ch-2 sp, ch 1) around; join with slip st to first dc, finish off: 48 dc and 16 ch-1 sps.
Rnd 4: With **right** side facing, join Tan with sc in any ch-1 sp *(see Joining With Sc, page 125)*; (ch 3, sc in next ch-1 sp) 3 times, ch 5, ★ sc in next ch-1 sp, (ch 3, sc in next ch-1 sp) 3 times, ch 5; repeat from ★ 2 times **more**; join with slip st to first sc: 16 sc and 16 sps.
Rnd 5: Slip st in first ch-3 sp, ch 3, 2 dc in same sp, 3 dc in each of next 2 ch-3 sps, (3 dc, ch 3, 3 dc) in next ch-5 sp, ★ 3 dc in each of next 3 ch-3 sps, (3 dc, ch 3, 3 dc) in next ch-5 sp; repeat from ★ 2 times **more**; join with slip st to first dc, finish off: 60 dc and 4 ch-3 sps.
Rnd 6: With **right** side facing, join Blue with slip st in any corner ch-3 sp; ch 3, (dc, ch 2, 2 dc) in same sp, ★ dc in each dc across to next corner ch-3 sp, (2 dc, ch 2, 2 dc) in corner ch-3 sp; repeat from ★ 2 times **more**, dc in each dc across; join with slip st to first dc: 76 dc and 4 ch-2 sps.

Rnd 7: Ch 3, dc in next dc, (2 dc, ch 3, 2 dc) in next corner ch-2 sp, ★ dc in each dc across to next corner ch-2 sp, (2 dc, ch 3, 2 dc) in corner ch-2 sp; repeat from ★ 2 times **more**, dc in each dc across; join with slip st to first dc, finish off: 92 dc and 4 ch-3 sps.

ASSEMBLY

With Blue and working through **inside** loops, whipstitch Squares together forming 5 vertical strips of 8 Squares each *(Fig. 6b, page 126)*, beginning in center ch of first corner ch-3 and ending in center ch of next corner ch-3; then whipstitch strips together in same manner.

EDGING

Rnd 1: With **right** side facing, join Blue with slip st in any corner ch-3 sp; ch 3, (2 dc, ch 2, 3 dc) in same sp, ★ † dc in next 23 dc, (2 dc in next sp, dc in next joining, 2 dc in next sp, dc in next 23 dc) across to next corner ch-3 sp †, (3 dc, ch 2, 3 dc) in corner ch-3 sp; repeat from ★ 2 times **more**, then repeat from † to † once; join with slip st to first dc, finish off: 732 dc and 4 ch-2 sps.
Rnd 2: With **right** side facing, join Red with slip st in any corner ch-2 sp; ch 5, dc in same sp, ch 1, ★ skip next dc, (dc in next dc, ch 1, skip next dc) across to next corner ch-2 sp, (dc, ch 2, dc) in corner ch-2 sp, ch 1; repeat from ★ 2 times **more**, skip next dc, (dc in next dc, ch 1, skip next dc) across; join with slip st to third ch of beginning ch-5, finish off: 372 sps.
Rnd 3: With **right** side facing, join Tan with slip st in any corner ch-2 sp; ch 3, (dc, ch 2, 2 dc) in same sp, ★ 2 dc in each ch-1 sp across to next corner ch-2 sp, (2 dc, ch 2, 2 dc) in corner ch-2 sp; repeat from ★ 2 times **more**, 2 dc in each ch-1 sp across; join with slip st to first dc, finish off: 752 dc and 4 ch-2 sps.
Rnd 4: With **right** side facing, join Blue with slip st in any corner ch-2 sp; ch 3, (dc, ch 2, 2 dc) in same sp, ★ dc in each dc across to next corner ch-2 sp, (2 dc, ch 2, 2 dc) in corner ch-2 sp; repeat from ★ 2 times **more**, dc in each dc across; join with slip st to first dc, do **not** finish off: 768 dc and 4 ch-2 sps.
Rnd 5: Ch 3, dc in next dc, (2 dc, ch 2, 2 dc) in next corner ch-2 sp, ★ dc in each dc across to next corner ch-2 sp, (2 dc, ch 2, 2 dc) in corner ch-2 sp; repeat from ★ 2 times **more**, dc in each dc across; join with slip st to first dc, finish off.

GUIDING LIGHT

Patricia Zihala used a filet-like texture to bring about the foggy presence of these seaside saviors.

Finished Size: 71" x 79"

MATERIALS
Worsted Weight Yarn:
   63 ounces, (1,790 grams, 3,560 yards)
   Crochet hook, size I (5.50 mm) **or** size needed
      for gauge

GAUGE: 12 dc = 4"; 7 rows = 5"

Gauge Swatch: 4"w x 5¾"h
Ch 14 **loosely**.
Row 1: Dc in fourth ch from hook **(3 skipped chs count as first dc)** and in each ch across: 12 dc.
Rows 2-8: Ch 3 **(counts as first dc)**, turn; dc in next dc and in each dc across.
Finish off.

AFGHAN
Ch 215 **loosely**.
Row 1: Dc in back ridge of fourth ch from hook **(Fig. 1, page 125)** and each ch across **(3 skipped chs count as first dc)**: 213 dc.
Row 2 (Right side)**:** Ch 3 **(counts as first dc, now and throughout)**, turn; dc in next dc and in each dc across.
Row 3: Ch 3, turn; dc in next 4 dc, ★ ch 1, skip next dc, (dc in next dc, ch 1, skip next dc) 23 times, dc in next 5 dc; repeat from ★ across: 117 dc and 96 ch-1 sps.
Row 4: Ch 3, turn; dc in next 4 dc, ★ ch 1, (dc in next dc, ch 1) 23 times, dc in next 5 dc, ch 1, dc in next dc, (dc in next ch-1 sp and in next dc, ch 1, dc in next dc) 11 times, ch 1, dc in next 5 dc; repeat from ★ once **more**: 139 dc and 74 ch-1 sps.
Row 5: Ch 3, turn; dc in next 4 dc, ★ ch 1, dc in next dc, (dc in next ch-1 sp and in next dc, ch 1, skip next dc, dc in next dc) 11 times, ch 1, dc in next 5 dc, (ch 1, dc in next dc) twice, (dc in next ch-1 sp and in next dc) 20 times, ch 1, dc in next dc, ch 1, dc in next 5 dc; repeat from ★ once **more**: 179 dc and 34 ch-1 sps.

Row 6: Ch 3, turn; dc in next 4 dc, ★ ch 1, dc in next dc, ch 1, dc in Back Loop Only of next 41 dc **(Fig. 2, page 125)**, ch 1, working in **both** loops, dc in next dc, ch 1, dc in next 5 dc, ch 1, dc in next dc, (dc in next ch-1 sp and in next dc, ch 1, skip next dc, dc in next dc) 11 times, ch 1, dc in next 5 dc; repeat from ★ once **more**.
Row 7: Ch 3, turn; dc in next 4 dc, ★ ch 1, dc in next dc, (dc in next ch-1 sp and in next dc, ch 1, skip next dc, dc in next dc) 11 times, ch 1, dc in next 5 dc, ch 1, dc in next dc, ch 1, dc in Back Loop Only of next 41 dc, ch 1, working in **both** loops, dc in next dc, ch 1, dc in next 5 dc; repeat from ★ once **more**.
Rows 8-10: Repeat Rows 6 and 7 once, then repeat Row 6 once **more**.
Row 11: Ch 3, turn; dc in next 4 dc, ★ ch 1, dc in next dc, (dc in next ch-1 sp and in next dc, ch 1, skip next dc, dc in next dc) 11 times, ch 1, dc in next 5 dc, ch 1, (dc in next dc, ch 1) twice, skip next dc, dc in Back Loop Only of next 37 dc, ch 1, skip next dc, working in **both** loops, (dc in next dc, ch 1) twice, dc in next 5 dc; repeat from ★ once **more**: 175 dc and 38 ch-1 sps.
Row 12: Ch 3, turn; dc in next 4 dc, ★ ch 1, (dc in next dc, ch 1) twice, dc in Back Loop Only of next 37 dc, ch 1, working in **both** loops, (dc in next dc, ch 1) twice, dc in next 5 dc, ch 1, dc in next dc, (dc in next ch-1 sp and in next dc, ch 1, skip next dc, dc in next dc) 11 times, ch 1, dc in next 5 dc; repeat from ★ once **more**.
Row 13: Ch 3, turn; dc in next 4 dc, ★ ch 1, dc in next dc, (dc in next ch-1 sp and in next dc, ch 1, skip next dc, dc in next dc) 11 times, ch 1, dc in next 5 dc, ch 1, (dc in next dc, ch 1) twice, dc in Back Loop Only of next 37 dc, ch 1, working in **both** loops, (dc in next dc, ch 1) twice, dc in next 5 dc; repeat from ★ once **more**.
Rows 14-16: Repeat Rows 12 and 13 once, then repeat Row 12 once **more**; do **not** finish off.

Continued on page 80.

Row 17: Ch 3, turn; dc in next 4 dc, ★ ch 1, dc in next dc, (dc in next ch-1 sp and in next dc, ch 1, skip next dc, dc in next dc) 11 times, ch 1, dc in next 5 dc, ch 1, (dc in next dc, ch 1) 3 times, skip next dc, dc in Back Loop Only of next 33 dc, ch 1, skip next dc, working in **both** loops, (dc in next dc, ch 1) 3 times, dc in next 5 dc; repeat from ★ once **more**: 171 dc and 42 ch-1 sps.

Row 18: Ch 3, turn; dc in next 4 dc, ★ ch 1, (dc in next dc, ch 1) 3 times, dc in Back Loop Only of next 33 dc, ch 1, working in **both** loops, (dc in next dc, ch 1) 3 times, dc in next 5 dc, ch 1, dc in next dc, (dc in next ch-1 sp and in next dc, ch 1, skip next dc, dc in next dc) 11 times, ch 1, dc in next 5 dc; repeat from ★ once **more**.

Row 19: Ch 3, turn; dc in next 4 dc, ★ ch 1, dc in next dc, (dc in next ch-1 sp and in next dc, ch 1, skip next dc, dc in next dc) 11 times, ch 1, dc in next 5 dc, ch 1, (dc in next dc, ch 1) 3 times, dc in Back Loop Only of next 33 dc, ch 1, working in **both** loops, (dc in next dc, ch 1) 3 times, dc in next 5 dc; repeat from ★ once **more**.

Rows 20-22: Repeat Rows 18 and 19 once, then repeat Row 18 once **more**.

Row 23: Ch 3, turn; dc in next 4 dc, ★ ch 1, dc in next dc, (dc in next ch-1 sp and in next dc, ch 1, skip next dc, dc in next dc) 11 times, ch 1, dc in next 5 dc, ch 1, (dc in next dc, ch 1) 4 times, skip next dc, dc in Back Loop Only of next 29 dc, ch 1, skip next dc, working in **both** loops, (dc in next dc, ch 1) 4 times, dc in next 5 dc; repeat from ★ once **more**: 167 dc and 46 ch-1 sps.

Row 24: Ch 3, turn; dc in next 4 dc, ★ ch 1, (dc in next dc, ch 1) 4 times, dc in Back Loop Only of next 29 dc, ch 1, working in **both** loops, (dc in next dc, ch 1) 4 times, dc in next 5 dc, ch 1, dc in next dc, (dc in next ch-1 sp and in next dc, ch 1, skip next dc, dc in next dc) 11 times, ch 1, dc in next 5 dc; repeat from ★ once **more**.

Row 25: Ch 3, turn; dc in next 4 dc, ★ ch 1, dc in next dc, (dc in next ch-1 sp and in next dc, ch 1, skip next dc, dc in next dc) 11 times, ch 1, dc in next 5 dc, ch 1, (dc in next dc, ch 1) 4 times, dc in Back Loop Only of next 29 dc, ch 1, working in **both** loops, (dc in next dc, ch 1) 4 times, dc in next 5 dc; repeat from ★ once **more**.

Rows 26-28: Repeat Rows 24 and 25 once, then repeat Row 24 once **more**.

Row 29: Ch 3, turn; dc in next 4 dc, ★ ch 1, [(dc in next dc, ch 1) twice, skip next dc] 11 times, dc in next dc, ch 1, dc in next 5 dc, ch 1, (dc in next dc, ch 1) 5 times, skip next dc, dc in Back Loop Only of next 25 dc, ch 1, skip next dc, working in **both** loops, (dc in next dc, ch 1) 5 times, dc in next 5 dc; repeat from ★ once **more**: 141 dc and 72 ch-1 sps.

Row 30: Ch 3, turn; dc in next 4 dc, ★ ch 1, (dc in next dc, ch 1) 5 times, dc in Back Loop Only of next 25 dc, ch 1, working in **both** loops, (dc in next dc, ch 1) 5 times, dc in next 5 dc and in next ch-1 sp, (dc in next dc and in next ch-1 sp) 23 times, dc in next 5 dc; repeat from ★ once **more**: 189 dc and 24 ch-1 sps.

Row 31: Ch 3, turn; dc in next 56 dc, † ch 1, (dc in next dc, ch 1) 5 times, dc in Back Loop Only of next 25 dc, ch 1, working in **both** loops, (dc in next dc, ch 1) 5 times †, dc in next 57 dc, repeat from † to † once, dc in last 5 dc.

Row 32: Ch 3, turn; dc in next 4 dc, ★ ch 1, (dc in next dc, ch 1) 5 times, dc in Back Loop Only of next 25 dc, ch 1, working in **both** loops, (dc in next dc, ch 1) 5 times, dc in next 5 dc, ch 1, skip next dc, (dc in next dc, ch 1, skip next dc) 23 times, dc in next 5 dc; repeat from ★ once **more**: 141 dc and 72 ch-1 sps.

Row 33: Ch 3, turn; dc in next 4 dc, ★ ch 1, (dc in next dc, ch 1) 23 times, dc in next 5 dc, ch 1, (dc in next dc, ch 1) 5 times, dc in Back Loop Only of next 25 dc, ch 1, working in **both** loops, (dc in next dc, ch 1) 5 times, dc in next 5 dc; repeat from ★ once **more**.

Row 34: Ch 3, turn; dc in next 4 dc, ★ ch 1, (dc in next dc, ch 1) 5 times, dc in Back Loop Only of next 25 dc, ch 1, working in **both** loops, (dc in next dc, ch 1) 5 times, dc in next 5 dc, (ch 1, dc in next dc) twice, (dc in next ch-1 sp and in next dc) 20 times, ch 1, dc in next dc, ch 1, dc in next 5 dc; repeat from ★ once **more**: 181 dc and 32 ch-1 sps.

Row 35: Ch 3, turn; dc in next 4 dc, ★ ch 1, dc in next dc, ch 1, dc in Back Loop Only of next 41 dc, ch 1, working in **both** loops, dc in next dc, ch 1, dc in next 5 dc, ch 1, (dc in next dc, ch 1) 6 times, skip next dc, dc in Back Loop Only of next 21 dc, ch 1, skip next dc, working in **both** loops, (dc in next dc, ch 1) 6 times, dc in next 5 dc; repeat from ★ once **more**: 177 dc and 36 ch-1 sps.

Row 36: Ch 3, turn; dc in next 4 dc, ★ ch 1, (dc in next dc, ch 1) 6 times, dc in Back Loop Only of next 21 dc, ch 1, working in **both** loops, (dc in next dc, ch 1) 6 times, dc in next 5 dc, ch 1, dc in next dc, ch 1, dc in Back Loop Only of next 41 dc, ch 1, working in **both** loops, dc in next dc, ch 1, dc in next 5 dc; repeat from ★ once **more**.

Row 37: Ch 3, turn; dc in next 4 dc, ★ ch 1, dc in next dc, ch 1, dc in Back Loop Only of next 41 dc, ch 1, working in **both** loops, dc in next dc, ch 1, dc in next 5 dc, ch 1, (dc in next dc, ch 1) 6 times, dc in Back Loop Only of next 21 dc, ch 1, working in **both** loops, (dc in next dc, ch 1) 6 times, dc in next 5 dc; repeat from ★ once **more**.

Row 38: Repeat Row 36.

Row 39: Ch 3, turn; dc in next 4 dc, ★ ch 1, dc in next dc, ch 1, dc in Back Loop Only of next 41 dc, ch 1, working in **both** loops, dc in next dc, ch 1, dc in next 5 dc, ch 1, (dc in next dc, ch 1) 4 times, skip next ch-1 sp, working in Back Loops Only of each dc and each ch, dc in next 29 sts, ch 1, working in **both** loops, (dc in next dc, ch 1) 4 times, dc in next 5 dc; repeat from ★ once **more**: 185 dc and 28 ch-1 sps.

Row 40: Ch 3, turn; dc in next 4 dc, ★ ch 1, (dc in next dc, ch 1) 4 times, working in Back Loops Only, (dc in next dc, ch 1, skip next dc) twice, dc in next 21 dc, ch 1, (skip next dc, dc in next dc, ch 1) twice, working in **both** loops, (dc in next dc, ch 1) 4 times, dc in next 5 dc, ch 1, (dc in next dc, ch 1) twice, skip next dc, dc in Back Loop Only of next 37 dc, ch 1, skip next dc, working in **both** loops, (dc in next dc, ch 1) twice, dc in next 5 dc; repeat from ★ once **more**: 173 dc and 40 ch-1 sps.

Row 41: Ch 3, turn; dc in next 4 dc, ★ ch 1, (dc in next dc, ch 1) twice, dc in Back Loop Only of next 37 dc, ch 1, working in **both** loops, (dc in next dc, ch 1) twice, dc in next 5 dc, ch 1, (dc in next dc, ch 1) 6 times, working in Back Loops Only, dc in next 3 dc, ch 1, skip next dc, dc in next dc, ch 1, skip next dc, dc in next 9 dc, ch 1, skip next dc, dc in next dc, ch 1, skip next dc, dc in next 3 dc, ch 1, working in **both** loops, (dc in next dc, ch 1) 6 times, dc in next 5 dc; repeat from ★ once **more**: 165 dc and 48 ch-1 sps.

Row 42: Ch 3, turn; dc in next 4 dc, ★ ch 1, (dc in next dc, ch 1) 6 times, dc in Back Loop Only of next 3 dc, ch 1, working in **both** loops, dc in next dc, ch 1, dc in next 9 dc, ch 1, dc in next dc, ch 1, dc in Back Loop Only of next 3 dc, ch 1, working in **both** loops, (dc in next dc, ch 1) 6 times, dc in next 5 dc, ch 1, (dc in next dc, ch 1) twice, dc in Back Loop Only of next 37 dc, ch 1, working in **both** loops, (dc in next dc, ch 1) twice, dc in next 5 dc; repeat from ★ once **more**.

Row 43: Ch 3, turn; dc in next 4 dc, ★ ch 1, (dc in next dc, ch 1) twice, dc in Back Loop Only of next 37 dc, ch 1, working in **both** loops, (dc in next dc, ch 1) twice, dc in next 5 dc, ch 1, (dc in next dc, ch 1) 6 times, dc in Back Loop Only of next 3 dc, ch 1, working in **both** loops, dc in next dc, ch 1, dc in next 9 dc, ch 1, dc in next dc, ch 1, dc in Back Loop Only of next 3 dc, ch 1, working in **both** loops, (dc in next dc, ch 1) 6 times, dc in next 5 dc; repeat from ★ once **more**.

Row 44: Ch 3, turn; dc in next 4 dc, ★ ch 1, (dc in next dc, ch 1) 5 times, skip next ch-1 sp, working in Back Loop Only of each dc and each ch, dc in next 25 sts, ch 1, working in **both** loops, (dc in next dc, ch 1) 5 times, dc in next 5 dc, ch 1, (dc in next dc, ch 1) twice, dc in Back Loop Only of next 37 dc, ch 1, working in **both** loops, (dc in next dc, ch 1) twice, dc in next 5 dc; repeat from ★ once **more**: 177 dc and 36 ch-1 sps.

Row 45: Ch 3, turn; dc in next 4 dc, ★ ch 1, (dc in next dc, ch 1) twice, dc in Back Loop Only of next 37 dc, ch 1, working in **both** loops, (dc in next dc, ch 1) twice, dc in next 5 dc, ch 1, (dc in next dc, ch 1) 5 times, working in Back Loops Only, dc in next dc, ch 1, skip next dc, dc in next 21 dc, ch 1, skip next dc, dc in next dc, ch 1, working in **both** loops, (dc in next dc, ch 1) 5 times, dc in next 5 dc; repeat from ★ once **more**: 173 dc and 40 ch-1 sps.

Row 46: Ch 3, turn; dc in next 4 dc, ★ ch 1, (dc in next dc, ch 1) 6 times, working in Back Loops Only, dc in next dc, ch 1, skip next dc, dc in next 17 dc, ch 1, skip next dc, dc in next dc, ch 1, working in **both** loops, (dc in next dc, ch 1) 6 times, dc in next 5 dc, ch 1, (dc in next dc, ch 1) 3 times, skip next dc, dc in Back Loop Only of next 33 dc, ch 1, skip next dc, working in **both** loops, (dc in next dc, ch 1) 3 times, dc in next 5 dc; repeat from ★ once **more**: 165 dc and 48 ch-1 sps.

Row 47: Ch 3, turn; dc in next 4 dc, ★ ch 1, (dc in next dc, ch 1) 3 times, dc in Back Loop Only of next 33 dc, ch 1, working in **both** loops, (dc in next dc, ch 1) 3 times, dc in next 5 dc, ch 1, (dc in next dc, ch 1) 7 times, working in Back Loops Only, dc in next dc, ch 1, skip next dc, dc in next 13 dc, ch 1, skip next dc, dc in next dc, ch 1, working in **both** loops, (dc in next dc, ch 1) 7 times, dc in next 5 dc; repeat from ★ once **more**: 161 dc and 52 ch-1 sps.

Row 48: Ch 3, turn; dc in next 4 dc, ★ ch 1, (dc in next dc, ch 1) 8 times, working in Back Loops Only, dc in next dc, ch 1, skip next dc, dc in next 9 dc, ch 1, skip next dc, dc in next dc, ch 1, working in **both** loops, (dc in next dc, ch 1) 8 times, dc in next 5 dc, ch 1, (dc in next dc, ch 1) 3 times, dc in Back Loop Only of next 33 dc, ch 1, working in **both** loops, (dc in next dc, ch 1) 3 times, dc in next 5 dc; repeat from ★ once **more**: 157 dc and 56 ch-1 sps.

Row 49: Ch 3, turn; dc in next 4 dc, ★ ch 1, (dc in next dc, ch 1) 3 times, dc in Back Loop Only of next 33 dc, ch 1, working in **both** loops, (dc in next dc, ch 1) 3 times, dc in next 5 dc, ch 1, (dc in next dc, ch 1) 9 times, working in Back Loops Only, dc in next dc, ch 1, skip next dc, dc in next 5 dc, ch 1, skip next dc, dc in next dc, ch 1, working in **both** loops, (dc in next dc, ch 1) 9 times, dc in next 5 dc; repeat from ★ once **more**: 153 dc and 60 ch-1 sps.

Row 50: Ch 3, turn; dc in next 4 dc, ★ ch 1, (dc in next dc, ch 1) 10 times, working in Back Loops Only, dc in next dc, ch 1, (skip next dc, dc in next dc, ch 1) twice, working in **both** loops, (dc in next dc, ch 1) 10 times, dc in next 5 dc, ch 1, (dc in next dc, ch 1) 3 times, dc in Back Loop Only of next 33 dc, ch 1, working in **both** loops, (dc in next dc, ch 1) 3 times, dc in next 5 dc; repeat from ★ once **more**; do **not** finish off: 149 dc and 64 ch-1 sps.

Continued on page 82.

Row 51: Ch 3, turn; dc in next 4 dc, ★ ch 1, (dc in next dc, ch 1) 3 times, dc in Back Loop Only of next 33 dc, ch 1, working in **both** loops, (dc in next dc, ch 1) 3 times, dc in next 5 dc, ch 1, (dc in next dc, ch 1) 23 times, dc in next 5 dc; repeat from ★ once **more**.

Row 52: Ch 3, turn; dc in next 4 dc, ★ dc in next ch-1 sp, (dc in next dc and in next ch-1 sp) 23 times, dc in next 5 dc, ch 1, (dc in next dc, ch 1) 4 times, skip next dc, dc in Back Loop Only of next 29 dc, ch 1, skip next dc, working in **both** loops, (dc in next dc, ch 1) 4 times, dc in next 5 dc; repeat from ★ once **more**: 193 dc and 20 ch-1 sps.

Row 53: Ch 3, turn; dc in next 4 dc, ★ ch 1, (dc in next dc, ch 1) 4 times, dc in Back Loop Only of next 29 dc, ch 1, working in **both** loops, (dc in next dc, ch 1) 4 times, dc in next 57 dc; repeat from ★ once **more**.

Row 54: Ch 3, turn; dc in next 4 dc, ★ ch 1, skip next dc, (dc in next dc, ch 1, skip next dc) 23 times, dc in next 5 dc, ch 1, (dc in next dc, ch 1) 4 times, dc in Back Loop Only of next 29 dc, ch 1, working in **both** loops, (dc in next dc, ch 1) 4 times, dc in next 5 dc; repeat from ★ once **more**: 145 dc and 68 ch-1 sps.

Row 55: Ch 3, turn; dc in next 4 dc, ★ ch 1, (dc in next dc, ch 1) 4 times, dc in Back Loop Only of next 29 dc, ch 1, working in **both** loops, (dc in next dc, ch 1) 4 times, dc in next 5 dc, ch 1, dc in next dc, (dc in next ch-1 sp and in next dc, ch 1, dc in next dc) 11 times, ch 1, dc in next 5 dc; repeat from ★ once **more**: 167 dc and 46 ch-1 sps.

Row 56: Ch 3, turn; dc in next 4 dc, ★ ch 1, dc in next dc, (dc in next ch-1 sp and in next dc, ch 1, skip next dc, dc in next dc) 11 times, ch 1, dc in next 5 dc, ch 1, (dc in next dc, ch 1) 4 times, dc in Back Loop Only of next 29 dc, ch 1, working in **both** loops, (dc in next dc, ch 1) 4 times, dc in next 5 dc; repeat from ★ once **more**.

Row 57: Repeat Row 24.

Rows 58-85: Repeat Rows 29-56.

Row 86: Repeat Row 24.

Row 87: Ch 3, turn; dc in next 4 dc, ★ ch 1, dc in next dc, (dc in next ch-1 sp and in next dc, ch 1, skip next dc, dc in next dc) 11 times, ch 1, dc in next 5 dc, ch 1, (dc in next dc, ch 1) 5 times, skip next dc, dc in Back Loop Only of next 25 dc, ch 1, skip next dc, working in **both** loops, (dc in next dc, ch 1) 5 times, dc in next 5 dc; repeat from ★ once **more**: 163 dc and 50 ch-1 sps.

Row 88: Ch 3, turn; dc in next 4 dc, ★ ch 1, (dc in next dc, ch 1) 5 times, dc in Back Loop Only of next 25 dc, ch 1, working in **both** loops, (dc in next dc, ch 1) 5 times, dc in next 5 dc, ch 1, dc in next dc, (dc in next ch-1 sp and in next dc, ch 1, skip next dc, dc in next dc) 11 times, ch 1, dc in next 5 dc; repeat from ★ once **more**.

Row 89: Ch 3, turn; dc in next 4 dc, ★ ch 1, dc in next dc, (dc in next ch-1 sp and in next dc, ch 1, skip next dc, dc in next dc) 11 times, ch 1, dc in next 5 dc, ch 1, (dc in next dc, ch 1) 5 times, dc in Back Loop Only of next 25 dc, ch 1, working in **both** loops, (dc in next dc, ch 1) 5 times, dc in next 5 dc; repeat from ★ once **more**.

Rows 90-92: Repeat Rows 88 and 89 once, then repeat Row 88 once **more**.

Row 93: Ch 3, turn; dc in next 4 dc, ★ ch 1, dc in next dc, (dc in next ch-1 sp and in next dc, ch 1, skip next dc, dc in next dc) 11 times, ch 1, dc in next 5 dc, ch 1, (dc in next dc, ch 1) 6 times, skip next dc, dc in Back Loop Only of next 21 dc, ch 1, skip next dc, working in **both** loops, (dc in next dc, ch 1) 6 times, dc in next 5 dc; repeat from ★ once **more**: 159 dc and 54 ch-1 sps.

Row 94: Ch 3, turn; dc in next 4 dc, ★ ch 1, (dc in next dc, ch 1) 6 times, dc in Back Loop Only of next 21 dc, ch 1, working in **both** loops, (dc in next dc, ch 1) 6 times, dc in next 5 dc, ch 1, dc in next dc, (dc in next ch-1 sp and in next dc, ch 1, skip next dc, dc in next dc) 11 times, ch 1, dc in next 5 dc; repeat from ★ once **more**.

Row 95: Ch 3, turn; dc in next 4 dc, ★ ch 1, dc in next dc, (dc in next ch-1 sp and in next dc, ch 1, skip next dc, dc in next dc) 11 times, ch 1, dc in next 5 dc, ch 1, (dc in next dc, ch 1) 6 times, dc in Back Loop Only of next 21 dc, ch 1, working in **both** loops, (dc in next dc, ch 1) 6 times, dc in next 5 dc; repeat from ★ once **more**.

Row 96: Repeat Row 94.

Row 97: Ch 3, turn; dc in next 4 dc, ★ ch 1, dc in next dc, (dc in next ch-1 sp and in next dc, ch 1, skip next dc, dc in next dc) 11 times, ch 1, dc in next 5 dc, ch 1, (dc in next dc, ch 1) 4 times, skip next ch-1 sp, working in Back Loop Only of each dc and each ch, dc in next 29 sts, ch 1, working in **both** loops, (dc in next dc, ch 1) 4 times, dc in next 5 dc; repeat from ★ once **more**: 167 dc and 46 ch-1 sps.

Row 98: Ch 3, turn; dc in next 4 dc, ★ ch 1, (dc in next dc, ch 1) 4 times, working in Back Loops Only, (dc in next dc, ch 1, skip next dc) twice, dc in next 21 dc, ch 1, (skip next dc, dc in next dc, ch 1) twice, working in **both** loops, (dc in next dc, ch 1) 4 times, dc in next 5 dc, ch 1, dc in next dc, (dc in next ch-1 sp and in next dc, ch 1, skip next dc, dc in next dc) 11 times, ch 1, dc in next 5 dc; repeat from ★ once **more**: 159 dc and 54 ch-1 sps.

Row 99: Ch 3, turn; dc in next 4 dc, ★ ch 1, dc in next dc, (dc in next ch-1 sp and in next dc, ch 1, skip next dc, dc in next dc) 11 times, ch 1, dc in next 5 dc, ch 1, (dc in next dc, ch 1) 6 times, working in Back Loops Only, dc in next 3 dc, ch 1, skip next dc, dc in next dc, ch 1, skip next dc, dc in next 9 dc, ch 1, skip next dc, dc in next dc, ch 1, skip next dc, dc in next 3 dc, ch 1, working in **both** loops, (dc in next dc, ch 1) 6 times, dc in next 5 dc; repeat from ★ once **more**: 151 dc and 62 ch-1 sps.

Row 100: Ch 3, turn; dc in next 4 dc, ★ ch 1, (dc in next dc, ch 1) 6 times, dc in Back Loops Only of next 3 dc, ch 1, working in **both** loops, dc in next dc, ch 1, dc in next 9 dc, ch 1, dc in next dc, ch 1, dc in Back Loop Only of next 3 dc, ch 1, working in **both** loops, (dc in next dc, ch 1) 6 times, dc in next 5 dc, ch 1, dc in next dc, (dc in next ch-1 sp and in next dc, ch 1, skip next dc, dc in next dc) 11 times, ch 1, dc in next 5 dc; repeat from ★ once **more**.

Row 101: Ch 3, turn; dc in next 4 dc, ★ ch 1, dc in next dc, (dc in next ch-1 sp and in next dc, ch 1, skip next dc, dc in next dc) 11 times, ch 1, dc in next 5 dc, ch 1, (dc in next dc, ch 1) 6 times, dc in Back Loop Only of next 3 dc, ch 1, working in **both** loops, dc in next dc, ch 1, dc in next 9 dc, ch 1, dc in next dc, ch 1, dc in Back Loop Only of next 3 dc, ch 1, working in **both** loops, (dc in next dc, ch 1) 6 times, dc in next 5 dc; repeat from ★ once **more**.

Row 102: Ch 3, turn; dc in next 4 dc, ★ ch 1, (dc in next dc, ch 1) 5 times, skip next ch-1 sp, working in Back Loops Only of each dc and each ch, dc in next 25 sts, ch 1, working in **both** loops, (dc in next dc, ch 1) 5 times, dc in next 5 dc, ch 1, dc in next dc, (dc in next ch-1 sp and in next dc, ch 1, skip next dc, dc in next dc) 11 times, ch 1, dc in next 5 dc; repeat from ★ once **more**: 163 dc and 50 ch-1 sps.

Row 103: Ch 3, turn; dc in next 4 dc, ★ ch 1, dc in next dc, (dc in next ch-1 sp and in next dc, ch 1, skip next dc, dc in next dc) 11 times, ch 1, dc in next 5 dc, ch 1, (dc in next dc, ch 1) 5 times, working in Back Loops Only, dc in next dc, ch 1, skip next dc, dc in next 21 dc, ch 1, skip next dc, dc in next dc, ch 1, working in **both** loops, (dc in next dc, ch 1) 5 times, dc in next 5 dc; repeat from ★ once **more**: 159 dc and 54 ch-1 sps.

Row 104: Ch 3, turn; dc in next 4 dc, ★ ch 1, (dc in next dc, ch 1) 6 times, working in Back Loops Only, dc in next dc, ch 1, skip next dc, dc in next 17 dc, ch 1, skip next dc, dc in next dc, ch 1, working in **both** loops, (dc in next dc, ch 1) 6 times, dc in next 5 dc, ch 1, dc in next dc, (dc in next ch-1 sp and in next dc, ch 1, skip next dc, dc in next dc) 11 times, ch 1, dc in next 5 dc; repeat from ★ once **more**: 155 dc and 58 ch-1 sps.

Row 105: Ch 3, turn; dc in next 4 dc, ★ ch 1, dc in next dc, (dc in next ch-1 sp and in next dc, ch 1, skip next dc, dc in next dc) 11 times, ch 1, dc in next 5 dc, ch 1, (dc in next dc, ch 1) 7 times, working in Back Loops Only, dc in next dc, ch 1, skip next dc, dc in next 13 dc, ch 1, skip next dc, dc in next dc, ch 1, working in **both** loops, (dc in next dc, ch 1) 7 times, dc in next 5 dc; repeat from ★ once **more**: 151 dc and 62 ch-1 sps.

Row 106: Ch 3, turn; dc in next 4 dc, ★ ch 1, (dc in next dc, ch 1) 8 times, working in Back Loops Only, dc in next dc, ch 1, skip next dc, dc in next 9 dc, ch 1, skip next dc, dc in next dc, ch 1, working in **both** loops, (dc in next dc, ch 1) 8 times, dc in next 5 dc, ch 1, dc in next dc, (dc in next ch-1 sp and in next dc, ch 1, skip next dc, dc in next dc) 11 times, ch 1, dc in next 5 dc; repeat from ★ once **more**: 147 dc and 66 ch-1 sps.

Row 107: Ch 3, turn; dc in next 4 dc, ★ ch 1, dc in next dc, (dc in next ch-1 sp and in next dc, ch 1, skip next dc, dc in next dc) 11 times, ch 1, dc in next 5 dc, ch 1, (dc in next dc, ch 1) 9 times, working in Back Loops Only, dc in next dc, ch 1, skip next dc, dc in next 5 dc, ch 1, skip next dc, dc in next dc, ch 1, working in **both** loops, (dc in next dc, ch 1) 9 times, dc in next 5 dc; repeat from ★ once **more**: 143 dc and 70 ch-1 sps.

Row 108: Ch 3, turn; dc in next 4 dc, ★ ch 1, (dc in next dc, ch 1) 10 times, working in Back Loops Only, dc in next dc, ch 1, (skip next dc, dc in next dc, ch 1) twice, working in **both** loops, (dc in next dc, ch 1) 10 times, dc in next 5 dc, ch 1, dc in next dc, (dc in next ch-1 sp and in next dc, ch 1, skip next dc, dc in next dc) 11 times, ch 1, dc in next 5 dc; repeat from ★ once **more**: 139 dc and 74 ch-1 sps.

Row 109: Ch 3, turn; dc in next 4 dc, ★ ch 1, [(dc in next dc, ch 1) twice, skip next dc] 11 times, dc in next dc, ch 1, dc in next 5 dc, ch 1, (dc in next dc, ch 1) 23 times, dc in next 5 dc; repeat from ★ once **more**: 117 dc and 96 ch-1 sps.

Row 110: Ch 3, turn; dc in next dc and in each dc and each ch-1 sp across: 213 dc.

Row 111: Ch 3, turn; dc in next dc and in each dc across; finish off.

BUTTERFLY

A symbol of the earth's transformation from winter to spring, the butterfly is captured in this lovely afghan by Flora Leger. Variegated chain loops fringe the top and bottom edges.

Finished Size: 41" x 61½"

MATERIALS
Worsted Weight Yarn:
   Ecru - 38 ounces, (1,080 grams, 2,145 yards)
   Variegated - 16 ounces, (450 grams, 930 yards)
Crochet hook, size H (5.00 mm) **or** size needed
   for gauge
Yarn needle

GAUGE: Each Block = 20½" square
         In pattern, 15 sc and 15 rows = 4"

Gauge Swatch: 4" square
With Ecru, ch 16 **loosely.**
Row 1: With Ecru and working over one strand of Variegated, sc in second ch from hook and in each ch across.
Rows 2-15: With Ecru, ch 1, turn; working over Variegated, sc in each sc across.
Finish off.

BLOCK (Make 6)
Note: Block is worked using two strands of yarn, forming stitches with first color and working over one strand of second color, carrying yarn with normal tension across top of previous row.

With Ecru, ch 78 **loosely.**
Row 1 (Right side)**:** With Ecru and working over Variegated, sc in second ch from hook and in each ch across: 77 sc.
Note: Loop a short piece of yarn around any stitch to mark Row 1 as **right** side.
Row 2: With Ecru, ch 1, turn; working over Variegated, sc in each sc across.

Row 3: With Ecru, ch 1, turn; working over Variegated, sc in first 2 sc changing to Variegated in last sc made *(Fig. 5, page 126)*, working over Ecru, sc in next sc changing to Ecru, working over Variegated, sc in next sc changing to Variegated, working over Ecru, sc in next 4 sc changing to Ecru in last sc made, working over Variegated, sc in next sc changing to Variegated, working over Ecru, sc in next 2 sc changing to Ecru in last sc made, working over Variegated, sc in next 3 sc changing to Variegated in last sc made, ★ working over Ecru, sc in next 3 sc changing to Ecru in last sc made, working over Variegated, sc in next 3 sc changing to Variegated in last sc made; repeat from ★ 8 times **more**, working over Ecru, sc in next 5 sc changing to Ecru in last sc made, working over Variegated, sc in next sc changing to Variegated, working over Ecru, sc in next sc changing to Ecru, working over Variegated, sc in last 2 sc.

Note: Continue changing colors in same manner throughout, working over color not being used.

Rows 4-77: Ch 1, turn; following Chart, page 86, for color changes, sc in each sc across.

ASSEMBLY
With Ecru and using photo as a guide, page 85, weave Blocks together forming 2 vertical strips of 3 Blocks each *(Fig. 7, page 126)*; then weave strips together in same manner.

FRINGE
BOTTOM
With **right** side facing and working over beginning chs, join Variegated with slip st in end of first row; ch 20, skip next sc, (slip st in sp **before** next sc, ch 20) across, slip st in end of same row; finish off.

TOP
With **right** side facing and working across Row 77 of Blocks, join Variegated with slip st in end of Row 77; ch 20, skip next sc, (slip st in sp **before** next sc, ch 20) across, slip st in end of same row; finish off.

BUTTERFLY
CHART

Row
- 77
- 70
- 60
- 50
- 40
- 30
- 20
- 10
- 3
- 1
(Right side)

KEY

☐ - Ecru

▉ - Variegated

On **right** side rows, follow Chart from **right** to **left**.

On **wrong** side rows, follow Chart from **left** to **right**.

HARLEQUIN

C.A. Riley uses an adventurous approach to create this classic wrap. The daring diamonds are crocheted in rows by using one color of yarn while working over a second color.

Finished Size: 46" x 63"

MATERIALS
Worsted Weight Yarn:
Purple - 11½ ounces, (330 grams, 650 yards)
Green - 9½ ounces, (270 grams, 535 yards)
Blue - 9 ounces, (260 grams, 510 yards)
Brown - 9 ounces, (260 grams, 510 yards)
Tan - 7 ounces, (200 grams, 395 yards)
Red - 7 ounces, (200 grams, 395 yards)
Crochet hook, size J (6.00 mm) **or** size needed for gauge

Note: Each row is worked across the length of Afghan. Afghan is worked using two strands of yarn, forming stitches with first color and working over one strand of second color, carrying yarn with normal tension across top of previous row. Do **not** cut yarn unless instructed.

GAUGE: In pattern, 14 sts and 12 rows = 5"

Gauge Swatch: 5½"w x 2½"h
Ch 17 **loosely**.
Work same as Afghan for 6 rows.
Finish off.

Continued on page 88.

STITCH GUIDE

SINGLE CROCHET DECREASE
(abbreviated sc decrease)
Pull up a loop in next 2 hdc, YO and draw through all 3 loops on hook **(counts as one sc)**.
TRIPLE DECREASE (uses 3 hdc)
Pull up a loop in next 3 hdc, YO and draw through all 4 loops on hook **(counts as one sc)**.
HALF DOUBLE CROCHET DECREASE
(abbreviated hdc decrease) (uses next 2 sc)
★ YO, insert hook in **next** sc, YO and pull up a loop; repeat from ★ once **more**, YO and draw through all 5 loops on hook **(counts as one hdc)**.

AFGHAN

With Purple, ch 178 **loosely**.
Row 1: With Purple and working over one strand of Blue, hdc in third ch from hook **(2 skipped chs count as first hdc)** and in each ch across: 177 hdc.
Row 2 (Right side)**:** With Purple, ch 1, turn; working over Blue, sc in each hdc across.
Note: Loop a short piece of yarn around any stitch to mark Row 2 as **right** side.
Row 3: With Purple, ch 2 **(counts as first hdc, now and throughout)**, turn; working over Blue, hdc in next sc and in each sc across.
Row 4: With Purple, ch 1, turn; working over Blue, sc in each hdc across.
Rows 5 and 6: Repeat Rows 3 and 4.
Row 7: With Purple, ch 2, turn; working over Blue, hdc in next 7 sc, ch 1, ★ skip next sc, hdc in next 15 sc, ch 1; repeat from ★ across to last 9 sc, skip next sc, hdc in last 8 sc: 166 hdc and 11 ch-1 sps.
Row 8: With Purple, ch 1, turn; working over Blue, sc in first 6 hdc, ★ † sc decrease changing to Blue *(Fig. 5, page 126)*, working over Purple, 3 sc in next ch-1 sp working over carried strand below and changing to Purple in last sc, working over Blue, sc decrease †, sc in next 11 hdc; repeat from ★ 9 times **more**, then repeat from † to † once, sc in last 6 hdc: 177 sc.

Note: Continue to change colors in same manner throughout.

Row 9: With Purple, ch 2, turn; working over Blue, hdc in next 4 sc, ★ † hdc decrease, with Blue and working over Purple, 2 hdc in next sc, hdc in next sc, 2 hdc in next sc, with Purple and working over Blue, hdc decrease †, hdc in next 9 sc; repeat from ★ 9 times **more**, then repeat from † to † once, hdc in last 5 sc.

Row 10: With Purple, ch 1, turn; working over Blue, sc in first 4 hdc, ★ † sc decrease, with Blue and working over Purple, 2 sc in next hdc, sc in next 3 hdc, 2 sc in next hdc, with Purple and working over Blue, sc decrease †, sc in next 7 hdc; repeat from ★ 9 times **more**, then repeat from † to † once, sc in last 4 hdc.
Row 11: With Purple, ch 2, turn; working over Blue, hdc in next 2 sc, ★ † hdc decrease, with Blue and working over Purple, 2 hdc in next sc, hdc in next 5 sc, 2 hdc in next sc, with Purple and working over Blue, hdc decrease †, hdc in next 5 sc; repeat from ★ 9 times **more**, then repeat from † to † once, hdc in last 3 sc.
Row 12: With Purple, ch 1, turn; working over Blue, sc in first 2 hdc, ★ † sc decrease, with Blue and working over Purple, 2 sc in next hdc, sc in next 7 hdc, 2 sc in next hdc, with Purple and working over Blue, sc decrease †, sc in next 3 hdc; repeat from ★ 9 times **more**, then repeat from † to † once, sc in last 2 hdc.
Row 13: With Purple, ch 2, turn; working over Blue, ★ hdc decrease, with Blue and working over Purple, 2 hdc in next sc, hdc in next 9 sc, 2 hdc in next sc, with Purple and working over Blue, hdc decrease, hdc in next sc; repeat from ★ across.
Row 14: With Purple, ch 1, turn; working over Blue, pull up a loop in first 2 hdc, with Blue, YO and draw through all 3 loops on hook, working over Purple, ★ † 2 sc in next hdc, sc in next 11 hdc, 2 sc in next hdc, with Purple and working over Blue †, work triple decrease, with Blue and working over Purple; repeat from ★ 9 times **more**, then repeat from † to † once, sc decrease changing to Blue, cut Purple.
Row 15: With Blue, ch 2, turn; working over Green, hdc in next 15 sc, ch 1, ★ skip next sc, hdc in next 15 sc, ch 1; repeat from ★ across to last 17 sc, skip next sc, hdc in last 16 sc changing to Green in last hdc: 167 hdc and 10 ch-1 sps.
Row 16: With Green, ch 1, turn; working over Blue, 2 sc in first hdc, ★ † with Blue and working over Green, sc decrease, sc in next 11 hdc, sc decrease, with Green and working over Blue †, 3 sc in next ch-1 sp working over carried strand below; repeat from ★ 9 times **more**, then repeat from † to † once, 2 sc in last hdc: 177 sc.
Row 17: With Green, ch 2, turn; working over Blue, 2 hdc in next sc, ★ † with Blue and working over Green, hdc decrease, hdc in next 9 sc, hdc decrease, with Green and working over Blue, 2 hdc in next sc, hdc in next sc †, 2 hdc in next sc; repeat from ★ 9 times **more**, then repeat from † to † once.

Row 18: With Green, ch 1, turn; working over Blue, sc in first 2 hdc, 2 sc in next hdc, ★ † with Blue and working over Green, sc decrease, sc in next 7 hdc, sc decrease, with Green and working over Blue, 2 sc in next hdc †, sc in next 3 hdc, 2 sc in next hdc; repeat from ★ 9 times **more**, then repeat from † to † once, sc in last 2 hdc.

Row 19: With Green, ch 2, turn; working over Blue, hdc in next 2 sc, 2 hdc in next sc, ★ † with Blue and working over Green, hdc decrease, hdc in next 5 sc, hdc decrease, with Green and working over Blue, 2 hdc in next sc †, hdc in next 5 sc, 2 hdc in next sc; repeat from ★ 9 times **more**, then repeat from † to † once, hdc in last 3 sc.

Row 20: With Green, ch 1, turn; working over Blue, sc in first 4 hdc, 2 sc in next hdc, ★ † with Blue and working over Green, sc decrease, sc in next 3 hdc, sc decrease, with Green and working over Blue, 2 sc in next hdc †, sc in next 7 hdc, 2 sc in next hdc; repeat from ★ 9 times **more**, then repeat from † to † once, sc in last 4 hdc.

Row 21: With Green, ch 2, turn; working over Blue, hdc in next 4 sc, 2 hdc in next sc, ★ † with Blue and working over Green, hdc decrease, hdc in next sc, hdc decrease, with Green and working over Blue, 2 hdc in next sc †, hdc in next 9 sc, 2 hdc in next sc; repeat from ★ 9 times **more**, then repeat from † to † once, hdc in last 5 sc.

Row 22: With Green, ch 1, turn; working over Blue, sc in first 6 hdc, 2 sc in next hdc, with Blue and working over Green, work triple decrease, with Green and working over Blue, 2 sc in next hdc, ★ sc in next 11 hdc, 2 sc in next hdc, with Blue and working over Green, work triple decrease, with Green and working over Blue, 2 sc in next hdc; repeat from ★ 9 times **more**, sc in last 6 hdc, cut Blue.

Row 23: With Green and working over Tan, repeat Row 7.

Rows 24-30: Replacing Purple with Green and Blue with Tan, repeat Rows 8-14; at end of Row 30, cut Green.

Row 31: Replacing Blue with Tan and Green with Brown, repeat Row 15.

Rows 32-38: Replacing Green with Brown and Blue with Tan, repeat Rows 16-22; at end of Row 38, cut Tan.

Row 39: With Brown and working over Red, repeat Row 7.

Rows 40-46: Replacing Purple with Brown and Blue with Red, repeat Rows 8-14; at end of Row 46, cut Brown.

Row 47: Replacing Blue with Red and Green with Purple, repeat Row 15.

Rows 48-54: Replacing Green with Purple and Blue with Red, repeat Rows 16-22.

Row 55: With Purple and working over Red, repeat Row 7.

Rows 56-62: With Purple and replacing Blue with Red, repeat Rows 8-14; at end of Row 62, cut Purple.

Row 63: Replacing Blue with Red and Green with Brown, repeat Row 15.

Rows 64-70: Replacing Green with Brown and Blue with Red, repeat Rows 16-22; at end of Row 70, cut Red.

Row 71: With Brown and working over Tan, repeat Row 7.

Rows 72-78: Replacing Purple with Brown and Blue with Tan, repeat Rows 8-14; at end of Row 78, cut Brown.

Row 79: Replacing Blue with Tan and working over Green, repeat Row 15.

Rows 80-86: With Green and replacing Blue with Tan, repeat Rows 16-22; at end of Row 86, cut Tan.

Row 87: With Green and working over Blue, repeat Row 7.

Rows 88-94: Replacing Purple with Green and using Blue, repeat Rows 8-14; at end of Row 94, cut Green.

Row 95: With Blue and and replacing Green with Purple, repeat Row 15.

Rows 96-102: Replacing Green with Purple and using Blue, repeat Rows 16-22, do **not** cut colors.

Row 103: Repeat Row 7.

Row 104: With Purple, ch 1, turn; working over Blue, sc in each hdc and in each ch-1 sp across working over carried strand below: 177 sc.

Row 105-108: Repeat Rows 3 and 4 twice; at end of Row 108, cut Blue.

Row 109: With Purple, ch 1, do **not** turn; working from **left** to **right**, work reverse sc in each sc across *(Figs. 8a-d, page 127)*; finish off.

Trim: With **right** side facing and working in free loops of beginning ch *(Fig. 3b, page 126)*, join Purple with slip st in ch at base of last hdc; ch 1, working from **left** to **right**, work reverse sc in each ch across; finish off.

Holding 7 strands of corresponding color together, each 17" long, add fringe in end of each hdc row across short edges of Afghan *(Figs. 9a & b, page 127)*.

RIBBONS

Bessie Ann Persinger worked her "ribbed bands" against a black background for an eye-catching result.

Finished Size: 45½" x 65"

MATERIALS
Worsted Weight Yarn:
Variegated - 46 ounces,
(1,310 grams, 2,670 yards)
Black - 18 ounces, (510 grams, 1,015 yards)
Crochet hook, size H (5.00 mm) **or** size needed
for gauge

GAUGE: In pattern, 16 sts = 4"; Rows 3-14= 4¾"

Gauge Swatch: 4"w x 4½"h
With Black, ch 17 **loosely**.
Work same as Afghan for 12 rows.

Note: Each row is worked across length of Afghan. When joining yarn and finishing off, leave an 8" end to be worked into fringe.

STITCH GUIDE

JOINING WITH DC
When instructed to join with dc, begin with a slip knot on hook. YO, holding loop on hook, insert hook in **or** around stitch indicated, YO and pull up a loop, (YO and draw through 2 loops on hook) twice.

WORKING AROUND VERTICAL STRAND
When instructed to work **around** vertical strand of dc, YO, insert hook from **back** to **front** under top loops of dc indicated, then from **front** to **back** under top loops of **next** dc *(Fig. A)*, YO and pull up a loop, (YO and draw through 2 loops on hook) twice.

Fig. A

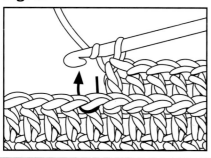

AFGHAN
With Black, ch 261 **loosely**.

Row 1 (Right side)**:** Sc in second ch from hook and in each ch across; finish off: 260 sc.

Note: Loop a short piece of yarn around any stitch to mark Row 1 as **right** side.

Rows 2 and 3: With **right** side facing, join Black with sc in first sc *(see Joining With Sc, page 125)*; sc in next sc, sc in Back Loop Only of next sc *(Fig. 2, page 125)* and each sc across to last 2 sc, sc in **both** loops of last 2 sc; finish off.

Row 4: With **right** side facing and working in both loops, join Variegated with dc in first sc; dc in next sc, dc in Back Loop Only of next sc and each sc across to last 2 sc, dc in **both** loops of last 2 sc; finish off.

Row 5: With **right** side facing and working **around** vertical strand of each dc *(Fig. A)*, join Variegated with dc **around** first dc; dc **around** next dc and each dc across; finish off.

Row 6: With **right** side facing and working in both loops, join Black with sc in first dc; sc in next dc and in each dc across; finish off.

Repeat Rows 4-6 until Afghan measures approximately 45" from beginning ch, ending by working Row 6.

Last 2 Rows: With **right** side facing and working in both loops, join Black with sc in first sc; sc in next sc, sc in Back Loop Only of next sc and each sc across to last 2 sc, sc in **both** loops of last 2 sc; finish off.

Holding 3 strands of Variegated yarn and 3 strands of Black yarn together, each 16" long, add additional fringe in each dc row across short edges of Afghan *(Figs. 9a & b, page 127)*.

LOG CABIN CHRISTMAS

Working in rows instead of rounds, Carole G. Wilder imitates the granny square to
create fresh-looking evergreens topped with stars made of gold-colored thread.

Finished Size: 47½" x 62½"

MATERIALS
Worsted Weight Yarn:
Dk Green - 18 ounces, (510 grams, 1,015 yards)
Burgundy - 13 ounces, (370 grams, 735 yards)
Green - 10½ ounces, (300 grams, 595 yards)
Red - 6½ ounces, (180 grams, 370 yards)
Dk Burgundy - 2½ ounces, (70 grams, 140 yards)
Bedspread Weight Cotton Thread (size 10):
125 yards
Crochet hook, size H (5.00 mm) **or** size needed
for gauge
Steel crochet hook, size 3 (2.10 mm)
Yarn needle
Tapestry needle

GAUGE: Each Square = 7½"

Gauge Swatch: 1½" diameter
Work same as Foundation Rnd.

SQUARE (Make 48)
Foundation Rnd (Right side)**:** With Dk Burgundy and
using large size hook, ch 4, 2 dc in fourth ch from
hook, ch 2, (3 dc in same ch, ch 2) 3 times; join with
slip st to top of beginning ch, finish off: 4 ch-2 sps.
Note #1: Loop a short piece of yarn around any stitch
to mark Foundation Rnd as **right** side.

Note #2: Remainder of Square will be worked in rows
using large size hook throughout.

Row 1: With **wrong** side facing, join Red with slip st
in any ch-2 sp; ch 3 **(counts as first dc, now and
throughout)**, 2 dc in same sp, ch 1, (3 dc, ch 2, 3 dc)
in next ch-2 sp, ch 1, 3 dc in next ch-2 sp, leave
remaining sp unworked: 3 sps.
Row 2: Ch 2, turn; 3 dc in next ch-1 sp, ch 1, (3 dc,
ch 2, 3 dc) in next ch-2 sp, ch 1, 3 dc in next ch-1 sp,
ch 2, skip next 2 dc, slip st in last dc; finish off: 5 sps.
Row 3: With **wrong** side facing, join Dk Green with
slip st in first ch-2 sp made on Row 2; ch 3, 2 dc in
same sp, ch 1, 3 dc in next sp on Foundation Rnd
(same sp as last 3 dc worked on Row 1), ch 1, (3 dc,
ch 2, 3 dc) in next ch-2 sp, ch 1, 3 dc in next sp (same
sp as first 3 dc worked on Row 1), ch 1, 3 dc in last
ch-2 sp on Row 2 changing to Green in last dc *(Fig. 5,
page 126)*.

Row 4: Ch 2, turn; (3 dc in next ch-1 sp, ch 1) twice,
(3 dc, ch 2, 3 dc) in next ch-2 sp, (ch 1, 3 dc in next
ch-1 sp) twice, ch 2, skip next 2 dc, slip st in last dc;
finish off: 7 sps.
Row 5: With **wrong** side facing, join Burgundy with
slip st in first ch-2 sp made on Row 4; ch 3, 2 dc in
same sp, ch 1, (3 dc in next sp, ch 1) twice, (3 dc,
ch 2, 3 dc) in next corner ch-2 sp, (ch 1, 3 dc in next
sp) 3 times.
Row 6: Ch 2, turn; (3 dc in next ch-1 sp, ch 1) 3
times, (3 dc, ch 2, 3 dc) in next corner ch-2 sp, (ch 1,
3 dc in next ch-1 sp) 3 times, ch 2, skip next 2 dc,
slip st in last dc; finish off: 9 sps.
Row 7: With **wrong** side facing, join Dk Green with
slip st in first ch-2 sp made on Row 6; ch 3, 2 dc in
same sp, ch 1, (3 dc in next sp, ch 1) 3 times, (3 dc,
ch 2, 3 dc) in next corner ch-2 sp, (ch 1, 3 dc in next
sp) 4 times changing to Green in last dc.
Row 8: Ch 2, turn; (3 dc in next ch-1 sp, ch 1) 4
times, (3 dc, ch 2, 3 dc) in next corner ch-2 sp, (ch 1,
3 dc in next ch-1 sp) 4 times, ch 2, skip next 2 dc,
slip st in last dc; finish off: 11 sps.
Row 9: With **wrong** side facing, join Red with slip st
in first ch-2 sp made on Row 8; ch 3, 2 dc in same sp,
ch 1, (3 dc in next sp, ch 1) 4 times, (3 dc, ch 2, 3 dc)
in next corner ch-2 sp, (ch 1, 3 dc in next sp) 5 times.
Row 10: Ch 2, turn; (3 dc in next ch-1 sp, ch 1) 5
times, (3 dc, ch 2, 3 dc) in next corner ch-2 sp, (ch 1,
3 dc in next ch-1 sp) 5 times, ch 2, skip next 2 dc,
slip st in last dc; finish off: 13 sps.
Row 11: With **wrong** side facing, join Dk Green with
slip st in first ch-2 sp made on Row 10; ch 3, 2 dc in
same sp, ch 1, (3 dc in next sp, ch 1) 5 times, (3 dc,
ch 2, 3 dc) in next corner ch-2 sp, (ch 1, 3 dc in next
sp) 6 times.
Row 12: Ch 2, turn; (3 dc in next ch-1 sp, ch 1) 6
times, (3 dc, ch 2, 3 dc) in next corner ch-2 sp, (ch 1,
3 dc in next ch-1 sp) 6 times, ch 2, skip next 2 dc,
slip st in last dc; finish off: 15 sps.

Continued on page 94.

ASSEMBLY

Using Placement Diagram as a guide, join Squares together forming 6 vertical strips of 8 Squares each as follows:

Holding two Squares with **wrong** sides together, working through **inside** loops of stitches **and** across end of rows, and matching colors as needed, sew Squares together beginning in second ch of first corner ch-2 and ending in first ch of next corner ch-2.

Sew strips together in same manner.

PLACEMENT DIAGRAM

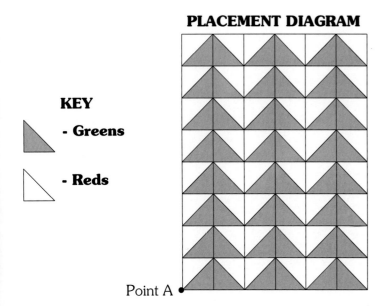

KEY

◣ - Greens

◺ - Reds

Point A •

EDGING

Rnd 1: With **right** side facing, join Green with slip st in corner ch-2 sp at Point A; ch 3, dc in same sp, † work 177 dc evenly spaced across to next corner ch-2 sp, (2 dc, ch 2, 2 dc) in corner ch-2 sp, work 237 dc evenly spaced across to next corner ch-2 sp †, (2 dc, ch 2, 2 dc) in corner ch-2 sp, repeat from † to † once, 2 dc in same sp as first dc, ch 2; join with slip st to first dc: 844 dc and 4 ch-2 sps.
Rnd 2: Ch 3, ★ dc in next dc and in each dc across to next corner ch-2 sp, (2 dc, ch 2, 2 dc) in corner ch-2 sp; repeat from ★ around; join with slip st to first dc, finish off: 860 dc.
Rnd 3: With **right** side facing, join Red with slip st in any corner ch-2 sp; ★ † ch 3, skip next 2 dc, (slip st in next dc, ch 3, skip next 2 dc) across to next corner ch-2 sp †, slip st in corner ch-2 sp; repeat from ★ 2 times **more**, then repeat from † to † once; join with slip st to first slip st, finish off.

STAR (Make 24)

Holding two strands of thread together and using small size hook, ch 4; join with slip st to form a ring.
Rnd 1 (Right side)**:** Ch 3, 9 dc in ring; join with slip st to first dc.
Note: Mark Rnd 1 as **right** side.
Rnd 2: ★ † Ch 5, working in back ridge of chs **(Fig. 1, page 125)**, slip st in second ch from hook, sc in next ch, hdc in next ch, dc in last ch, skip next dc †, slip st in next dc; repeat from ★ 3 times **more**, then repeat from † to † once; join with slip st to same st as joining slip st, finish off.

Using one strand of thread and photo as a guide for placement, page 93, sew Stars to Afghan.

DIAGONAL STRIPES

Using an unusual variation on a timeless design, Beryl Kuhr incorporated these block stitch stripes to make a bold throw.

Finished Size: 42" x 62"

MATERIALS
Worsted Weight Yarn:
  Brown - 26 ounces, (740 grams, 1,470 yards)
  Burgundy - 11 ounces, (310 grams, 620 yards)
  Teal - 6 ounces, (170 grams, 340 yards)
  Crochet hook, size J (6.00 mm) **or** size needed for gauge

GAUGE: 4 Blocks = 5"

Gauge Swatch: 6" x 6" x 8½"
Work same as Afghan Body for 7 rows.

Continued on page 96.

SYMBOL CROCHET CHART

KEY

- ○ - chain
- ● - slip st
- ⊤ - double crochet

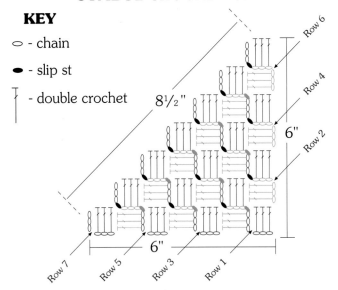

8½"

6"

6"

Row 6
Row 4
Row 2

Row 7 Row 5 Row 3 Row 1

STITCH GUIDE

BEGINNING BLOCK
Ch 6 **loosely**, turn; dc in fourth ch from hook and in next 2 chs.

BLOCK
Slip st in ch-3 sp of next Block, ch 3, 3 dc in same sp.

AFGHAN BODY

Note: Afghan Body is worked diagonally from corner to corner.

Row 1: With Brown, ch 6 **loosely**, dc in fourth ch from hook and in last 2 chs **(first Block made)**.

Row 2 (Right side)**:** Work Beginning Block, slip st around beginning ch of previous Block *(Fig. A)*, ch 3, 3 dc in same sp *(Fig. B)*: 2 Blocks.

Fig. A

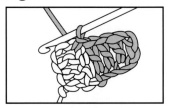

Fig. B

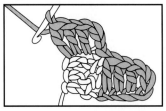

Note: Loop a short piece of yarn around any stitch to mark Row 2 as **right** side.

Row 3: Work Beginning Block, slip st in ch-3 sp of first Block, ch 3, 3 dc in same sp, work Block: 3 Blocks.

Rows 4-8: Work Beginning Block, slip st in ch-3 sp of first Block, ch 3, 3 dc in same sp, work Blocks across changing to Teal in last dc on Row 8 *(Fig. 5, page 126)*: 8 Blocks.

Row 9: Work Beginning Block, slip st in ch-3 sp of first Block, ch 3, 3 dc in same sp, work Blocks across changing to Burgundy in last dc: 9 Blocks.

Rows 10-13: Work Beginning Block, slip st in ch-3 sp of first Block, ch 3, 3 dc in same sp, work Blocks across changing to Teal in last dc on last row: 13 Blocks.

Row 14: Work Beginning Block, slip st in ch-3 sp of first Block, ch 3, 3 dc in same sp, work Blocks across changing to Brown in last dc: 14 Blocks.

Rows 15-22: Work Beginning Block, slip st in ch-3 sp of first Block, ch 3, 3 dc in same sp, work Block across: 22 Blocks.

Rows 23-49: Repeat Rows 9-22 once, then repeat Rows 9-21 once **more**: 49 Blocks.

Note: Rows 50-74 will have the same number of Blocks, **decreasing** on the left side and **increasing** on the right side to shape Afghan Body.

Row 50: Work Beginning Block, slip st in ch-3 sp of first Block, ch 3, 3 dc in same sp, work Blocks across to last Block, slip st in ch-3 sp of last Block; finish off.

Row 51: With **wrong** side facing, join Teal with slip st in ch-3 sp of first Block; ch 3, 3 dc in same sp, work Blocks across changing to Burgundy in last dc.

Row 52: Work Beginning Block, slip st in ch-3 sp of first Block, ch 3, 3 dc in same sp, work Blocks across to last Block, slip st in ch-3 sp of last Block.

Row 53: Turn; slip st in first 3 dc and in next ch-3 sp, ch 3, 3 dc in same sp, work Blocks across.

Rows 54 and 55: Repeat Rows 52 and 53 changing to Teal in last dc on last row.

Row 56: Repeat Row 50.

Row 57: With **wrong** side facing, join Brown with slip st in ch-3 sp of first Block; ch 3, 3 dc in same sp, work Blocks across.

Rows 58-63: Repeat Rows 52 and 53, 3 times.

Rows 64-71: Repeat Rows 50-57.

Rows 72-74: Repeat Rows 52 and 53 once, then repeat Row 52 once **more**.

Note: Rows 75-122 will decrease on **both** sides to shape Afghan Body.

Rows 75-78: Turn; slip st in first 3 dc and in next ch-3 sp, ch 3, 3 dc in same sp, work Blocks across to last Block, slip st in ch-3 sp of last Block: 45 Blocks. Finish off.

Row 79: With **wrong** side facing, join Teal with slip st in ch-3 sp of first Block; ch 3, 3 dc in same sp, work Blocks across to last Block, slip st in ch-3 sp of last Block; finish off: 44 Blocks.

Row 80: With **right** side facing, join Burgundy with slip st in ch-3 sp of first Block; ch 3, 3 dc in same sp, work Blocks across to last Block, slip st in ch-3 sp of last Block: 43 Blocks.

Rows 81-83: Repeat Rows 75-77: 40 Blocks. Finish off.

Row 84: With **right** side facing, join Teal with slip st in ch-3 sp of first Block; ch 3, 3 dc in same sp, work Blocks across to last Block, slip st in ch-3 sp of last Block: 39 Blocks.

Row 85: With **wrong** side facing, join Brown with slip st in ch-3 sp of first Block; ch 3, 3 dc in same sp, work Blocks across to last Block, slip st in ch-3 sp of last Block: 38 Blocks.

Rows 86-92: Turn; slip st in first 3 dc and in next ch-3 sp, ch 3, 3 dc in same sp, work Blocks across to last Block, slip st in ch-3 sp of last Block: 31 Blocks. Finish off.

Rows 93-120: Repeat Rows 79-92 twice; do **not** finish off: 3 Blocks.

Row 121: Turn; slip st in first 3 dc and in next ch-3 sp, ch 3, 3 dc in same sp, work Block, slip st in ch-3 sp of last Block: 2 Blocks.

Row 122: Turn; slip st in first 3 dc and in next ch-3 sp, ch 3, 3 dc in sme sp, slip st in ch-3 sp of last Block; finish off: one Block.

EDGING

Rnd 1: With **right** side facing, join Brown with sc in top of beginning ch-3 on Row 122 *(see Joining With Sc, page 125)*; working in end of rows and in sts across long edge, work 163 sc evenly spaced across to next corner; working in free loops of chs *(Fig. 3b, page 126)* and in end of rows across short edge, work 112 sc evenly spaced across to next corner; working in end of rows and in sts across long edge, work 164 sc evenly spaced across to next corner; working in end of rows and in sts across short edge, work 112 sc evenly spaced across; join with slip st to first sc: 552 sc.

Rnd 2: Ch 3, 5 dc in same st, skip next sc, slip st in next sc, skip next sc, ★ 6 dc in next sc, skip next sc, slip st in next sc, skip next sc; repeat from ★ around; join with slip st to top of beginning ch-3, finish off.

LOVE KNOTS

*Joyce Dale Truett used an openwork variation of a cross stitch
and a chain loop edging to fashion a simply lovely wrap.*

Finished Size: 45" x 60"

MATERIALS
Worsted Weight Yarn:
   62 ounces, (1,760 grams, 3,505 yards)
Crochet hook, size H (5.00 mm) **or** size needed
   for gauge

GAUGE: In pattern, 14 sc and 12 rows = 4"

Gauge Swatch: 4" square
Ch 15 **loosely**.
Work same as Afghan Body for 12 rows.
Finish off.

STITCH GUIDE

CROSS STITCH *(abbreviated Cross St)*
   (uses next 2 sc)
   Skip next sc, insert hook in next sc, YO and pull up
   a loop, insert hook in skipped sc, YO and pull up a
   loop (3 loops on hook), YO and draw through all
   3 loops on hook.

AFGHAN BODY
Ch 157 **loosely**.
Row 1 (Right side)**:** Sc in second ch from hook and in
each ch across: 156 sc.
Note: Loop a short piece of yarn around any stitch to
mark Row 1 as **right** side.
Row 2: Ch 3 **(counts as first hdc plus ch 1, now
and throughout)**, turn; working in Back Loops Only
(Fig. 2, page 125), (work Cross St, ch 1) across to last
sc, hdc in last sc: 79 sts and 78 ch-1 sps.

Row 3: Ch 1, turn; sc in both loops of each st and top
2 loops of each ch *(Fig. A)* across to last ch-1 sp, skip
last ch-1 sp, sc in last hdc: 156 sc.

Fig. A

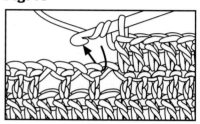

Row 4: Ch 3, turn; working in Back Loops Only,
(work Cross St, ch 1) across to last sc, hdc in last sc:
79 sts and 78 ch-1 sps.
Row 5: Ch 1, turn; working in both loops, sc in first
hdc, skip next ch-1 sp, sc in next Cross St and in top
2 loops of each ch and each st across: 156 sc.
Repeat Rows 2-5 until Afghan Body measures
approximately 59½" from beginning ch, ending by
working a **right** side row; do **not** finish off.

EDGING
Rnd 1: Ch 1, do **not** turn; 2 sc in top of last sc made;
work 206 sc evenly spaced across end of rows; working
in free loops of beginning ch *(Fig. 3b, page 126)*, 3 sc
in first ch, sc in each ch across to ch at base of last sc,
3 sc in ch at base of last sc; work 206 sc evenly spaced
across end of rows; working in sc across last row, 3 sc
in first sc, sc in each sc across and in same st as first sc;
join with slip st to first sc: 732 sc.
Rnd 2: Ch 35, ★ skip next sc, slip st in next sc, ch 35;
repeat from ★ around; join with slip st to same st as
joining.
Rnd 3: Ch 35, **turn**; working in **front** of Rnd 2 and
in skipped sc on Rnd 1, (slip st in next skipped sc,
ch 35) around; join with slip st to st at base of first
slip st, finish off.

BUDS & IVY

No-sew joinings and rows of sweet roses combine to form this charming afghan by Pat Gibbons.

Finished Size: 44" x 60½"

MATERIALS
Worsted Weight Yarn:
Lt Rose - 29 ounces, (820 grams, 1,640 yards)
Rose - 17½ ounces, (500 grams, 990 yards)
Green - 9 ounces, (260 grams, 510 yards)
Crochet hook, size H (5.00 mm) **or** size needed
for gauge

GAUGE: Each Strip = 4" wide
In pattern, (dc, ch 2) 4 times = 3¼"

Gauge Swatch: 2½"w x 6½"h
With Lt Rose, ch 23 **loosely.**
Work same as First Strip through Rnd 1.

STITCH GUIDE

CLUSTER
★ YO, insert hook in ch indicated, YO and pull up
a loop, YO and draw through 2 loops on hook;
repeat from ★ 2 times **more**, YO and draw
through all 4 loops on hook.

FIRST STRIP
With Lt Rose, ch 215 **loosely.**
Foundation Row: Dc in eighth ch from hook,
★ ch 2, skip next 2 chs, dc in next ch; repeat from ★
across: 70 sps.
Rnd 1 (Right side)**:** Slip st around post of last dc made,
ch 3 **(counts as first dc, now and throughout)**, dc
in same sp, place marker around post of same dc on
Foundation Row for Trim placement, (ch 3, 2 dc in
same sp) twice (after marker); working in sps across
beginning ch, (2 dc, ch 3, 2 dc) in each sp across to last
sp, (2 dc, ch 3) twice in last sp, place marker around
beginning ch after last dc worked for Trim placement,
(2 dc, ch 3, 2 dc) in same sp (after marker), (2 dc, ch 3,
2 dc) in each ch-2 sp across to last sp, 2 dc in last sp,
ch 3; join with slip st to first dc, finish off:
142 ch-3 sps.
Note: Loop a short piece of yarn around first dc made
to mark Rnd 1 as **right** side and bottom edge.
Rnd 2: With **right** side facing, join Rose with slip st in
ch-3 sp to left of joining; ch 3, (2 dc, ch 3, 3 dc) in
same sp, ch 1, (3 dc in next ch-3 sp, ch 1) across to
ch-3 sp **above** next marker, (3 dc, ch 3, 3 dc) in
ch-3 sp, ch 1, (3 dc in next ch-3 sp, ch 1) across; join
with slip st to first dc, finish off: 432 dc and 144 sps.

Trim: With **right** side facing and working around posts
of dc on Foundation Row, join Green with slip st
around dc marked for Trim placement at bottom edge;
ch 3, sc around next dc, [ch 6 **loosely**, slip st in second
ch from hook, sc in next ch, dc in next 2 chs, sc in last
ch **(leaf made)]** 3 times, slip st in ch at base of last sc
made on first leaf and around post of same dc on
Foundation Row, ★ (ch 3, sc around next dc) 4 times,
[ch 6 **loosely**, slip st in second ch from hook, sc in
next ch, dc in next 2 chs, sc in next ch **(leaf made)]** 3
times, slip st in ch at base of last sc made on first leaf
and around post of same dc on Foundation Row; repeat
from ★ across to next marker, ch 3, slip st around
beginning ch at marker; finish off: 18 3-leaf groups.
Last Rnd: With **right** side facing, join Lt Rose with sc
in ch-3 sp to left of joining on Rnd 2 **(see Joining
With Sc, page 125)**; ch 3, sc in same sp, ch 3, (sc,
ch 3) twice in next 69 ch-1 sps, sc in next ch-1 sp,
ch 3, place marker around ch-3 just made for joining
placement, sc in same sp, ch 3, (sc, ch 3) twice in each
sp around; join with slip st to first sc, finish off:
288 ch-3 sps.

REMAINING 10 STRIPS
Work same as First Strip through Trim:
18 3-leaf groups.
Last Rnd (Joining rnd)**:** With **right** side facing, join
Lt Rose with sc in ch-3 sp to left of joining on Rnd 2;
ch 3, sc in same sp, ch 3, (sc, ch 3) twice in next
69 ch-1 sps, sc in next ch-1 sp, ch 3, place marker
around ch-3 just made for joining placement, sc in same
sp, ch 3, (sc, ch 3) twice in next 3 sps, sc in next
ch-1 sp, ch 1, holding Strips with **wrong** sides together
and bottom edges at same end, sc in marked ch-3 sp on
previous Strip, ch 1, sc in same sp on **new Strip**,
★ ch 1, sc in next ch-3 sp on **previous Strip**, ch 1, sc
in next ch-1 sp on **new Strip**, ch 1, sc in next ch-3 sp
on **previous Strip**, ch 1, sc in same sp on **new Strip**;
repeat from ★ across to last ch-1 sp on **new Strip**,
ch 3, (sc, ch 3) twice in last ch-1 sp; join with slip st to
first sc, finish off.

FLOWER (Make 198)
With Rose, (ch 3, work Cluster in third ch from hook) 3
times; join with slip st to ch at base of first Cluster
made, finish off leaving a long end for sewing.

Sew one Flower to center of each 3-leaf group.

STAINED GLASS

*Capturing the kaleidoscope of an ornate window in a fine old house,
this afghan by Gail Smith is an intriguing home accent.*

Finished Size: 46½" x 63½"

MATERIALS
Worsted Weight Yarn:
Black - 30 ounces, (850 grams, 1,695 yards)
Variegated - 24 ounces, (680 grams, 1,390 yards)
Crochet hook, size J (6.00 mm) **or** size needed
for gauge

GAUGE: Each Motif = 6½"
(straight edge to straight edge)

Gauge Swatch: 3½" diameter
Work same as Motif through Rnd 3.

STITCH GUIDE

TREBLE CROCHET *(abbreviated tr)*
YO twice, insert hook in st indicated, YO and pull
up a loop (4 loops on hook), (YO and draw through
2 loops on hook) 3 times.
DOUBLE TREBLE CROCHET
(abbreviated dtr)
YO 3 times, insert hook in sc indicated, YO and
pull up a loop (5 loops on hook), (YO and draw
through 2 loops on hook) 4 times.

MOTIF (Make 72)
With Variegated, ch 5; join with slip st to form a ring.
Rnd 1 (Right side)**:** Ch 3 **(counts as first dc, now
and throughout)**, 11 dc in ring; join with slip st to
first dc: 12 dc.
Note: Loop a short piece of yarn around any stitch to
mark Rnd 1 as **right** side.
Rnd 2: Ch 1, sc in same st, ch 5, skip next dc, ★ sc in
next dc, ch 5, skip next dc; repeat from ★ around; join
with slip st to first sc: 6 ch-5 sps.
Rnd 3: Slip st in first ch-5 sp, ch 2 **(counts as first
hdc, now and throughout)**, 7 hdc in same sp, 8 hdc
in each ch-5 sp around; join with slip st to first hdc,
finish off: 48 hdc.
Rnd 4: With **right** side facing, join Black with slip st in
fifth hdc of any 8-hdc group; ch 3, 3 dc in same st,
working in **front** of Rnd 3, 2 dtr in next sc one rnd
below, ★ 4 dc in fifth hdc of next 8-hdc group on
Rnd 3, working in **front** of Rnd 3, 2 dtr in next sc one
rnd **below**; repeat from ★ around, skip last 4 hdc; join
with slip st to first dc, finish off: 36 sts.

Rnd 5: With **right** side facing, join Variegated with
slip st in third dc of any 4-dc group; ch 3, (2 dc, ch 2,
3 dc) in same st, skip next 2 sts, 3 dc in next dtr, skip
next 2 dc, ★ (3 dc, ch 2, 3 dc) in next dc, skip next
2 sts, 3 dc in next dtr, skip next 2 dc; repeat from ★
around; join with slip st to first dc, finish off: 54 dc and
6 ch-2 sps.
Rnd 6: With **right** side facing, join Black with sc in
any ch-2 sp *(see Joining With Sc, page 125)*; ch 2,
sc in same sp, ★ † skip next dc, sc in next 2 dc,
(working in **front** of Rnd 5, tr in next 2 skipped sts one
rnd **below**, skip next dc from last sc made, sc in next
2 dc) twice †, (sc, ch 2, sc) in next ch-2 sp; repeat from
★ 4 times **more**, then repeat from † to † once; join
with slip st to first sc, finish off: 72 sts and 6 ch-2 sps.

HALF MOTIF (Make 10)
With Variegated, ch 4; join with slip st to form a ring.
Row 1 (Right side)**:** Ch 3, 8 dc in ring, do **not** join:
9 dc.
Note: Mark Row 1 as **right** side.
Row 2: Ch 1, turn; sc in first dc, ch 4, skip next dc, sc
in next dc, ★ ch 5, skip next dc, sc in next dc; repeat
from ★ once **more**, ch 4, skip next dc, sc in last dc:
4 sps.
Row 3: Ch 2, turn; 3 hdc in first ch-4 sp, 8 hdc in
each of next 2 ch-5 sps, 3 hdc in next ch-4 sp, hdc in
last sc; finish off: 24 hdc.
Row 4: With **right** side facing, join Black with slip st
in first hdc; ch 3, dc in same st, working in **front** of
Row 3, 2 dtr in next sc one row **below**, ★ 4 dc in fifth
hdc of next 8-hdc group on Row 3, working in **front** of
Row 3, 2 dtr in next sc one row **below**; repeat from ★
once **more**, 2 dc in last hdc on Row 3; finish off:
18 sts.
Row 5: With **right** side facing, join Variegated with
slip st in first dc; ch 3, 2 dc in same st, skip next 2 sts,
3 dc in next dtr, ★ skip next 2 dc, (3 dc, ch 2, 3 dc) in
next dc, skip next 2 sts, 3 dc in next dtr; repeat from ★
once **more**, skip next dc, 3 dc in last dc; finish off:
27 dc and 2 ch-2 sps.

Continued on page 104.

Trim: With **right** side facing, join Black with sc in first dc; place marker around sc just made for joining placement, sc in same st and in next 2 dc, ★ (working in **front** of Row 5, tr in next 2 skipped sts one row **below**, skip next dc from last sc made, sc in next 2 dc) twice, (sc, ch 2, sc) in next ch-2 sp, skip next dc, sc in next 2 dc; repeat from ★ once **more**, working in **front** of Row 5, tr in next 2 skipped sts one row **below**, skip next dc from last sc made, sc in next 2 dc, working in **front** of Row 5, 2 tr in next skipped dc one row **below**, skip next dc from last sc made, 2 sc in each of last 2 dc, place marker around last sc made for joining placement; working in end of rows, 2 sc in each of first 2 rows, sc in next 2 rows, 2 sc in next row, sc in beginning ring, 2 sc in next row, sc in next 2 rows, 2 sc in each of last 2 rows; join with slip st to first sc, finish off: 55 sts and 2 ch-2 sps.

ASSEMBLY

Using Placement Diagram as a guide, join Motifs together forming 6 horizontal strips of 7 Motifs each **and** 5 horizontal strips of 6 Motifs and 2 Half Motifs each as follows:

With **wrong** sides together, working through both thicknesses and through **inside** loops only, join Black with slip st in second ch of first corner ch-2; slip st in each st across ending in first ch of next corner ch-2; then join strips together, beginning in marked sc on Half Motif and second ch of corresponding corner ch-2 on Motif and ending in next marked sc on Half Motif and first ch of next corner ch-2 on last Motif.

PLACEMENT DIAGRAM

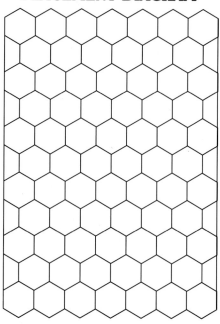

EDGING

Rnd 1: With **right** side facing, join Black with sc in any unworked ch-2 sp; 2 sc in same sp, sc evenly around entire Afghan working 3 sc in each unworked ch-2 sp around; join with slip st to first sc.
Rnd 2: Ch 1, sc in same st, 3 sc in next sc, sc in each sc around working 3 sc in center sc of each 3-sc group; join with slip st to first sc, finish off.

ROSES ON LACE

*With a unique no-sew joining method, this filigree floral garden
by Pat Gibbons exudes old-fashioned grace.*

Finished Size: 48" x 58"

MATERIALS
Worsted Weight Yarn:
    Ecru - 41 ounces, (1,160 grams, 2,315 yards)
    Green - 5 ounces, (140 grams, 285 yards)
    Rose - 3 ounces, (90 grams, 170 yards)
    Dk Rose - 3 ounces, (90 grams, 170 yards)
    Purple - 3 ounces, (90 grams, 170 yards)
    Blue - 3 ounces, (90 grams, 170 yards)
Crochet hook, size G (4.00 mm) **or** size needed for gauge

GAUGE: Each Square = 8"

Gauge Swatch: 3½" diameter
Work same as Rose.

STITCH GUIDE

CLUSTER (uses one sp)
★ YO twice, insert hook in ch-5 sp indicated, YO and pull up a loop, (YO and draw through 2 loops on hook) twice; repeat from ★ 3 times **more**, YO and draw through all 5 loops on hook.

Continued on page 106.

SQUARE (Make 30)

Note: Make the number of Squares indicated through Inner Petals in each of the following colors: Rose - 7, Dk Rose - 8, Purple - 7, and Blue - 8.

ROSE

With color indicated, ch 4; join with slip st to form a ring.

Rnd 1 (Right side): Ch 6 **(counts as first dc plus ch 3)**, (dc in ring, ch 3) 7 times; join with slip st to first dc: 8 ch-3 sps.

Note: Loop a short piece of yarn around any stitch to mark Rnd 1 as **right** side.

Rnd 2: Ch 1, (sc, hdc, dc, hdc, sc) in each ch-3 sp around; join with slip st to first sc: 8 petals.

Rnd 3: Ch 1, working **behind** petals and around posts of dc in Rnd 1, sc around first dc, ch 4, (sc around next dc, ch 4) around; join with slip st to first sc: 8 ch-4 sps.

Rnd 4: Ch 1, (sc, hdc, 3 dc, hdc, sc) in each ch-4 sp around; join with slip st to first sc: 8 petals.

Rnd 5: Ch 1, working **behind** petals and around posts of sc on Rnd 3, sc around first sc, ch 5, (sc around next sc, ch 5) around; join with slip st to first sc, finish off: 8 ch-5 sps.

INNER PETALS

Rnd 1: With **right** side facing and working around posts of dc on Rnd 1 **(below** sc on Rnd 3), join same color yarn with sc around post of any dc **(see Joining With Sc, page 125)**; ch 5, (sc around next dc, ch 5) around; join with slip st to first sc: 8 ch-5 sps.

Rnd 2: Ch 1, 5 sc in each ch-5 sp around; join with slip st to first sc, finish off: 40 sc.

BORDER

Rnd 1: With **right** side of Rose facing, join Green with slip st in any ch-5 sp on Rnd 5; ch 10, work (Cluster, ch 5, Cluster) in next ch-5 sp, ch 10, ★ slip st in next ch-5 sp, ch 10, work (Cluster, ch 5, Cluster) in next ch-5 sp, ch 10; repeat from ★ 2 times **more**; join with slip st to first slip st, finish off: 12 sps.

Rnd 2: With **right** side facing, join Ecru with sc in any ch-5 sp; 4 sc in same sp, ★ † 15 sc in next ch-10 sp, working **around** next slip st, sc in ch-5 sp on Rnd 5 of Rose, 8 sc in next ch-10 sp, drop loop from hook, insert hook from **front** to **back** in eighth sc worked in previous ch-10 sp, hook dropped loop and pull through, ch 1, 7 sc in same sp †, 9 sc in next ch-5 sp; repeat from ★ 2 times **more**, then repeat from † to † once, 4 sc in same sp as first sc; join with slip st to first sc.

Rnd 3: Ch 1, (sc, ch 3, sc) in same st, ch 6, skip next 4 sc, sc in sp **before** next sc, ch 6, skip next 6 sc, sc in next sc, ch 3, skip next ch-1, sc in next sc, ch 6, skip next 6 sc, sc in sp **before** next sc, ★ ch 6, skip next 4 sc, (sc, ch 3, sc) in next sc, ch 6, skip next 4 sc, sc in sp **before** next sc, ch 6, skip next 6 sc, sc in next sc, ch 3, skip next ch-1, sc in next sc, ch 6, skip next 6 sc, sc in sp **before** next sc; repeat from ★ 2 times **more**, ch 3, skip last 4 sc, dc in first sc to form last ch-6 sp: 24 sps.

Rnd 4: Ch 1, (sc, ch 3, sc) in same sp, ch 5, skip next ch-3 sp, (sc, ch 3, sc) in next ch-6 sp, ch 5, sc in next ch-6 sp, ch 5, (3 dc, ch 3, 3 dc) in next ch-3 sp, ch 5, sc in next ch-6 sp, ★ ch 5, (sc, ch 3, sc) in next ch-6 sp, ch 5, skip next ch-3 sp, (sc, ch 3, sc) in next ch-6 sp, ch 5, sc in next ch-6 sp, ch 5, (3 dc, ch 3, 3 dc) in next ch-3 sp, ch 5, sc in next ch-6 sp; repeat from ★ 2 times **more**, ch 2, dc in first sc to form last ch-5 sp: 32 sps.

Rnd 5: Ch 1, sc in same sp, ch 5, skip next ch-3 sp, (sc, ch 3, sc) in next ch-5 sp, ch 5, skip next ch-3 sp, (sc in next ch-5 sp, ch 5) twice, (3 dc, ch 3, 3 dc) in next ch-3 sp, ch 5, ★ (sc in next ch-5 sp, ch 5) twice, skip next ch-3 sp, (sc, ch 3, sc) in next ch-5 sp, ch 5, skip next ch-3 sp, (sc in next ch-5 sp, ch 5) twice, (3 dc, ch 3, 3 dc) in next ch-3 sp, ch 5; repeat from ★ 2 times **more**, sc in next ch-5 sp, ch 2, dc in first sc to form last ch-5 sp.

Rnd 6: Ch 1, (sc, ch 3) twice in same sp and in next ch-5 sp, skip next ch-3 sp, (sc, ch 3) twice in next 3 ch-5 sps, (3 dc, ch 3) twice in next ch-3 sp, ★ (sc, ch 3) twice in next 3 ch-5 sps, skip next ch-3 sp, (sc, ch 3) twice in next 3 ch-5 sps, (3 dc, ch 3) twice in next ch-3 sp; repeat from ★ 2 times **more**, (sc, ch 3) twice in last ch-5 sp; join with slip st to first sc, finish off: 56 ch-3 sps.

ASSEMBLY
SQUARE JOINING
Using Placement Diagram as a guide and starting at bottom edge, join Squares together forming 5 strips of 6 Squares each as follows:

FIRST 2 SQUARES
Row 1: With Ecru, ch 4 **loosely**, with **wrong** sides of two Squares facing, sc in any corner ch-3 sp on **first Square**, (2 dc, ch 3, 3 dc) in fourth ch from hook, sc in any corner ch-3 sp on **second Square**.
Rows 2-15: Turn; skip first sc, slip st in next 3 dc and in next ch-3 sp, ch 3, sc in next ch-3 sp on **same Square**, (2 dc, ch 3, 3 dc) in same ch-3 sp as last slip st, sc in next ch-3 sp on **adjacent Square**. Finish off.

PLACEMENT DIAGRAM

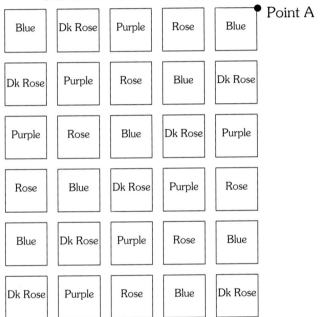

Point A

Blue	Dk Rose	Purple	Rose	Blue
Dk Rose	Purple	Rose	Blue	Dk Rose
Purple	Rose	Blue	Dk Rose	Purple
Rose	Blue	Dk Rose	Purple	Rose
Blue	Dk Rose	Purple	Rose	Blue
Dk Rose	Purple	Rose	Blue	Dk Rose

REMAINING 4 SQUARES
Row 1: With Ecru, ch 4 **loosely**, with **wrong** sides of next Square and previous Squares facing, sc in corner ch-3 sp to left of joining on **previous Square**, (2 dc, ch 3, 3 dc) in fourth ch from hook, sc in any corner ch-3 sp on **new Square**.
Rows 2-15: Turn; skip first sc, slip st in next 3 dc and in next ch-3 sp, ch 3, sc in next ch-3 sp on **same Square**, (2 dc, ch 3, 3 dc) in same ch-3 sp as last slip st, sc in next ch-3 sp on **adjacent Square**. Finish off.

STRIP JOINING
Row 1: With Ecru, ch 4 **loosely**, with **wrong** sides of strips facing and bottom edges at same end, sc in corner ch-3 sp to right of First Square joining on **first strip**, (2 dc, ch 3, 3 dc) in fourth ch from hook, sc in corresponding corner ch-3 sp on **adjacent strip**.
Rows 2-15: Turn; skip first sc, slip st in next 3 dc and in next ch-3 sp, ch 3, sc in next sp on **same strip**, (2 dc, ch 3, 3 dc) in same ch-3 sp as last slip st, sc in next sp on **adjacent strip**.
Row 16: Turn; skip first sc, slip st in next 3 dc and in next ch-3 sp, ch 3, sc in ch-3 sp of joining on **same strip**, (2 dc, ch 3, 3 dc) in same ch-3 sp as last slip st, sc in free loop of ch at base of next dc-group of joining on **adjacent strip** *(Fig. 3b, page 126)*.
Rows 17-31: Turn; skip first sc, slip st in next 3 dc and in next ch-3 sp, ch 3, sc in next sp on **same strip**, (2 dc, ch 3, 3 dc) in same ch-3 sp as last slip st, sc in next sp on **adjacent strip**.
Rows 32-95: Repeat Rows 16-31, 4 times. Finish off.

Repeat for remaining strips.

EDGING
With **right** side facing, join Ecru with slip st in corner ch-3 sp at Point A; ch 3, dc in same sp, (ch 2, 2 dc in same sp) twice, sc in next ch-3 sp, [(2 dc, ch 2, 2 dc) in next ch-3 sp, sc in next ch-3 sp] 6 times, † ★ skip next 2 dc, (2 dc, ch 2, 2 dc) in next dc, sc in next joining sc, (2 dc, ch 2, 2 dc) in next ch-3 sp, sc in next joining sc, (2 dc, ch 2, 2 dc) in next dc, sc in next ch-3 sp, [(2 dc, ch 2, 2 dc) in next ch-3 sp, sc in next ch-3 sp] 6 times; repeat from ★ across to next corner ch-3 sp, 2 dc in corner ch-3 sp, (ch 2, 2 dc in same sp) twice, sc in next ch-3 sp, [(2 dc, ch 2, 2 dc) in next ch-3 sp, sc in next ch-3 sp] 6 times †, repeat from † to † once **more**, ♥ skip next 2 dc, (2 dc, ch 2, 2 dc) in next dc, sc in next joining sc, (2 dc, ch 2, 2 dc) in free loop of ch at base of next dc-group of joining, sc in next joining sc, (2 dc, ch 2, 2 dc) in next dc, sc in next ch-3 sp, [(2 dc, ch 2, 2 dc) in next ch-3 sp, sc in next ch-3 sp] 6 times ♥, repeat from ♥ to ♥ across to next corner ch-3 sp, 2 dc in corner ch-3 sp, (ch 2, 2 dc in same sp) twice, sc in next ch-3 sp, [(2 dc, ch 2, 2 dc) in next ch-3 sp, sc in next ch-3 sp] 6 times, repeat from ♥ to ♥ across; join with slip st to first dc, finish off.

VANITY

With such a wonderful texture, this afghan has something to be vain about!
Marge Warner constructed this sensational piece by using single
crochet stitches behind chains skipped on previous rows.

Finished Size: 46½" x 60"

MATERIALS
Worsted Weight Yarn:
    47 ounces, (1,330 grams, 2,725 yards)
    Crochet hook, size I (5.50 mm) **or** size needed
    for gauge

GAUGE: In pattern, (sc, ch 1) 6 times = 3½";
        13 rows = 4"

Gauge Swatch: 11½"w x 4"h
Ch 40, place marker in eleventh ch from hook for
st placement.
Work same as Afghan for 13 rows.
Finish off.

AFGHAN

Ch 160, place marker in eleventh ch from hook for
st placement.
Row 1 (Right side)**:** Sc in second ch from hook,
★ ch 1, skip next ch, sc in next ch; repeat from ★
across: 80 sc.
Note: Loop a short piece of yarn around any stitch to
mark Row 1 as **right** side.
Row 2: Ch 1, turn; sc in first sc, (ch 1, sc in next sc)
across.
Row 3: Ch 1, turn; sc in first sc, (ch 1, sc in next sc)
twice, ch 6, skip next 2 ch-1 sps, working **around**
previous rows, sc in marked ch on beginning ch **below**
next ch-1, ch 6, skip next 2 sc on Row 2, sc in next sc,
★ (ch 1, sc in next sc) 5 times, ch 6, skip next
2 ch-1 sps, working **around** previous rows, sc in next
unworked ch on beginning ch **below** next ch-1, ch 6,
skip next 2 sc on Row 2, sc in next sc; repeat from ★
across to last 2 sc, (ch 1, sc in next sc) twice.

Row 4: Ch 1, turn; sc in first sc, ch 1, (sc in next sc,
ch 1) twice, working in **front** of next 2 ch-6 sps, (dc in
next skipped sc on Row 2, ch 1) 4 times, ★ (sc in next
sc on Row 3, ch 1) 6 times, working in **front** of next
2 ch-6 sps, (dc in next skipped sc on Row 2, ch 1) 4
times; repeat from ★ across to last 3 sc on Row 3, sc in
next sc, (ch 1, sc in next sc) twice.
Row 5: Ch 1, turn; sc in first sc, (ch 1, sc in next sc)
twice, ch 6, working in **front** of previous row, sc in sc
between next 2 ch-6 sps one row **below**, ch 6, skip
next 4 dc, sc in next sc, ★ (ch 1, sc in next sc) 5 times,
ch 6, working in **front** of previous row, sc in sc
between next 2 ch-6 sps one row **below**, ch 6, skip
next 4 dc, sc in next sc; repeat from ★ across to last
2 sc, (ch 1, sc in next sc) twice.
Row 6: Ch 1, turn; sc in first sc, ch 1, (sc in next sc,
ch 1) twice, working in **front** of next 2 ch-6 sps, (dc in
next skipped dc one row **below**, ch 1) 4 times, ★ (sc in
next sc, ch 1) 6 times, working in **front** of next
2 ch-6 sps, (dc in next skipped dc one row **below**,
ch 1) 4 times; repeat from ★ across to last 3 sc, sc in
next sc, (ch 1, sc in next sc) twice.
Repeat Rows 5 and 6 until Afghan measures
approximately 60" from beginning ch, ending by
working Row 6.
Last Row: Ch 1, turn; sc in first sc, ★ ch 1, skip next
ch-1 sp, sc in next st; repeat from ★ across; finish off.

Holding 8 strands of yarn together, each 17" long, add
fringe evenly spaced across short edges of Afghan
(Figs. 9c & d, page 127).

JAGUAR

If you're wild about classics, you'll love Carole G. Wilder's afghan celebrating the immortal beauty of the jaguar. Each square showcases a spot from the exotic cat, giving it all the "markings" of a timeless favorite!

Finished Size: 47½" x 63½"

MATERIALS
Worsted Weight Yarn:
    Tan - 40 ounces, (1,140 grams, 2,260 yards)
    Black - 9 ounces, (260 grams, 510 yards)
    Brown - 4 ounces, (110 grams, 225 yards)
Crochet hook, size I (5.50 mm) **or** size needed
    for gauge
Yarn needle

GAUGE SWATCH: 4" square
Work same as Square.

SQUARE (Make 165)
With Brown, ch 5 **loosely**.
Rnd 1 (Right side): Hdc in third ch from hook
(2 skipped chs count as first hdc) and in next ch,
3 hdc in last ch; working in free loops of beginning ch
(Fig. 3b, page 126), hdc in next 2 chs, 2 hdc in next
ch; join with slip st to first hdc, finish off: 10 hdc.
Note: Loop a short piece of yarn around any stitch to
mark Rnd 1 as **right** side.
Rnd 2: With **right** side facing, join Black with sc in
same st as joining *(see Joining With Sc, page 125)*;
sc in same st and in next 2 hdc, 2 sc in each of next
3 hdc, sc in next 2 hdc, 2 sc in each of last 2 hdc; join
with slip st to first sc, finish off: 16 sc.
Rnd 3: With **right** side facing, join Tan with slip st in
first sc to left of joining; ch 3 **(counts as first dc, now
and throughout)**, (dc, ch 2, 2 dc) in same st, ch 1,
skip next sc, 3 dc in next sc, ch 1, skip next sc, ★ (2 dc,
ch 2, 2 dc) in next sc, ch 1, skip next sc, 3 dc in next
sc, ch 1, skip next sc; repeat from ★ 2 times **more**;
join with slip st to first dc, do **not** finish off: 28 dc and
12 sps.

Rnd 4: Slip st in next dc and in next ch-2 sp, ch 3,
(dc, ch 3, 2 dc) in same sp, ch 1, (3 dc in next ch-1 sp,
ch 1) twice, ★ (2 dc, ch 3, 2 dc) in next ch-2 sp, ch 1,
(3 dc in next ch-1 sp, ch 1) twice; repeat from ★
2 times **more**; join with slip st to first dc, finish off:
40 dc and 16 sps.

ASSEMBLY
With Tan, using photo as a guide for placement,
page 111, and working through **inside** loops,
whipstitch Squares together forming 11 vertical strips of
15 Squares each *(Fig. 6b, page 126)*, beginning in
center ch of first corner ch-3 and ending in center ch of
next corner ch-3; then whipstitch strips together in
same manner.

EDGING
Rnd 1: With **right** side facing, join Black with slip st in
any corner ch-3 sp; ch 3, (dc, ch 2, 2 dc) in same sp,
ch 1, (2 dc in next sp, ch 1) across to next corner
ch-3 sp, ★ (2 dc, ch 2, 2 dc) in corner ch-3 sp, ch 1,
(2 dc in next sp, ch 1) across to next corner ch-3 sp;
repeat from ★ 2 times **more**; join with slip st to first dc,
finish off: 260 sps.
Rnd 2: With **right** side facing, join Brown with slip st
in any corner ch-2 sp; ch 3, (dc, ch 2, 2 dc) in same sp,
ch 1, (2 dc in next ch-1 sp, ch 1) across to next corner
ch-2 sp, ★ (2 dc, ch 2, 2 dc) in corner ch-2 sp, ch 1,
(2 dc in next ch-1 sp, ch 1) across to next corner
ch-2 sp; repeat from ★ 2 times **more**; join with slip st
to first dc, finish off.
Rnd 3: With Black, repeat Rnd 2.

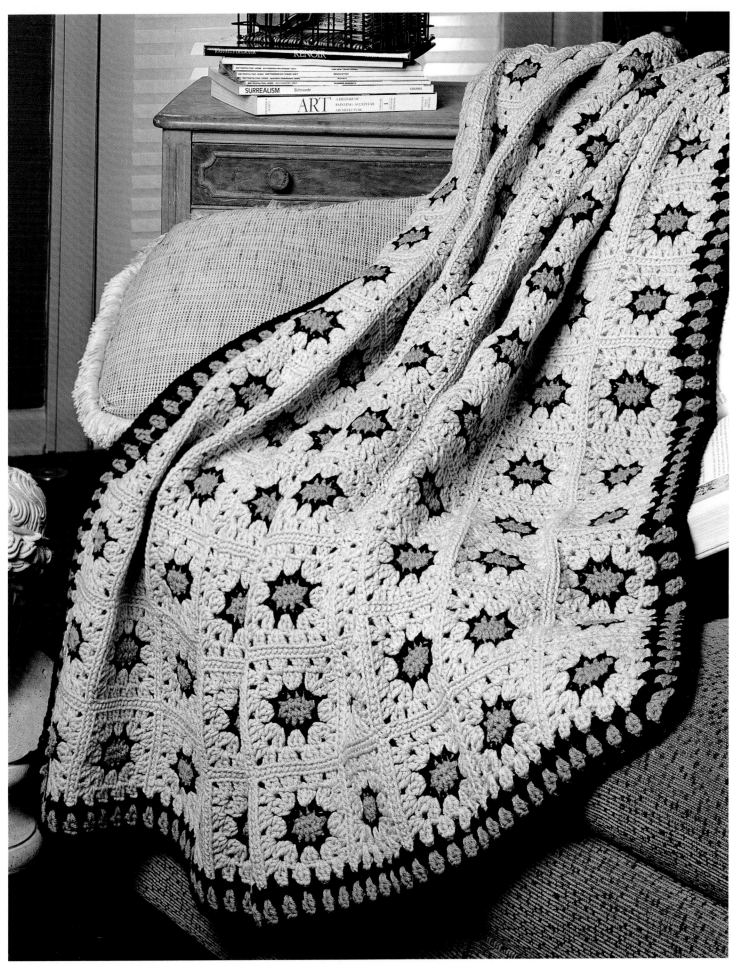

TRIPLE TREAT

If you like treble crochet, then this is the afghan for you! Ruthie Marks couldn't find a pattern that used only treble crochet, so she made her own design that "linked" the stitches together.

Finished Size: 42" x 60"

MATERIALS

Worsted Weight Yarn:
Lt Green - 14½ ounces, (410 grams, 820 yards)
Green - 12½ ounces, (350 grams, 710 yards)
Variegated - 11 ounces, (310 grams, 640 yards)
Crochet hook, size K (6.50 mm) **or** size needed
for gauge

GAUGE: In pattern, 11 Ltr = 3¾"; 4 rows = 4"

Gauge Swatch: 3¾"w x 4"h
With Lt Green, ch 15 **loosely**.
Work same as Afghan Body for 4 rows.
Finish off.

STITCH GUIDE

TREBLE CROCHET *(abbreviated tr)*
YO twice, insert hook in st indicated, YO and pull up
a loop (4 loops on hook), (YO and draw through
2 loops on hook) 3 times.
LINKED TREBLE CROCHET
(abbreviated Ltr)
Insert hook through upper horizontal bar on post of
previous st *(Fig. A)*, YO and pull up a loop, insert
hook through lower horizontal bar on post of same
st *(Fig. B)*, YO and pull up a loop, insert hook in
next st, YO and pull up a loop *(Fig. C)* (4 loops on
hook), (YO and draw through 2 loops on hook) 3
times *(Fig. D)*.

Fig. A

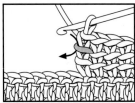

Fig. B

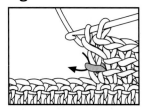

Fig. C

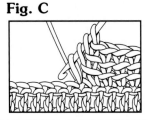

Fig. D

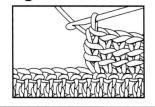

AFGHAN BODY

With Lt Green, ch 119 **loosely**.
Row 1: [Insert hook in second ch from hook, YO and
pull up a loop, (skip next ch, insert hook in next ch, YO
and pull up a loop) twice (4 loops on hook), (YO and
draw through 2 loops on hook) 3 times **(beginning Ltr
made)]**, work Ltr across *(Figs. A-D)*: 114 Ltr.
Row 2 (Right side): Ch 4, turn; insert hook in second
ch from hook, YO and pull up a loop, skip next ch,
insert hook in next ch, YO and pull up a loop, insert
hook in first Ltr, YO and pull up a loop, (YO and draw
through 2 loops on hook) 3 times, work Ltr across.
Note: Loop a short piece of yarn around any stitch to
mark Row 2 as **right** side.
Row 3: Ch 4, turn; insert hook in second ch from
hook, YO and pull up a loop, skip next ch, insert hook
in next ch, YO and pull up a loop, insert hook in first
Ltr, YO and pull up a loop, (YO and draw through
2 loops on hook) 3 times, work Ltr across changing to
Variegated in last Ltr *(Fig. 5, page 126)*.
Row 4: Ch 4, turn; insert hook in second ch from
hook, YO and pull up a loop, skip next ch, insert hook
in next ch, YO and pull up a loop, insert hook in first
Ltr, YO and pull up a loop, (YO and draw through
2 loops on hook) 3 times, work Ltr across changing to
Green in last Ltr.
Rows 5-7: Ch 4, turn; insert hook in second ch from
hook, YO and pull up a loop, skip next ch, insert hook
in next ch, YO and pull up a loop, insert hook in first
Ltr, YO and pull up a loop, (YO and draw through
2 loops on hook) 3 times, work Ltr across changing to
Variegated in last Ltr on last row.
Row 8: Repeat Row 4 changing to Lt Green in
last Ltr.
Rows 9-11: Repeat Rows 5-7.
Rows 12-59: Repeat Rows 4-11, 6 times; do **not**
finish off.

BORDER

Ch 1, turn; 3 sc in first Ltr, sc in each Ltr across to last
Ltr, 3 sc in last Ltr; 3 sc in end of each row across;
working in free loops of beginning ch *(Fig. 3b,
page 126)*, 3 sc in ch at base of first Ltr, sc in each ch
across to last ch, 3 sc in last ch; 3 sc in end of each row
across; join with slip st to first sc, finish off: 590 sc.

TRIM
FIRST SIDE
With **right** side facing and working across long edge, join Variegated with slip st in center sc of first corner 3-sc group; ch 4, tr in same st, (skip next 2 sc, 3 tr in next sc) across to within one sc of next corner 3-sc group, skip next 2 sc, 2 tr in center sc; finish off.

SECOND SIDE
Work same as First Side.

DESERT RAINBOW

This Navajo-inspired afghan by C.A. Riley will bring the subtle hues
and ambience of the Painted Desert to any setting.

Finished Size: 45½" x 62"

MATERIALS
Worsted Weight Yarn:
Tan - 34½ ounces, (980 grams, 1,950 yards)
Purple - 3 ounces, (90 grams, 170 yards)
Blue - 3 ounces, (90 grams, 170 yards)
Green - 3 ounces, (90 grams, 170 yards)
Yellow - 3 ounces, (90 grams, 170 yards)
Lt Rose - 3 ounces, (90 grams, 170 yards)
Rose - 3 ounces, (90 grams, 170 yards)
Crochet hook, size I (5.50 mm) **or** size needed
for gauge

*Note: Afghan is worked using two strands of yarn, forming stitches with first color and working over one strand of second color, carrying yarn with normal tension across top of previous row. Do **not** cut yarn unless instructed.*

GAUGE: In pattern, 10 Clusters and 8 rows = 4¼"

Gauge Swatch: 4½"w x 4¼"h
With Tan, ch 12 **loosely**.
Row 1: Working over Purple, hdc in second ch from hook, work Clusters across to last ch, hdc in last ch: 11 sts.
Rows 2-8: Ch 1, turn; hdc in first hdc, work Clusters across to last hdc, hdc in last hdc.
Finish off.

STITCH GUIDE

CLUSTER
YO, insert hook in same st as last st made, YO and pull up a loop, YO, insert hook in next st, YO and pull up a loop, YO and draw through all 5 loops on hook.

AFGHAN BODY
With Tan, ch 103 **loosely**.
Row 1 (Right side): With Tan and working over Purple, hdc in second ch from hook, work Clusters across to last ch, hdc in last ch: 102 sts.
Rows 2-4: With Tan, ch 1, turn; working over Purple, hdc in first hdc, work Clusters across to last hdc, hdc in last hdc.

Rows 5 and 6: With Tan, ch 1, turn; working over Purple, hdc in first hdc, work 40 Clusters changing to Purple in last Cluster made *(Fig. 5, page 126)*, working over Tan, work 20 Clusters changing to Tan in last Cluster made, working over Purple, work 40 Clusters, hdc in last hdc; at end of Row 6, cut Purple.

Note: Continue to change colors in same manner throughout, working over color not being used.

Rows 7 and 8: With Tan, ch 1, turn; working over Blue, hdc in first hdc, work 30 Clusters, with Blue, work 40 Clusters, with Tan, work 30 Clusters, hdc in last hdc; at end of Row 8, cut Blue.
Rows 9 and 10: With Tan, ch 1, turn; working over Green, hdc in first hdc, work 20 Clusters, ★ with Green, work 20 Clusters, with Tan, work 20 Clusters; repeat from ★ once **more**, hdc in last hdc; at end of Row 10, cut Green.
Rows 11 and 12: With Tan, ch 1, turn; working over Yellow, hdc in first hdc, work 10 Clusters, with Yellow, work 20 Clusters, with Tan, work 40 Clusters, with Yellow, work 20 Clusters, with Tan, work 10 Clusters, hdc in last hdc; at end of Row 12, cut Yellow.
Rows 13 and 14: With Tan, ch 1, turn; working over Rose, hdc in first hdc, with Rose, work 20 Clusters, with Tan, work 60 Clusters, with Rose, work 20 Clusters, with Tan, hdc in last hdc; at end of Row 14, cut Rose.
Rows 15 and 16: With Tan and replacing Yellow with Lt Rose, repeat Rows 11 and 12; at end of Row 16, cut Lt Rose.
Rows 17 and 18: With Tan and replacing Green with Purple, repeat Rows 9 and 10; at end of Row 18, cut Purple.
Rows 19 and 20: Repeat Rows 7 and 8.
Rows 21 and 22: With Tan and replacing Purple with Green, repeat Rows 5 and 6; at end of Row 22, cut Green.
Rows 23 and 24: With Tan and replacing Blue with Yellow, repeat Rows 7 and 8; at end of Row 24, cut Yellow.
Rows 25 and 26: With Tan and replacing Green with Rose, repeat Rows 9 and 10; at end of Row 26, cut Rose.
Rows 27 and 28: With Tan and replacing Yellow with Lt Rose, repeat Rows 11 and 12; at end of Row 28, cut Lt Rose.
Rows 29 and 30: With Tan and replacing Rose with Purple, repeat Rows 13 and 14; at end of Row 30, cut Purple.

Continued on page 116.

Rows 31 and 32: With Tan and replacing Yellow with Blue, repeat Rows 11 and 12; at end of Row 32, cut Blue.

Rows 33 and 34: Repeat Rows 9 and 10.

Rows 35 and 36: With Tan and replacing Blue with Yellow, repeat Rows 7 and 8; at end of Row 36, cut Yellow.

Rows 37 and 38: With Tan and replacing Purple with Rose, repeat Rows 5 and 6; at end of Row 38, cut Rose.

Rows 39 and 40: With Tan and replacing Blue with Lt Rose, repeat Rows 7 and 8; at end of Row 40, cut Lt Rose.

Rows 41 and 42: With Tan and replacing Green with Purple, repeat Rows 9 and 10; at end of Row 42, cut Purple.

Rows 43 and 44: With Tan and replacing Yellow with Blue, repeat Rows 11 and 12; at end of Row 44, cut Blue.

Rows 45 and 46: With Tan and replacing Rose with Green, repeat Rows 13 and 14; at end of Row 46, cut Green.

Rows 47 and 48: Repeat Rows 11 and 12.

Rows 49 and 50: With Tan and replacing Green with Rose, repeat Rows 9 and 10; at end of Row 50, cut Rose.

Rows 51 and 52: With Tan and replacing Blue with Lt Rose, repeat Rows 7 and 8; at end of Row 52, cut Lt Rose.

Rows 53-118: Repeat Rows 5-52 once, then repeat Rows 5-22 once **more**; at end of Row 118, do **not** cut Green.

Rows 119-122: With Tan, ch 1, turn; working over Green, hdc in first hdc, work Clusters across to last hdc, hdc in last hdc; at end of Row 122, cut Green; do **not** finish off Tan.

EDGING

Rnd 1: With Tan, ch 2 **(counts as first hdc, now and throughout)**, turn; working over second strand of Tan, hdc in same st and in each st across to last hdc, 3 hdc in last hdc; working in end of rows, skip first row, (2 hdc in next row, hdc in next row) across to last row, skip last row; working in free loops of beginning ch **(Fig. 3b, page 126)**, 3 hdc in first ch, hdc in next 100 chs, 3 hdc in next ch; working in end of rows, skip first row, (2 hdc in next row, hdc in next row) across to last row, skip last row, hdc in same st as first hdc; join with slip st to first hdc: 572 hdc.

Rnd 2: Ch 2, do **not** turn; work Clusters across to center hdc of next corner 3-hdc group, ★ hdc in same st as last Cluster made and in center hdc, work Clusters across to center hdc of next corner 3-hdc group; repeat from ★ 2 times **more**, hdc in same st as last Cluster made; join with slip st to first hdc: 576 sts.

Rnd 3: Ch 1, skip first hdc, ★ sc in next st, ch 1, working around last sc, sc in skipped st, skip next st; repeat from ★ around; join with slip st to first sc, finish off.

SEDONA STYLE

Crocheting since she was 9, Julene S. Watson has created numerous unique designs. The one shown here is a combination of rectangles that forms an image of "paving stones."

Finished Size: 47" x 69"

MATERIALS

Worsted Weight Yarn:
- Green - 32 ounces, (910 grams, 1,810 yards)
- Purple - 15 ounces, (430 grams, 850 yards)
- Rose - 14 ounces, (400 grams, 790 yards)

Crochet hook, size H (5.00 mm) **or** size needed for gauge

Yarn needle

GAUGE: Each Square = 3³⁄₄"
Each Rectangle = 3³⁄₄"w x 7¹⁄₂"h

Gauge Swatch: 3³⁄₄" square
Work same as Square.

STITCH GUIDE

> **TREBLE CROCHET** *(abbreviated tr)*
> YO twice, insert hook in st indicated, YO and pull up a loop (4 loops on hook), (YO and draw through 2 loops on hook) 3 times.

SQUARE (Make 14)

With Rose, ch 4; join with slip st to form a ring.

Rnd 1 (Right side)**:** Ch 3 **(counts as first dc, now and throughout)**, 2 dc in ring, ch 3, (3 dc in ring, ch 3) 3 times; join with slip st to first dc, finish off: 4 ch-3 sps.

Note: Loop a short piece of yarn around any stitch to mark Rnd 1 as **right** side.

Rnd 2: With **right** side facing, join Purple with slip st in any ch-3 sp; ch 3, (2 dc, ch 3, 3 dc) in same sp, ch 1, ★ (3 dc, ch 3, 3 dc) in next ch-3 sp, ch 1; repeat from ★ 2 times **more**; join with slip st to first dc, finish off: 24 dc and 8 sps.

Rnd 3: With **right** side facing, join Green with sc in any corner ch-3 sp *(see Joining With Sc, page 125)*; ch 3, sc in same sp, ch 3, sc in next ch-1 sp, ch 3, ★ (sc, ch 3) twice in next corner ch-3 sp, sc in next ch-1 sp, ch 3; repeat from ★ 2 times **more**; join with slip st to first sc, do **not** finish off: 12 ch-3 sps.

Rnd 4: Slip st in first ch-3 sp, ch 3, (2 dc, ch 3, 3 dc) in same sp, 3 dc in each of next 2 ch-3 sps, ★ (3 dc, ch 3, 3 dc) in next corner ch-3 sp, 3 dc in each of next 2 ch-3 sps; repeat from ★ 2 times **more**; join with slip st to first dc, finish off: 48 dc and 4 ch-3 sps.

RECTANGLE (Make 101)

With Rose, ch 4; join with slip st to form a ring.

Foundation Rnd (Right side)**:** Ch 6 **(counts as first dc plus ch 3)**, (3 dc, ch 3, 3 dc) in ring, ch 2, 2 dc in ring; join with slip st to first dc, do **not** finish off: 9 dc and 3 sps.

Note: Mark Foundation Rnd as **right** side.

Continued on page 118.

Row 1: Slip st in first ch-3 sp, ch 3, turn; (3 dc, ch 2, 3 dc) in next ch-2 sp, skip next 3 dc, dc in next ch-3 sp, leave remaining sts unworked: 8 dc and one ch-2 sp.

Rows 2-5: Ch 3, turn; (3 dc, ch 2, 3 dc) in next ch-2 sp, skip next 3 dc, dc in last dc.

Row 6: Ch 4, turn; 3 dc in next ch-2 sp, skip next 3 dc, tr in last dc; finish off.

Note: Begin working in rounds.

Rnd 1: With **right** side facing and working in end of rows, join Purple with slip st in end of Row 6; ch 3, (2 dc, ch 3, 3 dc) in same row, 3 dc in each of next 5 rows, (3 dc, ch 3, 3 dc) in next ch-3 sp on Foundation Rnd, ch 1, (3 dc, ch 3, 3 dc) in next ch-3 sp; working in end of rows, 3 dc in each of next 5 rows, (3 dc, ch 3, 3 dc) in last row, ch 1; join with slip st to first dc, finish off: 54 dc and 6 sps.

Rnd 2: With **right** side facing and working across long edge, join Green with sc in first corner ch-3 sp; ch 3, sc in same sp, ch 3, † (skip next 3 dc, sc in sp **before** next dc, ch 3) 6 times, (sc, ch 3) twice in next corner ch-3 sp, sc in next ch-1 sp, ch 3 †, (sc, ch 3) twice in next corner ch-3 sp, repeat from † to † once; join with slip st to first sc: 22 ch-3 sps.

Rnd 3: Slip st in first corner ch-3 sp, ch 3, (2 dc, ch 3, 3 dc) in same sp, 3 dc in each ch-3 sp across to next corner ch-3 sp, ★ (3 dc, ch 3, 3 dc) in corner ch-3 sp, 3 dc in each ch-3 sp across to next corner ch-3 sp; repeat from ★ 2 times **more**; join with slip st to first dc, finish off: 78 dc and 4 ch-3 sps.

ASSEMBLY

With Green, using Placement Diagram as a guide, matching sts, and working through **inside** loops, whipstitch Squares and Rectangles together *(Fig. 6b, page 126)*, beginning in center ch of first corner ch-3 **or** corresponding st and ending in center ch of next corner ch-3 **or** corresponding st.

EDGING

Rnd 1: With **right** side facing, join Green with sc in corner ch-3 sp at Point A; ch 3, sc in same sp, † 2 sc in next dc, sc in next dc and in each dc and each sp across to within one dc of next corner ch-3 sp, 2 sc in next dc, (sc, ch 3, sc) in corner ch-3 sp †, 2 sc in next dc, sc in next dc and in each dc and each sp across to next corner ch-3 sp, (sc, ch 3, sc) in corner ch-3 sp, repeat from † to † once, sc in each dc and in each sp across; join with slip st to first sc: 860 sc and 4 ch-3 sps.

Rnd 2: Slip st in first corner ch-3 sp, ch 3, (2 dc, ch 2, 3 dc) in same sp, ★ † skip next 2 sc, sc in next sc, skip next 2 sc, [(3 dc, ch 2, 3 dc) in next sc, skip next 2 sc, sc in next sc, skip next 2 sc] across to next corner ch-3 sp †, (3 dc, ch 2, 3 dc) in corner ch-3 sp; repeat from ★ 2 times **more**, then repeat from † to † once; join with slip st to first dc, finish off.

PLACEMENT DIAGRAM

Point A

ROSEBUD

Cathy Grivnow created these sweet folk-art florals by sewing together small squares of block stitches.

Finished Size: 41" x 57"

MATERIALS

Worsted Weight Yarn:
Ecru - 26 ounces, (740 grams, 1,470 yards)
Rose - 12 ounces, (340 grams, 680 yards)
Green - 6½ ounces, (180 grams, 370 yards)
Pink - 2 ounces, (60 grams, 115 yards)
Crochet hook, size H (5.00 mm) **or** size needed for gauge
Yarn needle

GAUGE: Each Small Square = 7¾";
Each Large Square = 17"

Gauge Swatch: 5¾" x 5¾" x 8¼"
Work same as Small Square for 7 rows.

Continued on page 120.

SYMBOL CROCHET CHART

KEY

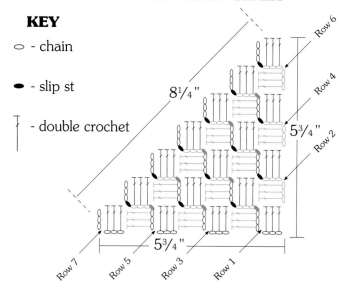

- ○ - chain
- ● - slip st
- ⊤ - double crochet

8¼"
5¾"
5¾"

Row 6
Row 4
Row 2
Row 7
Row 5
Row 3
Row 1

STITCH GUIDE

BEGINNING BLOCK
Ch 6 **loosely**, turn; dc in fourth ch from hook and in next 2 chs.
BLOCK
Slip st in ch-3 sp of next Block, ch 3, 3 dc in same sp.

SMALL SQUARE (Make 24)

Row 1 (Right side)**:** With Rose, ch 6 **loosely**, dc in fourth ch from hook and in next 2 chs changing to Green in last dc **(Fig. 5, page 126)**: one Block.
Note: Loop a short piece of yarn around any stitch to mark Row 1 as **right** side.
Row 2: Work Beginning Block, slip st around beginning ch of previous Block **(Fig. A)**, ch 3, 3 dc in same sp changing to Ecru in last dc **(Fig. B)**: 2 Blocks.

Fig. A

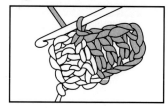

Fig. B

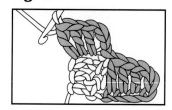

Note: Continue to change colors in same manner.

Row 3: Work Beginning Block, slip st in ch-3 sp of first Block, ch 3, 3 dc in same sp, work Block: 3 Blocks.
Row 4: Work Beginning Block, slip st in ch-3 sp of first Block, ch 3, 3 dc in same sp, with Green, work Block, with Ecru, work Block: 4 Blocks.
Row 5: Work Beginning Block, slip st in ch-3 sp of first Block, ch 3, 3 dc in same sp, work Block, with Green, work Block, with Ecru, work Block: 5 Blocks.
Row 6: Work Beginning Block, with Pink, slip st in ch-3 sp of first Block, ch 3, 3 dc in same sp, with Green, work 2 Blocks, with Ecru, work 2 Blocks: 6 Blocks.
Row 7: Work Beginning Block, slip st in ch-3 sp of first Block, ch 3, 3 dc in same sp, work 2 Blocks, with Green, work Block, with Ecru, work 2 Blocks: 7 Blocks.
Row 8: Work Beginning Block, slip st in ch-3 sp of first Block, ch 3, 3 dc in same sp, work 2 Blocks, ★ with Green, work Block, with Ecru, work Block; repeat from ★ once **more**: 8 Blocks.
Row 9: Work Beginning Block, with Pink, slip st in ch-3 sp of first Block, ch 3, 3 dc in same sp, with Green, work 2 Blocks, with Ecru, work 5 Blocks: 9 Blocks.
Row 10: Work Beginning Block, slip st in ch-3 sp of first Block, ch 3, 3 dc in same sp, work Block, with Rose, work 2 Blocks, with Ecru, work 2 Blocks, with Green, work Block, with Ecru, work 2 Blocks: 10 Blocks.
Row 11: Turn; slip st in first 3 dc and in next ch-3 sp, ch 3, 3 dc in same sp, work 2 Blocks, with Green, work Block, with Rose, work 3 Blocks, with Ecru, work 2 Blocks, slip st in ch-3 sp of last Block: 9 Blocks.
Row 12: Turn; slip st in first 3 dc and in next ch-3 sp, ch 3, 3 dc in same sp, work Block, with Rose, work 3 Blocks, with Ecru, work 3 Blocks, slip st in ch-3 sp of last Block: 8 Blocks.
Row 13: Turn; slip st in first 3 dc and in next ch-3 sp, ch 3, 3 dc in same sp, work 2 Blocks, with Rose, work Block, with Pink, work Block, with Rose, work Block, with Ecru, work Block, slip st in ch-3 sp of last Block: 7 Blocks.
Row 14: Turn; slip st in first 3 dc and in next ch-3 sp, ch 3, 3 dc in same sp, with Rose, work 3 Blocks, with Ecru, work 2 Blocks, slip st in ch-3 sp of last Block: 6 Blocks.

Row 15: Turn; slip st in first 3 dc and in next ch-3 sp, ch 3, 3 dc in same sp, work Block, with Rose, work 2 Blocks, with Ecru, work Block, slip st in ch-3 sp of last Block: 5 Blocks.

Row 16: Turn; slip st in first 3 dc and in next ch-3 sp, ch 3, 3 dc in same sp, work 3 Blocks, slip st in ch-3 sp of last Block: 4 Blocks.

Row 17: Turn; slip st in first 3 dc and in next ch-3 sp, ch 3, 3 dc in same sp, work 2 Blocks, slip st in ch-3 sp of last Block: 3 Blocks.

Row 18: Turn; slip st in first 3 dc and in next ch-3 sp, ch 3, 3 dc in same sp, work Block, slip st in ch-3 sp of last Block: 2 Blocks.

Row 19: Turn; slip st in first 3 dc and in next ch-3 sp, ch 3, 3 dc in same sp, slip st in ch-3 sp of last Block; finish off: one Block.

LARGE SQUARE (Make 6)

Holding Small Squares with **wrong** sides together, Row 1 in center, and matching colors as needed, sew 4 Small Squares together to form one Large Square.

BORDER

Rnd 1: With **right** side facing, join Ecru with sc in top of ch-3 in any corner (Row 19) *(see Joining With Sc, page 125)*; ch 2, sc in same st, ch 2, ★ † skip next 3 sts, sc in next st, ch 2, skip next 2 chs, (sc in next st, ch 2, skip next 3 sts, sc in next st, ch 2, skip next 2 chs) 9 times †, (sc, ch 2) twice in next ch; repeat from ★ 2 times **more**, then repeat from † to † once; join with slip st to first sc, finish off: 84 ch-2 sps.

Rnd 2: With **right** side facing, join Rose with slip st in any corner ch-2 sp; ch 3, (dc, ch 2, 2 dc) in same sp, 3 dc in each ch-2 sp across to next corner ch-2 sp, ★ (2 dc, ch 2, 2 dc) in corner ch-2 sp, 3 dc in each ch-2 sp across to next corner ch-2 sp; repeat from ★ 2 times **more**; join with slip st to top of beginning ch-3, finish off: 256 dc and 4 ch-2 sps.

ASSEMBLY

With Rose and working through **inside** loops, whipstitch Large Squares together forming 2 vertical strips of 3 Large Squares each *(Fig. 6b, page 126)*, beginning in second ch of first corner ch-2 and ending in first ch of next corner ch-2; then whipstitch strips in same manner.

EDGING

Rnd 1: With **right** side facing and working in Back Loops Only *(Fig. 2, page 125)*, join Rose with sc in first ch of upper right corner ch-2; ch 2, sc in next ch, † work 125 sc evenly spaced across to next corner ch-2, sc in next ch, ch 2, sc in next ch, work 185 sc evenly spaced across to next corner ch-2 †, sc in next ch, ch 2, sc in next ch, repeat from † to † once; join with slip st to first sc, finish off: 628 sc.

Rnd 2: With **right** side facing, join Green with sc in upper right corner ch-2 sp; (slip st, ch 3, 3 dc) in same sp, skip next 3 sc, (slip st, ch 3, 3 dc) in next sc, ★ † with Ecru, skip next 3 sc, (slip st, ch 3, 3 dc) in next sc, with Green, [skip next 3 sc, (slip st, ch 3, 3 dc) in next sc] twice †, repeat from † to † across to within 3 sc of next corner ch-2 sp, skip next 3 sc, (sc, slip st, ch 3, 3 dc) in corner ch-2 sp, skip next 3 sc, (slip st, ch 3, 3 dc) in next sc; repeat from ★ 2 times **more**, then repeat from † to † across to last 3 sc, skip last 3 sc; join with slip st to first sc changing to Ecru: 158 Blocks and 4 sc.

Rnd 3: Ch 3, **turn**; 3 dc in same st, with Pink, work Block, ★ † (with Ecru, work 2 Blocks, with Pink, work Block) across to within one Block of next corner sc, with Ecru, work Block †, (slip st, ch 3, 3 dc) in corner sc, with Pink, work Block; repeat from ★ 2 times **more**, then repeat from † to † once; join with slip st in sc at base of beginning ch-3: 162 Blocks.

Rnd 4: Turn; (slip st, ch 3, 3 dc) in first dc, † (slip st, ch 3, 3 dc) in ch-3 sp of same Block, work 32 Blocks, (slip st, ch 3, 3 dc) in first dc of next Block, (slip st, ch 3, 3 dc) in ch-3 sp of same Block, work 47 Blocks †, (slip st, ch 3, 3 dc) in first dc of next Block, repeat from † to † once; join with slip st in same st as first slip st changing to Rose: 166 Blocks.

Rnd 5: Turn; (slip st, ch 3, 3 dc) in first dc, † (slip st, ch 3, 3 dc) in ch-3 sp of same Block, work 47·Blocks, (slip st, ch 3, 3 dc) in first dc of next Block, (slip st, ch 3, 3 dc) in ch-3 sp of same Block, work 33 Blocks †, (slip st, ch 3, 3 dc) in first dc of next Block, repeat from † to † once; join with slip st in same st as first slip st, finish off.

WOVEN SQUARES

Let Julene S. Watson help you get "squared" away for the chilly months with this cozy geometric blanket!

Finished Size: 44" x 64"

MATERIALS

Worsted Weight Yarn:
Black - 28 ounces, (800 grams, 1,580 yards)
Rust - 7 ounces, (200 grams, 395 yards)
Teal - 7 ounces, (200 grams, 395 yards)
Purple - 6 ounces, (170 grams, 340 yards)
Coral - 6 ounces, (170 grams, 340 yards)
Green - 5 ounces, (140 grams, 285 yards)
Red - 5 ounces, (140 grams, 285 yards)
Crochet hook, size H (5.00 mm) **or** size needed for gauge
Yarn needle

GAUGE SWATCH: 2½" square
Work same as Square.

SQUARE

Note: Make the number of Squares specified in the colors indicated: Black - 175, Rust - 48, Teal - 46, Purple - 42, Coral - 40, Green - 37, and Red - 37.

Rnd 1 (Right side): With color indicated, ch 2; 8 sc in second ch from hook; join with slip st to first sc.
Note: Loop a short piece of yarn around any stitch to mark Rnd 1 as **right** side.
Rnd 2: Ch 1, (sc in same st, ch 1) twice, skip next sc, ★ (sc, ch 1) twice in next sc, skip next sc; repeat from ★ 2 times **more**; join with slip st to first sc: 8 ch-1 sps.
Rnd 3: Slip st in first ch-1 sp, ch 1, (sc in same sp, ch 1) twice, sc in next ch-1 sp, ch 1, ★ (sc, ch 1) twice in next ch-1 sp, sc in next ch-1 sp, ch 1; repeat from ★ 2 times **more**; join with slip st to first sc: 12 ch-1 sps.
Rnd 4: Slip st in first corner ch-1 sp, ch 1, (sc in same sp, ch 1) twice, (sc in next ch-1 sp, ch 1) twice, ★ (sc, ch 1) twice in next corner ch-1 sp, (sc in next ch-1 sp, ch 1) twice; repeat from ★ 2 times **more**; join with slip st to first sc: 16 ch-1 sps.
Rnd 5: Slip st in first corner ch-1 sp, ch 1, (sc in same sp, ch 1) twice, (sc in next ch-1 sp, ch 1) 3 times, ★ (sc, ch 1) twice in next corner ch-1 sp, (sc in next ch-1 sp, ch 1) 3 times; repeat from ★ 2 times **more**; join with slip st to first sc, finish off: 20 sc and 20 ch-1 sps.

ASSEMBLY

With matching color, using Placement Diagram as a guide, page 124, and working through **inside** loops, whipstitch Squares together forming 17 vertical strips of 25 Squares each *(Fig. 6b, page 126)*, beginning in first corner ch-1 and ending in next corner ch-1; then whipstitch strips together in same manner.

EDGING

With **right** side facing, join Black with slip st in ch-1 sp to left of upper corner ch-1 sp; ch 3, 3 dc in same sp, skip next ch-1 sp, (slip st, ch 3, 3 dc) in next ch-1 sp, † skip next 2 sc, (slip st, ch 3, 3 dc) in next joining, ★ [skip next sc and next ch-1 sp, (slip st, ch 3, 3 dc) in next ch-1 sp] twice, skip next sc, (slip st, ch 3, 3 dc) in next joining; repeat from ★ 14 times **more**, skip next sc and next ch-1 sp, [(slip st, ch 3, 3 dc) in next ch-1 sp, skip next ch-1 sp] 4 times, skip next 2 sc, (slip st, ch 3, 3 dc) in next joining, ♥ [skip next sc and next ch-1 sp, (slip st, ch 3, 3 dc) in next ch-1 sp] twice, skip next sc, (slip st, ch 3, 3 dc) in next joining ♥, repeat from ♥ to ♥ 22 times **more** †, skip next sc and next ch-1 sp, [(slip st, ch 3, 3 dc) in next ch-1 sp, skip next ch-1 sp] 4 times, repeat from † to † once, skip next sc and next ch-1 sp, [(slip st, ch 3, 3 dc) in next ch-1 sp, skip next ch-1 sp] twice; join with slip st to first slip st, finish off.

WOVEN SQUARES
PLACEMENT DIAGRAM

KEY

 - Red

- Rust

- Purple

- Teal

- Green

- Coral

- Black

GENERAL INSTRUCTIONS

ABBREVIATIONS

BPtr	Back Post treble crochet(s)
ch(s)	chain(s)
dc	double crochet(s)
dtr	double treble crochet(s)
exsc	extended single crochet(s)
FP	Front Post
FPdc	Front Post double crochet(s)
FPtr	Front Post treble crochet(s)
hdc	half double crochet(s)
LDC	Long Double Crochet(s)
Ltr	Linked treble crochet(s)
mm	millimeters
Rnd(s)	Round(s)
sc	single crochet(s)
sp(s)	space(s)
st(s)	stitch(es)
tr	treble crochet(s)
YO	yarn over

★ — work instructions following ★ as many **more** times as indicated in addition to the first time.

† to † or ♥ to ♥ — work all instructions from first † to second † **or** from first ♥ to second ♥ **as many** times as specified.

( ) or **[ ]** — work enclosed instructions **as many** times as specified by the number immediately following **or** work all enclosed instructions in the stitch or space indicated **or** contains explanatory remarks.

colon (:) — the number(s) given after a colon at the end of a row or round denote(s) the number of stitches you should have on that row or round.

GAUGE

Exact gauge is **essential** for proper size. Before beginning your project, make the sample swatch given in the individual instructions in the yarn and hook specified. After completing the swatch, measure it, counting your stitches and rows or rounds carefully. If your swatch is larger or smaller than specified, **make another, changing hook size to get the correct gauge**. Keep trying until you find the size hook that will give you the specified gauge.

JOINING WITH SC

When instructed to join with sc, begin with a slip knot on hook. Insert hook in stitch or space indicated, YO and pull up a loop, YO and draw through both loops on hook.

BACK RIDGE

Work only in loops indicated by arrows *(Fig. 1)*.

Fig. 1

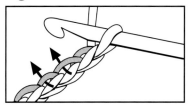

BACK OR FRONT LOOP ONLY

Work only in loop(s) indicated by arrow *(Fig. 2)*.

Fig. 2

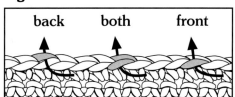

FREE LOOPS

After working in Back or Front Loops Only on a row or round, there will be a ridge of unused loops. These are called the free loops. Later, when instructed to work in the free loops of the same row or round, work in these loops *(Fig. 3a)*.

When instructed to work in free loops of a chain, work in loop indicated by arrow *(Fig. 3b)*.

Fig. 3a   **Fig. 3b**

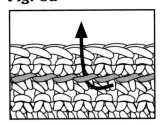 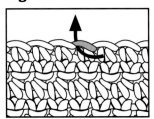

POST STITCH

Work around post of st indicated, inserting hook in direction of arrow *(Fig. 4)*.

Fig. 4

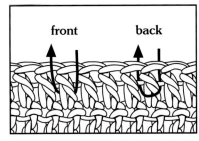

CHANGING COLORS

Work the last stitch to within one step of completion, hook new yarn *(Fig. 5)* and draw through all loops on hook. Cut old yarn and work over both ends unless otherwise specified.

Fig. 5

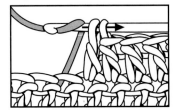

WHIPSTITCH

Holding two Strips, Motifs, or Squares with **wrong** sides together and beginning in stitch indicated, sew through both pieces once to secure the beginning of the seam, leaving an ample yarn end to weave in later. Working through **both** loops on **both** pieces *(Fig. 6a)* **or** through **inside** loop of each stitch on **both** pieces *(Fig. 6b)*, ★ insert the needle from front to back through the next stitch and pull yarn through; repeat from ★ across.

Fig. 6a   **Fig. 6b**

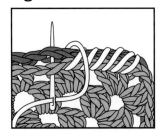 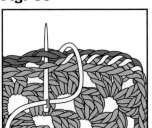

WEAVING SEAMS

With **right** side of two Panels or Blocks facing you, bottom edges at same end and edges even, sew through both pieces once to secure the beginning of the seam, leaving an ample yarn end to weave in later. Insert the needle from **right** to **left** through one strand on each piece *(Fig. 7)*. Bring the needle around and insert it from **right** to **left** through the next strand on both pieces. Continue in this manner, drawing seam together as you work.

Fig. 7

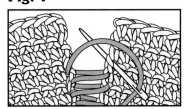

REVERSE SINGLE CROCHET

Working from **left** to **right**, ★ insert hook in stitch to right of hook *(Fig. 8a)*, YO and draw through, under and to left of loop on hook (2 loops on hook) *(Fig. 8b)*, YO and draw through both loops on hook *(Fig. 8c)* **(reverse sc made, *Fig. 8d*)**; repeat from ★ around.

Fig. 8a

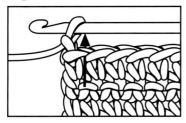

Fig. 8b

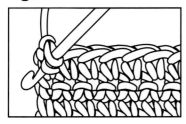

Fig. 8c

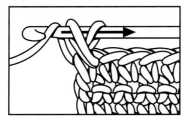

Fig. 8d

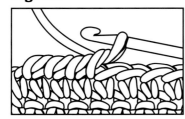

FRINGE

Cut a piece of cardboard 5" wide and half as long as fringe specified in individual instructions. Wind the yarn **loosely** and **evenly** around the cardboard lengthwise until the card is filled, then cut across one end; repeat as needed.

Hold together as many strands of yarn as specified in individual instructions; fold in half.

With **wrong** side facing and using a crochet hook, draw the folded end up through a stitch or space and pull the loose ends through the folded end *(Fig. 9a or 9c)*; draw the knot up **tightly** *(Fig. 9b or 9d)*. Repeat, spacing as specified in individual instructions.

Lay flat on a hard surface and trim the ends.

Fig. 9a

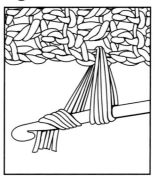

Fig. 9b

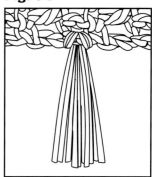

Fig. 9c

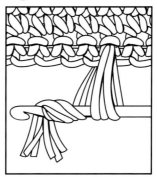

Fig. 9d

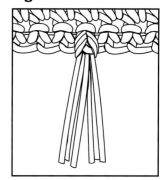

STRAIGHT STITCH

Straight Stitch is just what the name implies, a single, straight stitch. Come up at 1 and go down at 2 *(Fig. 10)*.

Fig. 10

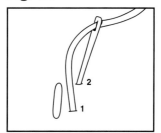

BASIC STITCH GUIDE

SLIP STITCH

Insert hook in st or sp indicated, YO and draw through st and through loop on hook *(Fig. 11)* **(slip stitch made, *abbreviated slip st)*.**

Fig. 11

SINGLE CROCHET

Insert hook in st indicated, YO and pull up a loop, YO and draw through both loops on hook *(Fig. 12)* **(single crochet made, *abbreviated sc)*.**

Fig. 12

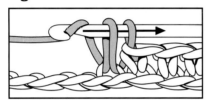

HALF DOUBLE CROCHET

YO, insert hook in st indicated, YO and pull up a loop, YO and draw through all 3 loops on hook *(Fig. 13)* **(half double crochet made, *abbreviated hdc)*.**

Fig. 13

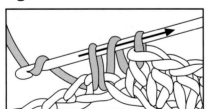

DOUBLE CROCHET

YO, insert hook in st indicated, YO and pull up a loop, YO and draw through 2 loops on hook *(Fig. 14a)*, YO and draw through remaining 2 loops on hook *(Fig. 14b)* **(double crochet made, *abbreviated dc)*.**

Fig. 14a   **Fig. 14b**

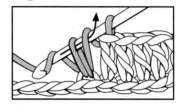 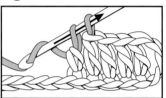

TREBLE CROCHET

YO twice, insert hook in st or sp indicated, YO and pull up a loop (4 loops on hook) *(Fig. 15a)*, (YO and draw through 2 loops on hook) 3 times *(Fig. 15b)* **(treble crochet made, *abbreviated tr)*.**

Fig. 15a   **Fig. 15b**

DOUBLE TREBLE CROCHET

YO 3 times, insert hook in st or sp indicated, YO and pull up a loop (5 loops on hook) *(Fig. 16a)*, (YO and draw through 2 loops on hook) 4 times *(Fig. 16b)* **(double treble crochet made, *abbreviated dtr)*.**

Fig. 16a   **Fig. 16b**

 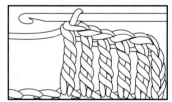

Afghans made and instructions tested by Janet Akins, Anitta Armstrong, Belinda Baxter, Pam Bland, JoAnn Bowling, Mike Cates, Marianna Crowder, Lee Ellis, Katie Galucki, Freda Gillham, Raymelle Greening, Jean Hall, Vicki Kellogg, Cheryl Knepper, Barbara Leslie, Kay Meadors, Peggy Pierpaoli, Dale Potter, Carla Rains, Teresa A. Smith, Donna Soellner, Clare Stringer, Margaret Taverner, and Carol Thompson.